VOID

Library of
Davidson College

The REAL Reason Why Johnny Still Can't Read

Books by Stanley L. Sharp

THE REAL REASON WHY JOHNNY STILL CAN'T READ
A GERMAN READING GRAMMAR
A SOLID FOUNDATION IN GERMAN
WORKBOOK TO A SOLID FOUNDATION IN GERMAN
WINNETOU (a German reader)

The REAL Reason Why Johnny Still Can't Read

Stanley L. Sharp

AN EXPOSITION-UNIVERSITY BOOK

Exposition Press   *Smithtown, New York*

To all of my former students:

University of Utah, 1928–1929
Stanford University, 1929–1946
College of San Mateo, 1946–1970
Morehouse College, 1970–1971

And to

TIRZAH

FIRST EDITION

© 1982 by Stanley L. Sharp

All rights reserved. No part of this book may be reproduced, in whole or in part, in any form or by any means, electronic or mechanical, including photocopying, recording, or by any information storage and retrieval system, without permission in writing from the publisher. Address inquiries to Exposition Press, Inc., 325 Rabro Drive, Smithtown, NY 11787-0817.

Library of Congress Catalog Card Number: 81-67491

ISBN 0-682-49771-1

Printed in the United States of America

Contents

	Acknowledgments	vii
	Preface	ix
1.	It Isn't the Method; It Isn't the Teacher	1
2.	Why Do Dictionaries Show Pronunciations of All Words?	11
3.	The Awful Written English Language	18
4.	The Cards Are Stacked against Johnny	32
5.	Three Handicaps—Sometimes Three Strikes	41
6.	Authorities Agree	53
7.	Try Again!	57
8.	How Our Irrational Spelling Developed (I)	65
9.	How Our Irrational Spelling Developed (II)	75
10.	Fifty-Five Common Ways to Spell Six Consonant Sounds	89
11.	Knotty Naughty Consonant Letters	99
12.	The Eyes Have It—Wrong!	109
13.	Those Insidious Schwa Spellings	115
14.	A Good Word for the Bad Speller	124
15.	The Second Great Big IF	136
16.	On a Silver Platter	147
17.	Their Name Is Sisyphus	162
18.	Low Test Scores	174
19.	English Has Many Fifth Wheels	178
20.	Marvelous Memories	188
21.	Clearing the Way	194
22.	Methods of Teaching Reading	197
23.	The Simultaneous Reading and Listening Method	205
24.	Support for the Method	210
25.	The Direct Method	217
26.	What Are the Alternatives?	226
27.	Help for Our Adult Illiterates	238
28.	The Truth—at Long Last	245
29.	The Teacher Is All	255
30.	It Is Up to You!	256

Acknowledgments

It is with considerable pleasure that I express my deep appreciation to all who have helped me with this project. Dozens of people have helped in one way or another, but I wish to single out for special mention the following individuals.

Tirzah Sharp, Dr. Timothy Steege, LeJeune and Jack Decker, Irene and William Given, Laura and George Manthey, David Steege, Dr. Leo Sides, Dr. Thomas A. Bailey, Marjorie Bigot, Sharon Brown, Susan Browne, Dr. Henry Cordes, Marcelle Crook, Dr. Kathryn Glenn, Richard Goodell, Wallace Hagamon, Louise Hazelton, Dr. Douglas Jenks, Gerald Kusebauch, Mary June McCue, Edward Mullen, Diane Musgrave, Gay Passell, Dr. Norbert Pfältzer, Nancy and Dr. Thomas Steege, Dr. F. W. Strothmann, David White, and Florence Wisner.

I also thank the excellent and helpful staff of the Cubberly School of Education Library and the staff of the Palo Alto Public Library.

Preface

Since illiteracy is a cruel, economic, social, and lifelong handicap to many millions of individuals in English-speaking countries, we ought to do everything in our power to eliminate it. If that should prove impossible, we ought to try to lower the numbers of those who are unable to read to an irreducible minimum.

We must be judicious in our approach and give a hearing to all who can make contributions. At the same time, we should separate the wheat from the chaff and not believe everything that is ever written about the subject of teaching reading.

One free-lance writer has set himself up as The Great Authority, and he is believed by vast numbers of readers, even by many who have never read his book. However, those who know the facts about the teaching of reading and have had training in linguistics and phonetics recognize his false claims and gross exaggerations for what they are: worthless and harmful.

I am speaking of Rudolf Flesch. When his *Why Johnny Can't Read* was published in 1955, I was alarmed and distressed but didn't feel qualified to write a reply, and I didn't have the time then to train myself. In 1971, when it was much too late to answer the book, I set about learning what I could. I studied the methods that have been used to teach reading and also the subject that teachers must teach: the relationships between words as they are written and as they are spoken.

In due course, I began to put down my findings in writing, and the results were a manuscript to which I had devoted nearly 30,000 hours. The publisher and I had just signed a contract when I learned, to my dismay, that Mr. Flesch had written a sequel, *Why Johnny* Still *Can't Read*. That book is the reason for this preface.

In my book you will find a number of references to the 1955 book, and because so many still believe what he wrote there, some three years ago I prepared a short chapter and reported on Flesch's false claims. (It is Chapter 28.)

What does the new *Johnny* book offer? For the most part it is simply a rehash of the first book, but it contains errors and omissions of scholarship even more flagrant than the first. Typical of gross exaggerations are these two claims: We learn on page sixty-two that our present literacy level has fallen to that of Albania and Burma, which, according to the *Reader's Digest Almanac* of 1981 is seventy! We learn on page two that in the 1990s, "We'll join the rank of such undereducated Third World countries as Saudi Arabia and Zambia." Zambia has a literacy level of twenty-eight, and Saudi Arabia one of fifteen. Are we really supposed to believe that in about twelve to eighteen years from now between 72 and 85 percent of all Americans will be unable to read?

In the 1955 book we were informed that 87 percent of all English words are spelled phonetically. People who know what the term "phonetic spelling" means also know that the number is outrageously high. But in his new book, Mr. Flesch would have us believe that an even greater number of English words are spelled phonetically, 97.4 percent! If that were true, children would have no trouble at all learning to read all those words. So Flesch would have us believe that children should have difficulty learning to read only 2.6 percent of our words!

Now comes the truly incredible: On pages ninety-eight and ninety-nine, he lists a total of 56 words, and they are, presumably, "the whole list" of difficult words! That is preposterous. For every one of Flesch's hard words, I can easily give him 100 common words that are equally as difficult for children to learn to read. If you will read Chapter 3 in this book, you will be convinced that Flesch is utterly wrong.

How did Flesch come up with that phantom figure of 97.4 percent? He gives it at least seven times and it cannot, therefore, be a misprint. He tells how he himself spent one afternoon making a count; he gives as a source a Margaret Bishop, who cannot possibly qualify as an expert; and, finally, he claims Paul and Jean Hanna and Richard Hodges produced the identical figure, right down to the decimal point. A miracle! That the latter group ever offered such a figure is pure fabrication. You will find in Chapter 4 of this book a description of a study by the Hannas, Hodges, and Edwin H. Rudorf, Jr. Flesch did not mention the volume in which the researchers made their report. If he were a true scholar, he would have gone to the original work. Instead, he was content with a brief summary in a short chapter in another book. I have scrutinized the chapter Flesch alluded to and have spent more than a hundred hours on the original, and I assure you the researchers couldn't possibly have arrived at the 97.4 figure. That is the reason I am obliged to state categorically that the figure is a falsehood.

So if you should read the new *Johnny* book, you must be careful not to believe everything. Because the following information is pivotal, I'll give another example. At least four times Mr. Flesch tells us there have been 124 studies in which phonics has been compared with the word-recognition method and that in every single one of them phonics has proved superior. That is not true. As you will find in Chapter 28 in this book, a good many studies report that the whole-word method won out. I'll not repeat what I said there, but if you will read it, you will find that Flesch conveniently overlooked important studies and major conclusions.

Another subject deserves your thoughtful consideration. Textbook publishers and authors maintain that they have introduced a great deal of phonics in their elementary readers. They are given support by one of the most highly regarded educators of today, Professor Jeanne Chall of Harvard. She made a survey of elementary reading series, and then she wrote a brochure, *"Reading, 1967–77: A Decade of Change and Promise."* In it she said, "Most of the published reading programs had a code (phonics) emphasis. Even those that are classified as meaning emphasis (whole word) had earlier and heavier decoding (phonics) programs in the first grade."

Flesch's entire book is based on his erroneous claim that 85 percent of all elementary reading series introduce and use almost no phonics! What he claims is just not true. Of course, he had to make the claim or he would have had nothing to write about. The general reading public has not seen and does not have access to the various reading series. Whom are you going to believe, Chall or Flesch?

Professor John J. DeBoer, who was editor of *Elementary English* at the time, wrote an editorial in April 1955. What he said then holds true today. He regretted Flesch's inflammatory statements, and he wrote, "Mr. Flesch's views are the more dangerous because they are superficially plausible to the uninformed and hold a spurious appeal to parents who are honestly worried about their children's reading." He stated further, "If Mr. Flesch has made no other contribution, he has illustrated how words can be used to prove that black is white."

I thoroughly agree with Dr. DeBoer when he said, "Let us have more facts and less angry rhetoric."

In this book I have endeavored to supply you with facts.

S.L.S.

June 15, 1981

CHAPTER 1

It Isn't the Method; It Isn't the Teacher

There are more than ten million adult illiterates in our country. If that figure is hard to comprehend, look at it this way:

The Rose Bowl in Pasadena seats almost 105,000 people. Suppose we gathered all the illiterates in the United States and seated them there. If we were to fill the Bowl once a day, it would take ninety-five days to accommodate them all; in other words, if we seated the first group on the first of January, the last group couldn't be seated until the fifth of April!

The number one problem in education is, and always has been, how to teach all our normal children to read. We do not yet know how to solve it. Indeed, very few know what causes our illiteracy rate to be so high.

In addition to the ten million illiterates in this country, there's a second group of unfortunate people even larger than the first: the thirteen million Americans who are classified as "functionally illiterate." That means they can read a few hundred words or possibly as many as three or four thousand, but are unable to function adequately as readers in a complex society. They are unable to read with full understanding such things as "help wanted" advertisements, application forms, job descriptions, or leasing agreements. If this group were combined with the illiterates, it would take 219 days to seat everyone in the Rose Bowl (from the first of January until the seventh of August) because the number of individuals in the U.S. who are either illiterate or functionally illiterate totals twenty-three million.

These were the findings of two nationwide studies conducted in the mid-seventies. The ten million figure was released by the National Center for Health Statistics on May 5, 1974. The next year the U.S. Office of Education issued the following report, which was published in the *New York Times* on October 30, 1975: "The results of the four-year study indicate that more than 23 million adults throughout the nation are functionally illiterate." (p. 45) This figure was repeated in the November 6, 1978 issue of *Newsweek*.

These statistics are even more distressing when we realize that illiteracy is almost nonexistent in many countries, for example, Finland, Hungary, Denmark, Norway, and Sweden, as well as among the native-born in Holland and the countries in which German is spoken.

So we ask ourselves—or we surely should—why is there such a great discrepancy? Why do so many of our children fail to learn to read? When the question is raised, we hear one of two stock answers. Critics claim either that our teachers are incompetent and are to blame, or that they use the wrong method to teach reading. Please withhold judgment for the time being as to teachers' competency. And as to method, what most critics don't know is that "the" teaching method is not just one method. In the past century and a half, educators have employed dozens of variations of methods and combinations of methods, and yet, regardless of the method, teachers have never been able to eliminate reading failures.

Our educators have employed methods that have been used successfully in Czechoslovakia, Germany, Scandinavia, France, Belgium, etc., but no matter what method they have used, they have never been successful with all beginners. Meanwhile, European educators have also copied the methods our teachers have used, and still they have met with relatively few failures.

A logical question arises: Why don't we copy the methods used to teach reading in Great Britain? But we have copied them, and teachers there have copied our methods.

Here we have clear proof that our methods are not to blame: Proportionately just as many children fail in Britain as here. Over the years I have read a good many issues of the *Times of London,* especially the Educational Supplement, and I have read there about the high rate of illiteracy in Great Britain. In 1974 I read that a TV series was to be started in the fall of 1975 to help illiterates learn to read. This story was picked up by the *San Francisco Chronicle.* On July 28, 1974, Michael Hellier reported that Parliament had been informed there were 3.5 million illiterates in Britain. Parliament thereupon ordered the British Broadcasting Corporation to take action and make an attempt to stamp out illiteracy. A good friend of mine living in London reported on the resulting TV series and sent me copies of the books which were written and published to support the program. This is not the place to comment, but later I'll give my reactions, for what they may be worth.

The figures on illiteracy in Great Britain quoted by Mr. Hellier are substantiated in several places, including a book, *The Initial Teaching Alphabet,* by the British-born educator John Downing. On page four is this statement: "The Ministry of Education statistics show that one in four English fifteen-year-olds are either backward or semi-literate."

It Isn't the Method; It Isn't the Teacher

The question as to which method or which combination of methods should be employed in the teaching of reading has been debated just as much in Britain as here. Lay persons there, just as here, have been inclined to criticize "the" method, not realizing that many methods and combinations of methods have been tried and found wanting.

Before leaving the question concerning how reading has been taught, we should consider at least briefly the method that almost all parents assume is the logical one and probably the only method which can possibly be successful—the phonic method. This is the approach by which children are taught the sound each letter spells and then, presumably, to read by sounding out the words, letter by letter.

This method is considered the only practical one not only by parents, but also by free-lance journalists and newspaper editors who support the assumption in articles and editorials at least once a year. Parents are told over and over again that it is the only possible way to teach reading successfully. They were told this by Rudolf Flesch in *Why Johnny Can't Read* (1955), and the book was so widely read that it remained on the best-seller list for 39 weeks. In addition, it was later condensed and appeared serially in a great number of newspapers. More than anything else that book and the condensation cemented in the minds of parents and other lay people the assumption that phonics must be used; and if it is, it is inevitable that all children will learn to read.

James Kilpatrick, a syndicated columnist and TV commentator, wrote that "Until the primacy of phonics is fully restored, the new federal millions (monies appropriated to improve the teaching of reading) are likely to go gurgling down the drain." (*Palo Alto Times,* June 1, 1974)

More recently, the Associated Press commissioned Kathryn Diehl and E. G. Hodenfeld to write a ten-part series of articles titled, "Johnny Still Can't Read." It was sold to nearly 300 newspapers and was published during August and September of 1976. The thrust of the articles was that Johnny still can't read because teachers still do not use intensified phonics. Among other things, the authors said:

1. "In English there are very few irregular words for which the rules don't apply."
2. English has (only) "a few easy-to-learn irregularities."
3. "Children learn to read words . . . by the way they SOUND." (The capital letters are in the original.)

When you read Chapter Three of this book, you will see how little the authors of that series of articles know about the written English language. There you will find five solid reasons why Johnny can't read. They prove the reverse of what the authors say is true of English; they must have thought they were writing about Finnish. In the same chapter you will find that

1. In English there are relatively few words for which rules do apply.
2. Written English has vast numbers of irregularities.
3. Children cannot sound out thousands of words—common words they must learn in order to become literate.

In short, in the one chapter you will discover how exceedingly difficult it is to learn to read English, no matter what method is used in teaching reading.

If it could be proved that "earlier generations read perfectly well," as Edith Efron, a *TV Guide* editor claimed (October 11, 1975, p. 5a), then my entire argument and thesis would be wrong. So we had better look into the ability to read by "earlier generations." Editor Efron named as her authority Rudolf Flesch, who said in his *Johnny* book "The teaching of reading never was a problem anywhere in the world until . . . about 1925." (p. 2)

If you will consult the Fourteenth Edition of the *Encyclopaedia Britannica* (1929), you will find an article on "Illiteracy" in volume 12. In it you will read that "about 60 percent of the world's population over ten years of age cannot read or write." (p. 94) Thus, some 820 million couldn't read or write. In the article you will find only these countries listed as having virtually no reading problems: Finland (one percent), Germany (one-half of one percent), Norway, and Sweden.

The writer of the article explains that no universal criterion had been established to define illiteracy, and for that reason no statistics were provided for Great Britain. For decades literacy was determined there by a person's being able to write his/her name on the marriage license! During the years 1841–1845 a third of the men and half of the women were not able to write their names on what was then a very important document.

In the United States we have relied largely on census figures. But in the past, census takers merely inquired if anybody in the household was unable to read. Even so, in 1910 when the population was less than half of what it is today census figures showed there were 5,516,163 persons over ten who couldn't read. This figure included 1.5 million native-born whites who were illiterate. (*The Literary Digest,* January 11, 1919, p. 27)

Figures for 1920 were roughly the same. In an article in *Current Opinion,* "Illiteracy in the United States," we read as follows: "The Federal Census Bureau (set the number of illiterates) at 4,931,905, but it asserted that the number is probably twice as great, since the census authorities accept the word of those who are counted without submitting them to an examination." (p. 344)

If you are a teacher and wonder if the teaching of reading was a problem in the past, you will do well to read Edmund Burke Huey's remarkable book, *The Psychology and Pedagogy of Reading*. It was published in 1908. Huey described at length the various teaching methods which had been used and were then being used, and there you will find that there is "nothing new under the sun." Yes, there were indeed reading problems. The book is so important that Macmillan reprinted it in 1968. I'll return to the book in a later chapter.

Now we should talk about our elementary teachers. They have a most difficult task: to teach children to read when the symbols of the language are much more unreliable than those of any other Western language. Teachers are too often blamed for reading failures, for being too stubborn to return to phonics, a system which failed in the nineteenth century. They are scapegoats. You will find that I champion them throughout this book. This is my advice to them:

Elementary teachers, arise! You have been criticized, attacked, and maligned much too often and much too long. Undeservedly you have been blamed for Johnny's failure to learn to read. Why hasn't someone from your ranks given the English-speaking world the facts and offered the real reason why Johnny can't read?

An example of unwarranted and vicious attacks on teachers is found, for example, in a column on the editorial page of the *San Francisco Chronicle* on September 18, 1978. The writer, Abe Mellinkoff, writes a daily column. In his column he told how children in San Francisco schools henceforth will be required to pass tests at the end of the third and eighth grades in order to move up to the next higher grade, and at the end of the high school experience before they will be awarded diplomas. (This regulation is a state requirement and is being matched in many states.) In the last paragraph comes the vicious attack: "Meanwhile a new and horrifying educational possibility has been raised. It could be, say some experts, that a lot of teachers are unqualified to teach and would be unable to pass their tests in reading, writing and arithmetic. If we're going to flunk the youngsters, it would be only fair to fire the teachers as well."

Please note that Mellinkoff failed to name the "experts." He probably does not know that all teachers in elementary schools in California have had to hold bachelor degrees for lo these many years and that for the past twelve years, before being employed as teachers they have had to have an additional college year and thus have studied five years in college. Surely every single one can read at least on third and eighth grade level. If you were to see how easy the reading material is on both levels, you would gasp to think that an intelligent columnist would stoop to make such a vilifying statement. Can teachers complete four or five successful years of college and not be able to pass a high school reading test? But let us assume for the sake of argument that of all the teachers in the school system perhaps a dozen were to fail the latter examination. If it were true, would that fact give Mr. Mellinkoff the right to cast aspersions on "a lot of teachers"? What are parents of children now in school supposed to believe? The seeds of doubt have been sown, and they are sure to sprout as weeds.

It is time for someone to stand up for our teachers (and for the failing children who are often blamed). Because seven members of my family are, or have been, elementary teachers, I have more than a passing interest in this matter. In many respects my background and training have qualified me to state the facts; and since nobody else has spoken out, I ask that you elementary teachers let me be your champion and proclaim and prove this truth:

> OF ALL THE MAJOR WESTERN LANGUAGES
> WRITTEN ENGLISH
> IS FAR AND AWAY
> THE HARDEST ONE TO LEARN TO READ

This truth, which is self-evident when one has the facts, should be common knowledge. Certainly all educated people, all college graduates, even high school graduates, all editors, all journalists who write about language and elementary teaching, all TV commentators, all people in high government positions, local, state, and federal, all teachers, school administrators, school board members, all college professors, all psychiatrists, all psychologists, all counselors, all members of the clergy, all poor spellers, and all people of good will should know this truth. Above all, parents who give their children or the children's teachers "a bad time" should be given the facts which are offered in this book. It should be assigned reading for all such parents. Anyone who will read with an open mind even half of this book, including the third chapter, will have a very good indication as to why it is so difficult to learn to read English. They will, I hope, never again blame all teachers or criticize slower learners.

Through the years many parents of poor readers have looked for a scapegoat. Usually they have ended up, as I said, finding it in the teacher or in the teaching method. What can they know about teaching methods? Where have they done their studying or their research? Why haven't they looked for the basic and real reason for the poor performance of their children? That is a question which I can answer. After working on this project in retirement exclusively for ten years, I know for a fact that not one parent in ten (and I imagine not one in a hundred) has any idea how irregular and inconsistent the spelling of our sounds is, how hard English is to learn to read, especially by slower learners, or how much easier the other alphabetic languages are. Parents assume that almost all of the sounds and words in English are spelled regularly and, consequently, should be easy to learn to read. Relatively few parents have had the necessary training in language to be able to arrive at really worthwhile judgments.

When the words of a language are spelled phonetically, that is, each letter spells only one sound, children who speak that language have little difficulty learning to read. And they do it amazingly fast. In other words, when the sounds of a language are spelled regularly and consistently, reading teachers "have it made," because the children in their classes learn to read the symbols relatively effortlessly and quickly. This is true in Finland and Hungary, because almost all of the words of Finnish and Magyar (Hungarian) are spelled phonetically. For that reason it is no wonder that the children there learn to read with relative ease and speed, a high percentage of them even before they start to school! That is also the basic reason for the very low rate of illiteracy in those countries. In due time I'll give more information about the two languages. This is a thought to ponder:

> *If our native language were Finnish instead of English, we would have far fewer failures and illiterates.*

There are many other languages which are relatively easy to learn to read, and among them are Dutch, German, and the Scandinavian languages. The children who speak one of those languages do not learn to read quite as rapidly or easily as children do in Finland and Hungary, and that is true because not so many of the words in those languages are spelled phonetically as in Finnish and Hungarian.

And yet, in comparison with children whose native language is English, children who speak Dutch, German, or Danish spend far less time and effort to become proficient in the reading of their respective languages.

Yes, I hear your protests. We can all point to adults and children who learned to read English with little difficulty and quite rapidly. But the fastest learners in the countries whose languages I have named learn with even less difficulty and much faster. Indeed, average learners in those countries learn about as fast as our fastest learners. This is not speculation; I will offer proof later.

Mencius, a grandson of Confucius, believed a person could attain the proper perspective in any situation by making comparisons. He said, "By weighing, we know what things are light and what heavy. By measuring, we know what things are long and what short. The relations of all things may be thus determined." In a like manner, by comparing written languages we can ascertain how much more difficult it is to learn to read one language than it is to learn to read another.

Of the Germanic languages, English is spoken by the greatest number of people. Since German is spoken by the next largest number, it is logical to use that language as a basis for comparison. You need not know a word of German to follow along with me; but you may be sure I will not give you wrong information to make my points. Too many German experts would jump on me with both feet. Besides, I have professional pride. I majored in German in college and also earned both the M.A. and Ph.D. degrees in German. In addition, I studied at five German universities, taking courses in phonetics in two; and I am the co-author of two college German grammars. Only as many comparisons as are absolutely necessary will be given; the point is not to prove that German is easy for German-speaking children to learn to read; it is to demonstrate how much more difficult it is for our children to learn to read English.

I urge all readers to try to see the problems connected with learning to read from the point of view of the average or, preferably, the slower learner. In that way you may discover things which you have not thought about for a long time and some which you may never have paid any attention to before. Mature, highly trained (and we are definitely that) readers find it exceedingly difficult to start where learners must.

In retrospect, it took me a distressingly long time to be able to do that. This was the first step: Although I had worked with languages (I began with the study of French and Spanish in high school, later became fluent in Dutch, and started the study of German in college), I didn't really realize how regular the spelling of German is until I attended a German university. There I set about getting for myself the best possible all-German dictionary. I went into a large bookstore near the university in Munich and asked where the all-German dictionaries were located. I spent a good deal of time examining all the dictionaries I could find, but not one of them gave what all of our good dictionaries give: respellings to indicate proper pronunciations. I asked a salesperson where the dictionaries containing that information were. He was amazed to think anybody would want such a German dictionary. Soon we had a cluster of university students around us. Then one of them said, "But German isn't like English. We don't need dictionaries to show us pronunciation; our conventional spelling does that. We have no need for your kind of dictionary."

It turned out there was a book showing "stage pronunciation," but as everybody pointed out with much gesticulating and loud talking— we were speaking German and they must have thought that would help a poor foreigner—that book showed actors what standard pronunciation

It Isn't the Method; It Isn't the Teacher

is. It wouldn't sound right on the stage for parents to have children with varying dialects, perhaps a Saxon, a Bavarian, a Swabian, and an Austrian dialect; all had to have a standard pronunciation to give the performance plausibility. But all of the people in the group assured me that they didn't own or need that book; they had no use for it!

(Now there is a pronunciation dictionary available, but as the editors state in the preface, the book will be used mostly by foreign students. It also shows the pronunciation of great numbers of foreign words which aren't widely used by the general population.) It took me a long time to get over my preconception and to accept Germans' statements that they don't need respellings.

As a matter of fact, since then I have been in Danish, Dutch, French, East German, West German, and Swiss homes of educated people in which there were no dictionaries at all of the native language.

Being preoccupied with German, I gave little thought to the idiosyncracies of English. I certainly proved the eighteenth century Scottish philosopher and historian David Hume was right when he said habit molds our thinking more powerfully than analysis does. As a child I had learned to read English relatively easily and assumed everybody should be able to do it also. Believing Hume to be correct, as I do, I am mindful of the gigantic task which lies before me. It took me decades to accept what I now know. Can I possibly change your thinking about the written English symbols in the brief time it will take you to read this book?

Now comes the second and critical step in my discovery. Possibly it will help you if I tell you about my "conversion." I had taught German for ten years at a prestigious university where only the best students were accepted, and then I transferred to teach at a community college where all people eighteen years of age and older were admitted. My role there was to teach English and not German. We ran the gamut from the very poorest "students" to excellent students who had reasons, often financial, for taking their first two years at a community college.

In my first year there we were attempting the impossible in the English department: to teach English to all students on a university level. To be sure, half of them took what is "humorously" called "bonehead" English, but the sole purpose of the course was to prepare students to take university-level freshman composition, and many young people on that level got nothing out of it because it was over their heads. As chairman-elect of the department, I proposed in my first year that we increase the number of levels to four and to teach practical English in the two lower levels. My colleagues didn't relish the idea of teaching either of the two lower levels, but they already had the very poor students in their classes. When I reminded them they were badly watering down university-level courses and would continue to do so as long as the poorer students remained (and usually failed or were given courtesy D grades), my colleagues agreed with me and the new levels were established the next fall. I assigned myself a section at the lowest level.

If I had continued to teach German at the university level and had never taught English to young people at the lowest level, I would never have made my GREAT DISCOVERY: English is hard to learn to read! In my first lowest-level class I discovered I had some young people who had graduated from high school but had never read a single adult book, in or out of class. They simply could not read well enough. Every member of the class was eager to learn, and those young people demonstrated and proved much to me. For example, they proved that people can know the alphabet and still not be able to find a whole lot of words in a dictionary!

Although I was gradually awakening to the facts about the way we spell our sounds (and, hence, our words), I couldn't believe it when Rolf Johnson, professor of English at the University of Illinois, wrote in *The American Mercury:*

> It has been estimated that 80 percent (or about a half million) of the words in English are not spelled phonetically. As a result, dictionaries must use one combination of symbols to show the spelling of a word, another to show its pronunciation. It is evident, therefore, that English is not one language, but two—a written one and a spoken one.

Professor Johnson gave his article the title, "Should the Spelling of English Be Streamlined?" It was published in September, 1948.

At noontime several English teachers ate lunch together, and we often talked about the problems of teaching English. A couple of months after the article by Professor Johnson appeared, a colleague brought it to the group and read it aloud to us. While we munched on our sandwiches, we chewed on the article. As I recall, all of us thought the estimate of 80 percent of our words not being spelled phonetically was absurdly high. Today, after many years of experience with students struggling with English, and ten years wrestling with the subject of this book, I confess I was wrong, and I am sure Professor Johnson was right.

If you will read this book with an open mind, I am convinced you will agree with me that the reason for the inordinate numbers of illiterates in this country isn't necessarily the method or the teacher or the child. In all probability it is the difficult language. Therefore, it is no wonder Johnny can't read.

CHAPTER 2

Why Do Dictionaries Show Pronunciations of All Words

A mother was complaining to me about her boy's inability to spell. She said he wouldn't sound out the words and he simply did not, or would not, listen carefully enough. I told her I sympathized with her and her son because they both had real problems. I said her problem was in not being able to comprehend her boy's problem. That puzzled her, and she asked me what I meant. Well, I said I'd try to clarify my statement. I asked her to pretend she was in the second grade and, as a child, to sound out the word "beauty." She promptly said, "/b/ /yoo/ /tē/."

She made the same mistake most adults do. We adults see our words after the fact, as it were. She was thinking of the sounds, not of the six letters in "beauty," each one of which is supposed to represent a sound. If the word were spelled "butee," children would have an infinitely better chance to sound it out, moving along letter by letter. As it is, the letters *e* and *a* are in the way and serve no phonetic function at all.

When she wanted another example, I asked her if the average child in the second grade, on the basis of the printed letters, could sound out her name. (It is *Virginia*.) She tentatively tried /vĭ/, /vĭr/ and shook her head and then continued, /jĭn/ /ĭ/ /ā/ (/ă/) and decided a child couldn't be expected to sound it out.

In just two or three minutes she was able to see her boy's problems in a different light. She asked me for more examples. I wrote down three difficult words:

    bouquet   bureau   bureaucracy

For a moment we went on a detour. She asked me if the correct pronunciation of "bouquet" is /bō kā′/ or /boo kā′/. I replied that dictionaries give both pronunciations and added that her question and my answer were further proof that many of our words cannot be sounded out.

Careful listening doesn't help us with a high percentage of our words. Certainly at least ten of the letters in the three words can't be sounded out!

For a minute or two I watched Virginia trying to sound the words out to herself, and then she suddenly protested, "But those are French words!" "Well," I answered, "Yes and no. To be sure, they came from French, but now they are English words. Are we going to say that our children and all who learn to read English don't have to learn the words we borrowed?" I then explained how English borrowed approximately three-fourths of all its words; and about a fourth of the words we use frequently came from French, and our forebears failed to naturalize many thousands of French, Latin, and Greek words English borrowed, too often leaving them with their original foreign spellings and too seldom translating them, which at one time could have been done by using basic native elements. I had selected the three words (and beauty and Virginia) for the very reason that they not only were borrowed, but they quickly and convincingly reveal one of the fundamental reasons for our unphonetic spelling: they do not follow the conventions of what ought to be regular English spelling. Thus, though the words might be spelled phonetically in their original languages, their spelling much too often is unphonetic *in English*.

Virginia wanted to know if there are some native words which can't be sounded out. I assured her there are great numbers of them, and when she wanted a half dozen, I quickly wrote down these nine words: *English, tongue, one, women, laugh, flood, business, ought,* and *dead*. Her first reaction was that those words would be easier to sound out than the "French" words. At home she had an excellent dictionary, the *American Heritage Dictionary,* and she said she would look up the respellings. Two days later, she called me. She had written down the respellings to show her husband; she had changed her mind completely and now understood her boy's problem. This is what she found and would have found in other quality dictionaries:

English	/ĭng′glĭsh/	tongue	/tŭng/	one	/wŭn/
women	/wĭm′ĭn/	laugh	/lăf/	flood	/flŭd/
business	/bĭz′nĭs/	ought	/ôt/	dead	/dĕd/

Actually the pronunciation of "women" was not shown in her dictionary, but she had found it in a friend's *Webster's New World Dictionary*. She had come to the conclusion that the nine English words were no easier to sound out than the five "foreign" words which I had given her.

It would be difficult, probably impossible, for you to rid yourself even temporarily of the images of the conventional spellings of these nine words, but if you were able to do so, you would see how easy it

Why Do Dictionaries Show Pronunciations of All Words?

would be for children to learn to read them (and all other words) if their phonetic respellings were their only spellings. Imagine now that you had never once seen the conventional spellings and that you had seen only the spellings as you see them here:

ingglish tung wunn wimmin laff fludd biznis ott dedd

No matter how odd they look, it becomes at once apparent that IF the words were spelled conventionally as they are now respelled, we could easily "sound them out" and read (and remember) them.

In the group of respelled words we find excellent correspondence between letters and sounds, and that is what phonetic spelling is. Isn't it curious: As the words are rewritten, they look as if an illiterate person had written them. That tells how bad our conventional spelling is. After you have read this book, I think you will agree with this statement:

CONVENTIONAL SPELLINGS HINDER MANY CHILDREN FROM LEARNING TO READ VAST NUMBERS OF ENGLISH WORDS

You will find that in huge numbers of words our spelling does not correspond to our sounds. That is the real reason why Johnny can't read and why millions of English-speaking people are illiterate.

Once we have learned how words are written and have read them perhaps forty or fifty times, we no longer pay any attention to the way sounds are spelled in known words. We are intent upon getting meaning, which is, after all, the goal of our reading. Our many years of reading and our conditioning are the reasons for the inability of most adult readers to see why it is hard to learn to read English.

We'll continue to add large numbers of illiterates to our vast army of them if we don't get nearly everybody to see and accept the real cause of failures. Constructive steps to reduce illiteracy must be based on facts.

Why are most people reluctant to admit they don't really have any idea what phonetic spelling is? In my efforts to see how much the average person-in-the-street knows about the subjects of this book, I have discussed them with many people, most of whom have come up to ask questions after I have spoken on the general topic or some specific phase. Not even a half dozen have said they don't know what phonetic spelling is. When I have asked if their first names are spelled phonetically—of course I have asked only those who should have said no—almost every one has considered the question for a moment and then answered yes. People must be made to realize that lack of knowledge of phonetics is not a disgrace. In fact, phonetic spelling isn't even defined well in our most-often used dictionaries, not even in five recent college edition dictionaries.

So what *is* phonetic spelling? It is the spelling of each identifiable sound one way (and only one way), and the using of each letter or combination of letters to represent only one sound. In any good recent college dictionary you will find between 120 thousand and 140 thousand examples of phonetic spelling. However, these phonetically spelled words are the *re*spellings which immediately follow conventional spellings. In other words, the respellings, which show how words are pronounced, are phonetic spellings. It follows, then, that words spelled the same way in conventional spellings and respellings are spelled phonetically. All other words are not. Here are a few words where spellings coincide:

bat boil chin drip livid met mount ship tent up

Now let's apply the definition to five names:

John   Rhoda   Pauline   Louise   Sarah

They are not spelled phonetically because of these irregularities:

Jo*h*n: The letter *h* performs no phonetic function.
R*h*oda: Again, the letter *h* tells the reader nothing. The *a* does not spell /ā/ or /ă/ and is, therefore, irregular.
Pa*u*line: Should the letter *o* or the combination of *a* plus *u* spell /ô/? (Compare "Polly.") In any case, the letter *i* does not represent /ī/ or /ĭ/; it spells /ē/, and we can't accept it. And what does the letter *e* spell?
L*ou*ise: The combination *ou* is supposed to spell the diphthong sounds /ou/, as in *out*; again we find the letter *i* spells /ē/; the letter *s* should spell /s/, but here it spells /z/; and the letter *e* spells nothing at all.
Sara*h*: The second letter *a* spells neither /ā/ nor /ă/; and the *h* again performs no phonetic function.

This is the criterion I assume my friends and acquaintances have used: they have asked themselves if people would be able to spell their names if they heard them. Since the answer is yes, their answer has also been yes. Because most people rarely hear and perhaps never use the term "phonetic spelling," it is not to be expected that they will know what it means. Here is an interesting illustration of what I am talking about, but in a place where one certainly would not expect to find it. In the "Education" section of *Time* (January 9, 1956, p. 54) a writer says, ". . . circumference can be spelled phonetically thousands of ways." Wow! That is a highly regrettable misuse of the word "phonetically."

Why Do Dictionaries Show Pronunciations of All Words?

What the writer meant was that by using all variations of spelling possibilities the word can be "spelled" in a great number of ways. Here are four possibilities, two boring and two fairly imaginative:

Simple:

ssercumference

sser (as in canva*sser*)

surrcumference

surr (as in *surr*ender)

Imaginative:

psorcomephorance

psor (as in *psor*iasis)
come (as in *come*)
phor (as in cam*phor*)

ance (as in dist*ance*)

cir–
–cum–
–fer–

–ence–

swercomffarants

swer (as in an*swer*)
com (as in *com*fort)
ff (as in di*ff*er)
ar (as in marg*ar*ine)
ants (as in inf*ants*)

While such toying with our language may be diverting, if we stop to consider the matter earnestly, we readily understand why there are so many millions of poor spellers in the English-speaking world. Concomitantly it explains why so many beginners fail to learn to read. In any event, the word "circumference" cannot be spelled *phonetically* thousands of ways, not even a half dozen ways! Since it may be pronounced in either of two ways, with three syllables or four, it can be spelled phonetically two ways also, but only two ways, one if you pronounce it in three syllables, and one if you pronounce it in four: /sər kŭm′ frəns/ and /sər kŭm′ fər əns/. (The symbol /ə/ will be explained in the next chapter.)

How can I be positive of my phonetic spelling of the word? In my five college dictionaries the word is respelled as I gave it above, and the respellings are the same in all five dictionaries.

Alphabetic writing was conceived and developed so that each symbol would stand for a sound regularly and consistently. Phonetic spelling follows that principle.

It is only natural for us to believe that most of our words are spelled phonetically because they should be. Who among lay persons would dispute the claim that six-sevenths of all English words are spelled regularly, that is, phonetically? Thus, in 1955, when Rudolf Flesch in *Why Johnny Can't Read* asserted that three or four researchers working independently had made counts of all the words in the English language to ascertain how many of our words are spelled phonetically, readers accepted as gospel truth the conclusion that only "about 13 percent of all English words are partly irregular in their spelling." (p. 13)

Generally accepted, universally known facts require no references.

We know, for instance, that the sun rises in the east; we know that hot air rises; we know that ice is cold to the touch. But we do NOT know that 87 percent of our words are spelled phonetically; and if someone asserts that three or four researchers working independently have come to such a conclusion, then the writer owes it to his readers to give them sources in order that they may learn who the researchers were, what their credentials were, what criteria they used, how they made their counts, and the like. That one qualified researcher would come up with such an absurd figure would be hard to believe; but that four or even three researchers would arrive at the same ridiculous result boggles the mind. We must get out our salt shaker for our grain of salt. As you read Chapter Three, please keep in mind the figure of 13 percent of irregularly spelled words. You might also remember Professor Johnson's estimate of 80 percent.

Naturally, I fully realize how reluctant we are to believe that our symbols representing our sounds are badly flawed and defective; and we are likely to go on the defensive when we are given the unwelcome information.

Please let me establish once and for all this important point: The majority, probably the great majority, of the *letters* on any given page of print will spell correctly the sounds they are designated to spell, and this fact leads us to the false assumption that as many as 87 percent of all our *words* are spelled phonetically. We can see how this operates with twelve additional names:

| Helen | Dorothy | Margaret | Laura | Susan | Karen |
| Thomas | Timothy | Richard | William | Kenneth | Michael |

At first glance some of the names seem to be spelled phonetically; and adults bearing them have heard, spoken, seen, and written them so often that to them they certainly seem to be spelled phonetically. Well, about 70 percent of the letters spell sounds phonetically; but not one of the names, as we'll see later, is spelled phonetically.

I spent some thirty to forty hours counting the words that are spelled phonetically on 20 pages each of five dictionaries, a total of 100 pages, and then I suddenly realized that if I were to give my results, it would appear as if I were trying to set myself up as some kind of authority, which I am not. I can make the point more convincingly, I believe, by telling you of the many languages whose dictionaries do not need to respell all or most of their words to tell how their words are pronounced. If only 13 percent of our words are not spelled phonetically, is it not a gigantic waste of money, labor, paper, ink, and space to give unnecessary respellings for the remaining 87 percent of our words?

Why Do Dictionaries Show Pronunciations of All Words?

This information is significant. Axel Wijk, a Swedish scholar and English expert, notes in his *Rules of Pronunciation of the English Language,* "Such information (showing pronunciation) is not normally considered necessary in dictionaries for other European languages, for example, for French, Italian, Spanish, German, Dutch, Danish, Swedish, Russian, Polish, Finnish, Hungarian, etc." (p. 7) On the same page he tells why English dictionaries do give pronunciations: "It is a generally recognized fact that the English language presents far greater difficulties (because of) the fact that the confused and irregular spelling of the language offers such poor guidance as to its pronunciation."

Here are the words of an American scholar, Stuart Robertson, whose book, *The Development of Modern English,* has been widely used in advanced college English classes. He wrote:

> We possess a language that appears, on the printed page, in a form so different from the way in which it is spoken that the only adequate way for the dictionary to indicate the pronunciation of Modern English words is to respell them in a phonetic alphabet. (p. 274)

Professor Frederick G. Cassidy revised Robertson's book, but he left the quotation unchanged. (p. 335)

If you will make a count on ten to twenty pages in a dictionary of words for which (a) no phonetic respelling is necessary, and (b) phonetic respelling is needed, you will have your own thoughts about someone who says 87 percent of our words are spelled phonetically.

We owe it to all English-speaking children, their teachers, and their parents to make known the truth about our written symbols.

CHAPTER 3

The Awful Written English Language

FIVE FATEFUL FLAWS

These are five basic reasons why Johnny can't read:

REASON #1. A major flaw in written English is the lack of enough vowel symbols (letters) to spell (represent) all of the vowel sounds. We have only five vowel letters with which to spell nineteen sounds! (The letter *y* when used as a vowel merely duplicates the spelling of other letters.) To be sure, when we accept the spelling of both "long" and "short" sounds by each of the five letters, we have taken care of ten of the sounds. But that still leaves nine, or 47 percent, of our vowel sounds with no designated symbols to represent them. That is highly illogical, because each sound should be represented by its own letter.

People who don't know better would assume the two dots (the umlaut) over the German vowel letters *a, o,* and *u (ä, ö, ü)* make that language more difficult for German-speaking children to learn. Quite the contrary. Those letters with the umlaut spell six of German's 17 vowel sounds, three "long" and three "short," and they do it fairly consistently and regularly. English would be much easier if similar symbols had been developed and were used to spell the sounds for which we have no symbols.

Table 1 shows what we are talking about:

Table 1

Symbols Used by a Majority of Recent College Edition
Dictionaries to Show the Pronunciation of Vowels

SYMBOL	KEY WORDS	SYMBOL	KEY WORDS
ă	g*a*p, *a*dd	ā	p*a*per, f*a*ble, m*a*de, m*ai*d, g*ay*
ä	f*a*ther, st*a*r	â	c*a*re, ch*ai*r, th*e*re
ĕ	*e*nd, t*e*n	ē	w*e*, s*ea*t, happ*y*

The Awful Written English Language

Symbol	Key Words	Symbol	Key Words
ĭ	it, big, lift	ī	bite, by, buy
ŏ	odd, hot	ō	no, toast, low
ô	all, saw, bought, caught	o͞o	tool, rule, to, you
o͝o	took, pull, wolf, could	yo͞o	use, few
ŭ	pup, wonder, couple	û	term, firm, worm, burn, learn
yo͝o	fury, Europe	ə	ago, agent, clarity, melon, circus, ethyl
ər	liar, waiter, elixir, author, sulphur, zephyr		

Diphthongs

oi	oil, joy	ou	out, cow

Here are some of the ways three of those vowel sounds for which we have no designated symbol are spelled in English, and we'll also see a few of the ways a consonant sound which has no exclusive symbol is spelled.

A. We'll begin with *the most frequently heard vowel sound in the English language.* If you say in a natural way the words "banana" and "Alabama," you will hear that the letter *a* spells (represents) two different sounds, /ă/ in the three stressed (accented) syllables, and an indistinct, vague, obscure sound in the four unstressed syllables. The sound we are talking about is heard only in unstressed syllables; its phonetic symbol is /ə/.

The name of this neutral, colorless sound is "schwa" (/shwä/—/ä/ as in father), and it came into English from Hebrew by way of German. To my knowledge no widely used dictionary* before World War II used the symbol to show the pronunciation of the most often heard sound in our language! And yet it is not something that recently sneaked into English as a result of slovenly speech habits. According to language experts, it was heard in Britain long before Columbus discovered America. Professor Albert H. Marckwardt in his *Introduction to the English Language* tells how the schwa has been in English since about the eleventh century. (p. 284)

About 150 years ago, Horace Mann examined all words beginning with the letter *a* in his *Worcester Dictionary* and found that almost half of the 3,000 words, when spoken, began with the schwa sound, as they do today. (My count in a recent dictionary indicated 47 percent.) We hear it, for example, in *a*back, *a*bandon, *a*bate, *a*bbreviate, etc.

*The huge (23-volume) *New English Dictionary,* commonly known as the *Oxford English Dictionary,* has employed the schwa symbol ever since the first volume, 1888, but has used it very sparingly, e.g., in words ending in *-tion* as in *action.*

Beginning, as I recall, with the *American College Dictionary* in 1947, dictionaries have been using in their phonetic respelling of words a special symbol to designate the sound, an inverted *e*, /ə/. Now all standard dictionaries use it. Thus, you will find these pronunciation respellings: /ə băk′/, /ə băn′ dən/, /ə bāt′/, and /ə brē′ vē āt/. Banana and Alabama are shown as /bə năn′ ə/ and /ăl ə băm′ ə/.

Unfortunately, we don't always spell the sound with the letter *a*. We have fifteen common ways to spell it, and, all told, more than thirty different ways! You will read more about the spellings in a later chapter. But it is self-evident that *a, e,* and *i* spell the schwa sound in these words:

dist*a*nce	/dĭs′ təns/	compl*e*ment	/kŏm′ plə mənt/
insist*e*nce	/ĭn sĭs′ təns/	compl*i*ment	/kŏm′ plə mənt/

Here are sample words in which the six vowel letters, including *y*, spell the schwa sound:

a: *a*lone, Chin*a; e*: m*e*tallic, statem*e*nt; *i*: san*i*ty, eas*i*ly; *o*: c*o*mmence, butt*o*n; *u*: s*u*bmit, walr*u*s; *y*: ph*y*sician, meth*y*l

Now prepare yourself for a real shock: In view of the fact that we do not have a special symbol, no special letter, to spell the sound in conventional writing, *every written word in which the schwa sound is heard when spoken is spelled unphonetically.*

If you will refer to any good recent dictionary, you will find confirmation of what I am about to say. But make sure it is a recent dictionary. The *Merriam-Webster* Unabridged didn't begin to use the schwa symbol until the Third Edition (1961); and not until the Seventh Edition of the *Collegiate* (1963) was it used there. This is what you will find in any good recent dictionary: The schwa sound is heard at least once in a big majority of our words of two or more syllables; it is heard twice in many thousands of words, as in *A*lask*a*, *a*musem*e*nt, *a*partm*e*nt, m*a*j*o*rity, princip*a*l, tel*e*visi*o*n, etc.; and it is heard in at least several hundred words three times, as in *a*cc*o*mm*o*dati*o*n, *a*ss*a*ssinati*o*n, categ*o*ric*a*l, c*o*mmissi*o*n*e*r, c*o*nditi*o*n*a*l, and c*u*rric*u*l*u*m.

We adults see in the schwa a major spelling problem, but children learning to read find it a major reading problem because words in which the one sound is spelled so many ways simply CANNOT BE SOUNDED OUT.

Already we see how utterly false and absurd the statements are which I quoted from the Associated Press series of articles. Here they are again:

1. "In English there are very few irregular words for which the rules don't apply."

The Awful Written English Language

2. "English has (only) a few easy-to-learn irregularities."
3. "Children learn to read words . . . by the way they SOUND."

As I said, the series was sold to, and appeared in, nearly 300 newspapers. Readers must have believed what they read, for that is what they wanted to believe. Pity the reading teachers, the parents, and especially the slower beginners.

The schwa sound is spoken in other Germanic languages. In fact, it is heard more often on a relative basis in German than in English. But in German it is spelled *just one way;* the letter *e* spells it.

B. A second vowel sound for which English writing has no designated symbol is heard in the words "h*ea*rd," "w*o*rd," and "c*u*rrent." Most current dictionaries use the symbol /û/ in phonetic respelling to show pronunciation. Here is a sentence put together in which nine different spellings stand for the one sound:

H*e*rb   h*ea*rd   dist*u*rbed   n*u*rse   M*y*rtle's
f*i*rst   t*e*rse   w*o*rd: "C*ou*rage."

In phonetic respelling we find these transcriptions:

/hûrb/ /hûrd/ /dĭs tûrbd′/ /nûrs/ /mûr′ təlz/
/fûrst/ /tûrs/ /wûrd/ /kûr′ ĭj/

The /û/ sound is spoken much less frequently than the obscure schwa sound, but it is heard in at least a thousand words, and, regrettably, the various spellings of the sound cannot be postponed for long in the reading procedure because a number of words in which it is heard are needed early, e.g., h*e*r, g*i*rl, l*ea*rn, *ea*rly, h*ea*rd, f*i*rst, w*o*rd, w*o*rk, b*i*rd, d*i*rt, sh*i*rt, sk*i*rt, h*u*rt, b*u*rn, t*u*rn, etc.

You will see how it is impossible to tell learners which vowel spells the sound when you see the following words. Read along:

e	*ea*	*i*	*o*	*ou*	*u*	*y*
b*e*rth	*ea*rth	b*i*rth	w*o*rth			
f*e*rn	*ea*rn			adj*ou*rn	t*u*rn	
h*e*rd	h*ea*rd	b*i*rd	w*o*rd		c*u*rd	B*y*rd
p*e*rch	s*ea*rch	b*i*rch			ch*u*rch	
r*e*versed	reh*ea*rsed	th*i*rst	w*o*rst		b*u*rst	

Our /û/ sound is spelled sixteen ways, seven of which are common spellings. It is clear that no word in which the sound is uttered can be spelled phonetically; and just as with all words containing the schwa sound, each word must be learned and memorized. Unfortunately, we cannot establish a rule and tell our children that when they see the letter *r* following any vowel letter the latter represents the /û/ sound. Just look at these words:

Presumed Rule	Does Not Apply	Presumed Rule	Does Not Apply
earn	ear, pear	heard	swear, rear
her	heresy, heredity	word	cord, ford
work	cork, fork	worm	form, norm

In addition, the following words and the ones they represent do not fit into the pattern either: there; merit, very; fire, virile, miracle, spirit; forest, moral, sorry; cure, during, sure, etc.

German does not have the identical sound; but as a basis for comparison, the closest German sound is spelled in just two ways.

C. A third vowel sound for which we have no designated letter seems to have two accepted symbols. It is the /oo/ sound heard in food and truth. But the double o combination is not reserved to spell the one sound exclusively, for we find it spells /ō/ in brooch, /oŏ/ in foot, /ŭ/ in blood, and /ô/ or /ō/ in door. Nor is the letter u reserved to spell just that one sound. In fact, it spells a total of ten sounds, as you will see in a later chapter. In reality, there are more than thirty ways to spell the /oo/ sound, of which twelve are fairly common. You have seen two, and here are ten more: chew, do, glue, group, rude, shoe, sleuth, suit, through, and two.

In comparison with our twelve common ways to spell the /oo/ sound, we find that German has three ways.

D. The spellings of consonant sounds are more regular than those of the vowels, but they are less regular than most people think. Later you will find two chapters dealing with their spellings. Here we'll consider the consonant sound with the most spellings. English has seven consonant sounds for which no single letter symbols were set aside or developed. In order to spell those sounds, we are obliged to use combinations of consonant letters, called consonant digraphs, or to use combinations of a consonant letter and a vowel letter. (This strange spelling will be explained later.) Would you care to guess which one sound all of these letters spell: *c, ce, ch, ci, s, t,* and *ti?* If I add *sh, ss,* and *ssi,* the answer is given; they all spell /sh/, and only one spelling can be, and is, a phonetic spelling. Dictionaries all use the /sh/ spelling and that is the accepted spelling for the sound. Thus, in the following words the sound is not spelled phonetically: oceanic, ocean, chef, special, insurance, fissure, Russia, satiate, caution, etc.

We have some eighteen fairly common ways to spell the sound and ten less common ways, a total of twenty-eight, all of which will be exemplified later. In contrast to our eighteen common ways, German has only three to spell the /sh/ sound.

You have seen in brief outline how we have forty-six common ways to spell just four of our forty-four sounds. If we compare the spellings

The Awful Written English Language

of the three sounds that are heard both in English and in German, we find that English has thirty-nine common ways to spell them and German has only seven common ways. That means English has 5.5 times as many as German; and there we have one of the major reasons why so many of all English-speaking children find it difficult, even impossible, to learn to read.

REASON #2. Each of our vowel letters spells too many sounds, and more than half of the spellings are irrational. Under Reason #1 your mind was in control and you were able to examine objectively how four sounds are spelled so many ways, and you were able to accept the information rather easily. However, when we reverse the procedure and explore the sounds our letters represent, you will find you are facing a formidable task. Unless you are a great exception, you will find that Hume was correct: habit molds our thinking more than analysis does. You have read thousands of words hundreds—and many of them thousands—of times and, as a result, you have become so conditioned to the spellings that in your thinking they should and must be spelled as they are. In short, they have become a part of your life, part of your daily habits. It will truly be difficult for you to see the many irregularities and especially to see them as abnormalities.

Having said that, I request you again to try to see the spelling problems through the eyes of a poor learner, say, Ichabod, who has considerably less than average ability. But he is not so incapable that he would not be able to learn to read all words in which each symbol (letter) represents one sound, as in Finnish. Indeed, when a letter spells only two sounds (as is generally true of the vowel letters in other Germanic languages), he will master them quite readily because half of them are easy; they spell their names: *a* in b*a*ker, *e* in sh*e*, *i* in *i*dea, *o* in g*o*, and *u* in m*u*sic. Perhaps Ichabod could learn the sounds the vowels spell if, say, they spelled an average of three sounds each. But our six vowel letters, including *y*, spell an average of TEN sounds each!

Here are some of the sounds spelled by *a*, *e*, *i*, and *o:*

(a) The letter *a* spells twelve sounds. We think first of /ā/ in r*a*zor, /ă/ in h*a*nd, and /ə/ in *a*bout. And then come three spellings which seem to be perfectly normal; we have lived with them all our lives: /ä/ in f*a*r, /â/ in b*a*re, and /ô/ in *a*ll. You now read words containing these sounds spelled by the letter *a* just as easily and quickly as you do the spelling of the "long" and the "short" sounds. But Ichabod doesn't and can't. Even the modified definition of phonetic spelling is that each vowel letter may spell two sounds; therefore, four of the six spellings used so far are irregular, that is, unphonetic, and for that reason are much harder to learn.

The letter *a* also spells these two sounds: /ĕ/ in quite a few words, such as *a*nybody, custom*a*ry, diction*a*ry, m*a*ny, m*a*rshmallow, station*a*ry, etc. (No wonder we have trouble spelling station*a*ry and station*e*ry correctly.) The letter *a* also spells /ī/ (or *a-e* does) in many words. We hear it distinctly in D*e*nnis the Men*ace* and in cabb*age*, im*age*, watt*age*, neckl*ace*, and priv*ate*. It also spells /ər/ in begg*a*r; /ŏ/ in w*a*tch; /ŭ/ in unstressed w*a*s, th*a*t, etc.; and /ē/ in Isr*a*el.

In Chapter 5 you will see how the letter *a* alone and in combination with other letters spells sixteen (!) of our nineteen vowel sounds in 114 ways! More than half of the spellings are common ones that we see often.

(b) The letter *e* spells nine sounds, including /ē/ in m*e* and /ĕ/ in d*e*n. But the big surprise is that it spells /ĭ/ in thousands of words! You hear it, of course, in *E*ngland and *E*nglish. It is fairly easy to detect in pr*e*tty and coll*e*ge, but since the subject is so important, it will be necessary to devote a chapter to it. There you will find that I simply report what you will find in the dictionary. The letter *e* also spells different sounds in many other words: /ā/ in caf*e* and su*e*de; /ä/ in several recent borrowings from French, e.g., *e*ntree and *e*nsemble; /â/ in th*e*re and wh*e*re; /û/, as you have seen, e.g., in cl*e*rk and p*e*rson; and /ə/, as you have also seen, in heav*e*n and it*e*m. Of course we must add /ər/ because it is found in many words, as in mast*e*r.

(c) The letter *i* spells /ī/ in *i*dentify and /ĭ/ in d*i*d. As we discussed earlier, it also spells /û/, as in s*i*r and c*i*rcle and /ə/, as in intell*i*gent and per*i*l. That is four representations. In addition, it spells /ē/ in vast numbers of words, as in am*i*able, id*i*om, magaz*i*ne, mart*i*ni, obed*i*ent, or*i*ent, and sk*i*. It also spells /y/, as we can plainly hear in begon*i*a, on*i*on, opin*i*on, sen*i*or, etc. Does it spell /ă/ or /ä/ in l*i*ngerie and *i*ngenue? Finally, add /ər/, as in elix*i*r.

(d) The letter *o* represents ten sounds. We are acquainted with four: /ō/ in *o*ld, /ŏ/ in s*o*ften, /ə/ in c*o*nfirm, and /û/ in w*o*rse. We quickly recognize these additional spellings: /o͞o/ in wh*o*; /ô/ in n*o*rth; /o͝o/ in w*o*man; /ĭ/ in w*o*men; /ər/ in mot*o*r; and /ŭ/ in s*o*n. This latter spelling is so bizarre that its development is described in Chapter 8. To be sure, this phenomenon is found in fewer than 300 words, but, regrettably, most of them have to be learned early in the reading program because the spelling is found in words of high frequency. Here are a few samples:

| br*o*ther | c*o*mpany | d*o*ve | fr*o*nt | M*o*nday | m*o*ney |
| m*o*nth | m*o*ther | n*o*thing | *o*ne | *o*ther | st*o*mach |

Think also of L*o*ndon. Isn't English w*u*nderful—sorry, w*o*nderful?

In examples you have seen how four vowel letters spell forty sounds; surely thirty-five of the spellings are found in essential words. When I say the four letters spell forty sounds, you might rightly protest and

The Awful Written English Language 25

say we don't have that many vowel sounds. Exactly. There is horrible overlapping of spelling, which compounds learning difficulties enormously. For instance, children have to learn the spelling of twelve sounds by the letter *a*, but they must also learn that the letter *e* spells nine of those same sounds, that the letter *i* spells six of the sounds the letter *a* spells, and six which the letter *o* spells, and so forth. This irrational overlapping is without any doubt one of our major problems in learning to read.

In German, the same four letters spell not more than ten sounds in words which children learn to read in their first four or five years of school, and overlapping of spelling by those same four letters is virtually nonexistent. If we subtract in both languages the easy spellings, that is, those in which the letters "say their names" (the "long" sounds), we find that English-speaking children have to learn thirty-one common hard spellings for the four letters; in contrast, German-speaking children have to learn not more than five or six.

REASON #3. An ambush to which we trained readers pay little attention but which must contribute materially to the cause of the failure of many children is our considerable use of combinations of two vowel letters to spell a single vowel sound. We have seen and written many of the combinations so frequently that they have become second nature to us. And yet they have to be extremely difficult to master. Here are three samples which spell six sounds: *ai* /ā/ in *ai*d, /ĕ/ in ag*ai*n; *ey* /ā/ in th*ey,* /ē/ in vall*ey; ei* /â/ in h*ei*r, /ĭ/ in w*ei*rd. We call such combinations vowel digraphs, and we find that they spell sounds in even more ways than our single vowel letters do. In the first place, there are so many more of them, more than 50 (!); and whereas our single vowel letters spell sounds in an unreasonably high number of ways, 60, our 50 (plus) digraphs spell sounds in 3 × 60, or 180 ways!

Vowel digraphs do *not* fill a phonetic spelling need; they do not fill a single gap; they do not spell any sound that single vowel letters alone cannot and do not spell. Phonetically, they merely duplicate, unnecessarily, the work of our single vowel letters. The subject is of vital importance and will be treated more fully later. There you may read how I counted the vowel combinations in several places, including the front page of a copy of the *New York Times*. On the one page I found a total of 442 digraphs; so you see we are dealing with a very real problem, an inordinate number of spellings of sounds which our children must master if they are going to become readers. There were 29 different digraph spellings among the 442 digraphs, and they spelled sounds 57 ways. These additional samples will indicate what children must learn:

Sounds	Digraphs in Words	Sounds	Digraphs in Words
/ā/	matin*ee*, v*ei*n	/ē/	c*ei*ling, ch*ie*f
/ĭ/	forf*ei*t, bu*i*ld	/ĕ/	h*ea*d, g*ue*st

You cannot readily see the troubles youngsters have learning digraph spellings. They appear to be so easy—and are to us. Ichabod tries to read, "Their friends ate a hearty and nourishing breakfast" and has good and obvious cause for tears. Indeed, digraphs are a source of tears for great numbers of children learning to read.

Not counting the three duplications, among the fifty-four words in the preceding paragraph there are twenty-two digraphs spelling sounds eighteen ways. Two of the most active ones, *ea* and *ou* jointly spell sounds in twelve different ways in those four sentences. You, as an accomplished reader, take digraphs in stride because you have over-learned most of the spellings. If you are not a genius, it took you quite some time to master them, and there really are many of them on any printed page of your newspaper, magazine, or book. You will see just how easy they are for you if you count all of them on the front page of your newspaper. Unless you are a trained proofreader, you probably will miss many on the first reading and even a few on the second.

My extensive research indicates that in English nineteen of our more than fifty digraphs are used very often, and they spell sounds fifty-one ways. I have also counted digraph spellings on fifty pages of German prose and found confirmation of what I had already known: German doesn't have half as many digraphs as English and uses only eight of them extensively, three of which are simply doubled letters, *aa, ee, oo*. Of equal, probably more, importance is the fact that each of the eight digraphs in German spells *only one sound*. But in English, each of the two digraphs named above, *ea* and *ou,* spells eight sounds!

It is necessary to touch lightly on a minor problem. Just when average learners begin to feel comfortable with vowel digraphs, a new element arises. They know *read, reed, reap,* and *hygiene*. Then suddenly the combinations no longer serve as digraphs to spell a single sound; both letters have phonetic value. Compare:

r*ea*d	r*ea*djust	r*ee*d	r*ee*ducate
r*ea*p	r*ea*ppear	hyg*ie*ne	hyg*ie*nic

REASON #4. A major obstacle along the rocky path leading to learning to read is the lack of a rule telling our learners when a vowel letter represents a "long" or a "short" sound. Unfortunately, then, we cannot teach our beginners that a vowel letter spells a "long" sound when it is followed by a single consonant, for it would be misleading. In several Germanic languages this is a basic and fairly reliable rule. It certainly is not true in most of our short three and four letter words, e.g., *bag, bed, hip, lot, but; that, them, this, stop, shut,* etc.

If in words of two or more syllables our writing (spelling)

The Awful Written English Language

followed the rule, children could simply apply it. Take these sample words. Do the letters in italics represent "long" or "short" sounds:

appar*a*tus   *a*pricot   f*e*tid   f*e*tish   g*a*la
l*e*ver   long-l*i*ved   p*a*tently   pl*a*cate   pr*e*sentation
r*a*tion   s*a*dist   s*i*necure   s*o*lstice.

Good current dictionaries show both "long" and "short" sounds for all of them. We often learn one "correct" pronunciation of a word and then become confused, sometimes irritated, when we discover a second one is just as "correct." If we had a rule, soon one pronunciation would be standard. Our brains, our memories, and our ears are not at fault; it's our language.

If we had the rule, we couldn't have such dual pronunciations or such possibilities as we find in these sample words. Read along:

"Short"	"Long"	"Short"	"Long"
n*a*tional	n*a*tion	n*a*tural	n*a*ture
ten*a*city	ten*a*cious	r*a*venous	r*a*ven
*a*vid	D*a*vid	c*a*vern	c*a*ve
s*a*tin	S*a*tan	s*a*livate	s*a*lient
d*e*vil	*e*vil	*e*ver	f*e*ver
l*e*gend	l*e*gal	s*e*ven	*e*ven
r*e*gimen	r*e*gal	r*e*gicide	r*e*gent
diab*e*tic	diab*e*tes	arthr*i*tic	arthr*i*tis
forg*i*ving	str*i*ving	l*i*ver	d*i*ver
s*i*lica	s*i*lent	s*i*mulate	s*i*multaneous
s*o*litary	s*o*ber	S*o*lomon	s*o*lo

A few years ago I started to make a list of words in which a vowel letter spells a "short" sound when followed by a single consonant. There was no challenge, especially when I turned to a dictionary and merely copied a whole lot of words. I soon stopped because I had twelve hundred well-known words on the list. Here are additional samples in which the sound would be "long" if we had a reliable rule:

a	*e*	*i*	*o*	*u*
b*a*lance	bl*e*mish	b*i*gamy	b*o*tany	b*u*gaboo
b*a*nish	ch*e*mistry	ch*i*sel	m*o*dify	p*u*nish
c*a*rol	cl*e*ver	cont*i*nue	dep*o*sit	d*u*cat

When two or more consonants follow a vowel, the sound spelled by the vowel—Praise the Lord—is usually short. I take delight in reporting one pleasant fact. We don't need a large number of examples because we can find them everywhere: Ch*a*tter, l*e*tter, l*i*tter, *o*tter, b*u*tter; *a*nd, s*e*nd, t*i*mber, b*o*nd, b*u*ndle. It is too bad this happy situation is marred by great numbers of exceptions. Here is a generous baker's dozen of samples:

*a*ncient	c*a*ble	c*o*bra	d*u*plicate	c*o*ld	fl*a*grant	j*o*lt
l*i*brary	m*i*nd	*o*nly	p*u*trid	r*o*ll	v*a*grant	y*o*lk

Probably these additional examples will be a more effective way to demonstrate what children have to learn. Here we have a number of word pairs where the vowel is "short" in some words and "long" in others, even though two consonants follow. Read along:

"Short"	"Long"	"Short"	"Long"
*a*nger	d*a*nger	c*a*ste	b*a*ste
ch*a*stize	ch*a*sten	fl*a*nge	str*a*nge
s*a*crifice	s*a*cred	ch*i*ldren	ch*i*ld
Chr*i*stmas	Chr*i*st	k*i*ndred	k*i*nd
m*i*ldew	m*i*ld	l*i*nt	p*i*nt
w*i*lderness	w*i*ld	w*i*nd	w*i*nd
b*o*ther	b*o*th	h*o*stage	h*o*st
p*o*llen	sw*o*llen	r*o*ster	p*o*ster

If we do justice to the subject of "long" or "short" sounds and if we are fair to our learners, we must remember the vowel sounds which are neither "long" nor "short," and they are found in thousands of words. Here are a few samples in the second, third, and fourth columns. Read along:

/ă/	/ô/, /ŏ/	/ä/	/ô/
r*a*nt	w*a*nt	b*a*rn	w*a*rn
b*a*ffle	w*a*ffle	c*a*rd	w*a*rd
c*a*mp	sw*a*mp	ch*a*rm	w*a*rm
g*a*sh	w*a*sh	m*a*rble	w*a*rble
c*a*tch	w*a*tch	sh*a*rp	w*a*rp
gr*a*sp	w*a*sp	/ŭ/	/o͞o/
sh*a*ll	h*a*ll	br*u*sh	b*u*sh
inf*a*llible	f*a*ll	p*u*tter	p*u*tter

REASON #5. There is another major flaw in English: We have no set location where the stress (accent) falls on our words, and we have few meaningful rules to tell us where it belongs. Who can name two or three? Or just one? It would make considerably less difference if our heavy stress didn't exert such a dominant influence on vowel sounds in syllables preceding and/or following the stress, where, as a result, we generally hear the schwa sound. It would be a great help to readers if the spelling changed along with the sound(s). With a small number of words the spelling does follow the sound. Compare pron*ou*nce and pron*u*nciation. But as a general rule this does not follow, and since we have no special symbol to represent the schwa sound, our slower learners are in trouble.

This is what I mean. We say *Canada* /kăn′ə də/ and we say *Canadian* /kə nā′ dē ən/. Note what happens to the first two vowel sounds. To us, who have heard the sounds and seen the letters they spell all of our adult lives, nothing could be more natural. To learners, at least to would-be learners of Ichabod's ability, nothing could be more unnatural. In *Canada* the first *a* represents /ă/ and the second represents /ə/, but in *Canadian* the sounds are different; the first *a* now spells /ə/ and the second spells /ā/. This is frustrating to learners because it is irrational.

How fortunate it is for the Ichabods in Finland and Hungary, where words are stressed on the first syllable and no schwa sound ever follows the stress. But learners speaking Germanic languages other than English are also fortunate because even when there is a shift in stress on related words, the sounds remain essentially unchanged. We'll use as examples the words *monotone* and *monotonous* and their German counterparts, which, like our words, were also borrowed from Latin. But see how easy it is for children learning to read German:

English		German	
monotone	/mŏn′ə tōn/	monoton	/mō nō tōn′/
monotony	/mə nŏ′tə nē/	Monotonie*	/mō nō tō nē′/

As you can see, English has three sound changes; German has none.

In accordance with my statement that I'd keep the emphasis on English, I'll merely tell you that German's *Horizont* and *horizontal* maintain the same three vowel sounds. But we don't hear the relationship between *horizon* and *horizontal* and for that reason do not connect the idea that horizontal means parallel to the horizon. Note the three vowel changes:

horizon	/hə rī′ zən/	/ə/	/ī/	/ə/
horizontal	/hô rə zŏn′ təl/	/ô/	/ə/	/ŏ/

There are great numbers of pairs of words in which the spelling remains unchanged but two sounds are different, as in the following samples:

*The German digraph *ie* always spells /ē/.

*a*ppendix	*a*ppendectomy	/ə/, /ĕ/; /ă/, /ə/
*a*pply	*a*pplication	/ə/, /ī/; /ă/, /ə/
comb*i*ne	comb*i*nation	/ə/, /ī/; /ŏ/, /ə/
c*o*nsole	c*o*nsolation	/ə/, /ō/; /ŏ/, /ə/
med*i*cine	med*i*cinal	/ĕ/, /ə/; /ə/, /ĭ/
p*a*c*i*fic	p*a*c*i*fist	/ə/, /ī/; /ă/, /ə/

There aren't great numbers of related words in which three different sounds are heard and in which the spelling remains constant when there is a shift in stress, but in a later chapter I'll offer twenty pairs. You have seen two and here are three more:

*a*n*a*lysis	/ə năl′ ə sĭs/	/ə/ /ă/ /ə/
*a*n*a*lyst	/ăn′ ə lĭst/	/ă/ /ə/ /ĭ/
c*a*t*a*strophe	/kə tăs′ trə fē/	/ə/ /ă/ /ə/
c*a*t*a*strophic	/kăt′ ə strŏ′fĭk/	/ă/ /ə/ /ŏ/
p*a*r*a*lyze	/pă′ rə līz/	/ă/ /ə/ /ī/
p*a*r*a*lysis	/pə răl′ ə sĭs/	/ə/ /ă/ /ə/

Because of the state of affairs which I have been describing, all readers of English are able to recognize more words than they can pronounce. I can recall five words whose pronunciations were hard for me to learn, in part because I hadn't heard them often enough and in part because I had not yet acquired the dictionary habit. These are the words:

anathema   atavistic   cacophony   clandestine   respite

We rarely hear *clandestine*, but when we do, we probably hear a mispronunciation more often than the correct one. I well remember how I used the word *respite* in class in my third or fourth year of teaching. I made it rhyme with *despite*. After class, a number of students—I can even remember the names of three of them—rushed up to tell me that the correct pronunciation is /rĕs′ pĭt/.

A daughter volunteered a word she had mislearned, *hyperbole*. She had thought, as you probably have guessed, that it is /hī′ pər bōl/ until she heard it pronounced /hī pûr′ bə lē/. She was glad that she hadn't ever tried to use the word. (Of course if she had, many listeners would probably have thought her pronunciation was correct.) We are all reluctant to use in speech a number of words which we know from reading but not from sound. In a language whose words are spelled phonetically that problem does not arise.

The Awful Written English Language

Surely some of the six words given above have been mispronounced millions of times in the last ten years. And they will undoubtedly be mispronounced millions of times in the next ten years.

As I said before, this subject, the location of the stress and the distressing effects it has on our learners, will be taken up in more detail later. Meanwhile, however, I should like to share with you the experience of a boy, Loren. His grandfather was in an accident and became an invalid. Loren learned to say and read the word /ĭn′ və lĭd/. Then he saw the word stamped on his grandfather's driver's license. He read the word there and said, /ĭn′ və lĭd/ and wondered why everybody laughed. We automatically think /ĭn văl′ ĭd/ in that situation. We have good memories, haven't we?

The location of the stress is important because learners can read words many times and still not know how they are pronounced. This is by no means an original thought. I have read it repeatedly. For instance, in 1905 Otto Jespersen, a great Danish philologist and authority on the English language wrote, "If we know the sounds of a word (in English) we can't know how to spell it; if we know the spelling, we can't know how to pronounce it." *Essentials of English Grammar* (p. 11)

* * *

Because hundreds of thousands of our words are not spelled phonetically the title of this chapter is richly deserved:

/thə/   /ôf′ əl/   /rĭt′ ən/   /ĭng′ glĭsh/   /lăng′ gwĭj/

CHAPTER 4

The Cards Are Stacked against Johnny

A computer study of 17,310 commonly used English words, which was made at Stanford University, revealed how truly wretched the spelling of English is. The words were not chosen for their irregularities; the sole criterion was frequency of use. The single goal of the researchers was to find better ways to teach spelling.

Such a study of the words of Finnish, Hungarian, Modern Turkish, Italian, or Hawaiian would be a waste of time and money. The reason, of course, is that spelling in those languages follows the sounds. For instance, the editors of the Berlitz book, *Finnish for Travellers,* write, "It (Finnish spelling) is entirely phonetic." (p. 7)

The Stanford study may or may not have shown better ways to teach spelling, but the things it brought to light about the spelling of English words beggar belief. It was a major effort of considerable importance. The four researchers who conducted the experiment had the brilliant idea of utilizing what was then a million dollar machine, a computer, to do the work which otherwise would have taken thousands of hours of workers' time to perform. It would also have been a tedious task. A grant from the U.S. Department of Health, Education and Welfare made the study financially possible.

Wisely, the investigators made a trial run, a pilot study, with 565 words. This was completed at the Stanford University Computation Center. Based on the experiences acquired there, trained personnel at the Service Bureau Corporation of Palo Alto, California, coded the words and took over the computer operation.

Expressed in the simplest terms, the programmers began with the phonetic respelling of the group of words and, by developing rules, attempted to reconcile the differences between the phonetic and conventional spellings of the words.

If 87 percent of our words were spelled phonetically, as Mr. Flesch contended in his *Johnny* book, then approximately 87 percent of the 17,310 words should have been spelled correctly by the computer with certainly not more than, say, 90 rules (to spell 44 sounds and two diphthongs). Additional rules (the ways sounds are spelled) would, naturally, have been needed in order to spell a sound or two in each of the remaining 13 percent of the words. So if 90 rules took care of six-sevenths of the words, surely those same rules plus 40 to 45 additional rules should have taken care of the remaining one-seventh of the words. That means the researchers would have needed a total of, say, 90 plus 45, or 135 rules to spell the words conventionally.

However, the programmers needed more than twice that many rules, more than 270! In fact, they developed 308 rules, 308 ways to spell the words on the list. If we break the number down, we find that the computer program used an average of 6.7 ways to spell each English sound!

But now comes the bombshell:

With 308 rules the computer spelled only 49 percent of the words correctly! That is right, not even half of the 17,310 words!

The computer spelled 8,463 words correctly and misspelled 8,847. Unbelievable as it may seem, this information is not in error. You may read it on page 119 of the report, which you will find in a gigantic volume with the title, *Phoneme-Grapheme Correspondences as Cues to Spelling Improvement.*

Flesch's claim that 87 percent of our words are spelled phonetically is a cruel hoax. A man who would write a book based on such a premise is revealed here as knowing very little about his subject. The evidence offered in the computer study is plain and irrefutable. If that claim and several other equally erroneous assertions in the *Johnny* book had not been accepted so widely as being the last word in providing the solution to our reading problems, they would not have been so harmful. It would also be much better if the reading public had not been so gullible.

What distresses me more than anything else about the computer study is the fact that very few educators and even fewer parents know about it. It proved conclusively that English has an immense number of words which are difficult to learn to spell and, consequently, to learn to read. Here was news that should have been, and still should be, trumpeted from the housetops. Here is information that should be given to every teacher of reading and to every parent whose child is learning to read. At the very least, the investigators should have tried to get the results of their study published in newspapers, weekly newsmagazines, educational journals, and popular magazines.

It is an enigma to me that the pilot study did not reveal how inadequate 308 rules would be. I myself, without the benefit of a computer, have collected more than twice that many ways to spell our sounds. Some 650 rules would be needed to spell most of the words.

And what rules could be developed to spell such words as *choir, colonel, eighth,* and *one?* An amusing aspect of the study is found with those four words and 84 more: they were simply set aside—swept under the rug, as it were—and no effort was made to develop rules to spell them! These additional words will show you what the problem was: *asthma, chamois, mediocre,* and *poignant.* If the researchers could throw out 88 words, children in school (and secretaries) should have the right to do the same thing with the words which they find hardest!

You must not gain the impression that a group of inexperienced researchers or immature bunglers conducted the study. All of the investigators had had considerable experience in the subject of teaching spelling. One had supervised two doctoral dissertations, and one had written a dissertation on the subject himself. They were Paul R. Hanna, Jean S. Hanna, Richard E. Hodges, and Edwin H. Rudorf, Jr. Nor was there any pressure of time. The four began their work in earnest in January, 1963, and their findings were published in 1966.

Let us consider some of the feats which the team and their computer specialists were able to achieve. First, here are samples of words which the machine spelled correctly:

/ə bŭv′/ spelled *above; o* spelled /ŭ/, and the *e* was wasted;
/ă′ kwē əs/ spelled *aqueous;* the *u* spelled /w/;
/ăv′ ər ij/ spelled *average;* the *a–e* did not result in /ā/;
/ăv′ ər ĭs/ spelled *avarice; i–e* did not spell /ī/.

Second, another impressive accomplishment was the spelling of a number of homophones (homonyms), such as these:

| bridal, bridle | capital, capitol | cast, caste | flour, flower |
| for, fore | halve, have | hour, our | peace, piece |

Third, by developing six rules for the spelling of the /û/ sound, the programmers prepared the machine to spell these words correctly:

e: div*e*rt; *i*: th*i*rd; *o*: w*o*rk; *u*: ch*u*rn; *ea*: y*ea*rn; *ou*: sc*ou*rge

It is easy to criticize those who established the spelling rules used to program the computer, but if you will spend as many hours as I have studying the errors the computer made in spelling, you will come to an overwhelming conclusion: The human mind is indeed marvelous to think it can cope with our unreliable visual symbols. Perhaps if I offer you a fairly sizable number of samples where the computer failed, you will get an inkling of what I mean.

The Cards Are Stacked against Johnny

In Rows, A, D, G, I, K, M, and O are words in their conventional spelling. In Rows B, E, H, J, L, N, and P are the same words as misspelled by the computer. In Rows C and F you have samples to show why the computer failed.

A.	ashen	bosom	breezy	cheese	chisel
B.	ation	boosum	breasy	cheas	chizzle
C.	ration	good	easy	fleas	drizzle
D.	hurry	tassel	trouble	two	wrought
E.	hery	tassle	trubble	tew	raut
F.	her	tussle	bubble	crew	auto
G.	alligator	appetite	arrow	attorney	bachelor
H.	alagater	apetight	aro	aterny	batchaler
I.	calves	chute	corrode	could	cuckoo
J.	cavs	shoot	coroad	cood	cookew
K.	cynicism	discipline	horrible	kangaroo	kimono
L.	sinasism	disaplin	horable	cangarew	comona
M.	metal	none	pretty	receipt	recipe
N.	mettle	nun	prity	reseat	resapee
O.	scene	stopped	tomb	tricycle	voiced
P.	sean	stopt	toom	trisickle	voist

If you are a bit mystified by the computer spellings and if you protest that they are not phonetic spellings, you are quite right, and therein lies our problem in the spelling of English words. The point of departure was the correct phonetic spelling of each word. But the experiment was to learn the various ways our sounds are spelled conventionally. Take the word *could*. The vowel sound /o͝o/ is spelled by *oo* in a good many words, such as *book, foot, hook, good, look,* and *stood*. Therefore, it is understandable that the machine came up with *cood*.

After that explanation, here are a few additional samples. I suggest that you cover up columns two and four and try to work out the words from the misspelled computer words in columns one and three:

Computer:	Dictionary:	Computer:	Dictionary:
butishan	beautician	efitionsy	efficiency
fiteeg	fatigue	geperdy	jeopardy
nolege	knowledge	manikin	mannequin
nesaseraly	necessarily	paratioot	parachute
fasishan	physician	fisasist	physicist
sisers	scissors	sicom	succumb
sifalice	syphilis	tecneak	technique

If the spelling *efitionsy* seems far-fetched, we must remember that we have many hundreds of words in which *-tion* spells /shən/, and *sy* are the last letters in courte*sy* and fanta*sy*. The *-lice* in *sifalice* is just as logical (or illogical) as it is in accomp*lice* and ma*lice*.

The investigators pointed out that with more rules more words would have been spelled correctly. I came across the study about six years ago and at the time I believed them. However, it gradually dawned on me that with more rules the computer would have had more choices and could easily have wound up with just as many, or even more, errors. I'll give you a few illustrations.

One of the rules for the spelling of the /ī/ sound was the spelling *igh*. On the master list there are at least eighty words in which *igh* spells /ī/, as in *light, might, night,* and *right*. Yet in some words, such as *high* and *thigh*, the computer did not use the *igh* spelling; it used *hy* and *thy*. But even worse, the computer used *-igh* to spell the /ī/ sound in at least sixty-one words in which we do not use that spelling. *Despite* came out *despight*, *quite* was *quight*, and *satellite* was *satalight*. I was amused when I saw that *typewriter* became *tiprighter*, but the spelling which made me chuckle was the one given for *dynamite*. It turned out to be *dynamight*!

On the master list there are at least sixty-seven other words in which *gh* "helps" to spell eight sounds, whose spellings we see in these sample words; /ô/ *bought, caught;* /ō/ *though;* /ŭ/ *tough;* /ou/ *bough;* /o͞o/ *through;* /ā/ *weight;* /ī/ *height;* and /ă/ *laugh*. Of the sixty-seven words the computer spelled only one correctly. No wonder our children have a rough time learning to spell and to read words in which the *gh* spelling is found.

Actually, the machine was given only the two most often used spellings of the /f/ sound, *f* and *ff*. (p. 1105) We have at least seven ways to spell it, of which the combination *ph* is used third most frequently and is found in 242 words in the study. (p. 77) Examples: *ph*one, sym*ph*ony, *ph*otogra*ph*. Obviously all the words in which the /f/ sound occurs where it is not spelled by *f* or *ff* were misspelled. Perhaps if the five rules that were withheld had been developed, *bluff, buff,* and *gruff*, which were correctly spelled, might have been spelled *bluph, buph,* and *gruph* by the computer.

Here is the best evidence that added rules would have resulted in confusion. Fifteen rules were developed to spell the /sh/ sound. Of course *ti* spells /sh/ in many words in conventional spelling: *conventional, station, tuition*. These misspelled words were given the same spelling: *pation, ratial, tiampew, tianeal*. If you are unable to "decode" the words, here they are in recognizable spelling: *passion, racial, shampoo,* and *chenille*. This one is easier: *ishue (issue)*. As we know, the letter *t* alone spells /sh/ in a number of words, e.g., nego*t*iate, substan*t*iate, vi*t*iate. That reminder prepares you for partner*t*ip *(partnership)*.

The point is clear: the more ways there are to spell a sound, the more chances there are for error.

One more striking example should suffice. Although there are thirty-six (!) ways to spell the /ā/ sound, a few of the words having rarer spellings are not words of sufficiently high frequency to make the master list. Nevertheless, children in high school will undoubtedly be expected to spell all the words in the following group and, therefore, know these eight spellings of /ā/. But in the study no rules were developed for them; consequently, not one of these 24 words, all of which are on the master list of 17,310 words, was spelled correctly:

br*ea*k, gr*ea*t, st*ea*k; caf*e*, *e*lite, m*e*lee;
d*ei*gn, f*ei*gn, r*ei*gn; *eigh*t, fr*eigh*t, w*eigh*t;
conv*ey*, h*ey*, ob*ey*; br*ai*se, pr*ai*se, w*ai*ve

Often the computer, searching among the possibilities, didn't do any better than many of our children (and adults) do trying to dredge up correct spellings from their memories. For instance:

1. The sounds *ee* and *ea* got confused: b*ea*d and ch*ea*p came out b*ee*d and ch*ee*p; and sp*ee*ch and sw*ee*t came out sp*ea*ch and sw*ea*t (!)

2. Many words in which *i* very clearly spells /ē/ came out misspelled. L*i*ter, mot*i*f and sard*i*ne look like children's spellings: l*e*ter, mot*ie*f, and sard*ea*n.

3. Many words spelled *ie* came out *ea:* f*ie*ld as f*ea*ld, and f*ie*nd as f*ea*nd.

4. The spelling of the consonant sound /ch/ was also amusing. Words ending in *-ch* came out looking like Du*tch* and sti*tch:* mu*tch*, su*tch*, ri*tch*, and whi*tch*.

Because so many errors made by the machine look like human errors, I commented on the fact to my computer specialist friends. They laughed at me for saying that; they said the errors *were* human errors.

It will now come as no surprise to you to read that the computer did worse than badly with the spelling of "demons." I took the list of one hundred words which was compiled many years ago by W. Franklin Jones from fifteen million running words of theme writing by young people. The machine must go to the foot of the class; it did miserably, spelling only 29 words correctly! Here are a dozen of the 71 words the computer misspelled: *which, their, meant, many, friend, some, been, always, women, done, here, write.*

As bad as the results of the computer study were, I am thoroughly convinced that if a different dictionary had been used to provide phonetic spellings, the computer would have misspelled a great many more words.

Here is my reasoning. The team of investigators selected a dictionary, the Sixth Edition of the *Merriam-Webster Collegiate,* which was badly out of date. The changes in the pronunciation respellings in the Third, Fourth, Fifth, and Sixth editions were minimal. But between the Six and the Seventh editions there were literally many thousands of changes; and thousands of the changes were corrections. I am saying there were thousands of errors in the pronunciation respellings in the Sixth Edition! Pronunciation between 1900 and 1963 had certainly not changed very much. But there was a change in policy, in principle: Prior to the Seventh Edition, the editors began with letters and the printed words; and in giving pronunciation respellings, they tried to adhere as closely as possible to the conventional spelling, to make the "phonetic" spelling fit the letters rather than the sounds. The result was what might be expected, stilted "eye" pronunciations which were possibly correct in theory but not carried out in practice.

However, in preparing the Third Edition of the *Merriam-Webster Unabridged Dictionary* (1961), upon which the Seventh Edition of the *Collegiate* (1963) was based, the editors followed the opposite principle. They began, not with the printed words, but with sounds, with words spoken in connected discourse. The tape recorder was of great assistance because it could be used to record pronunciations from various parts of the country, and it could be listened to over and over again. (See page 5a of the Preface to the Seventh.) The goal now was to offer in the pronunciation respellings representations of sounds that were as accurate and correct as possible. Speakers were thinking not primarily of the way words are spelled, but of the thoughts expressed by words so that they spoke the words normally. In other words, pronunciation respellings in 1961 and 1963 became what they always should have been: truly phonetic respellings. No longer were the pronunciations given considered to be prescriptive; they were and are now descriptive.

Here are four areas where vast numbers of changes, most of them corrections, were made in the Seventh Edition.

1. The final sound /ē/. A goodly number of people in one small area of the country pronounce or pronounced the final sound in words like lad*y* and chimn*ey* as /ĭ/, not /ē/. For that reason the Sixth (and earlier editions) gave the respellings as /lā′ dĭ/ and /chĭm′ nĭ/. Can you hear yourself saying:

/bā′bĭ/ for bab*y*   /sĭ′tĭ/ for cit*y*   /fŭ′nĭ/ for funn*y*
/mŭ′nĭ/ for mon*ey*   /moo̅′vĭ/ for mov*ie*   /kôf′ĭ/ for coff*ee*

The former "phonetic" respellings now seem to be, and were, absurd. The Seventh made the corrections and shows the spellings to represent /ē/. To give you an idea of the number of words involved, I examined the words in the computer study of 17,310 words and found 1,687 words in which the Sixth gave the /ĭ/ sound and the Seventh changed to the /ē/ sound. If there are 130,000 entries in the Seventh, think how many respellings had to be corrected from /ĭ/ to /ē/.

2. The letter *i* spelling /ē/. In the Sixth we find that the letter *i* was supposed to spell the /ĭ/ sound in at least many hundreds, perhaps thousands, of words where it actually spells the /ē/ sound. Thus, *radius* /rā′dĭ ŭs/ and *radio* /rā′ dĭ ō/ have been corrected in the Seventh to /rā′ dē əs/ and /rā′ dē ō/. Surely you will agree (with all newer dictionaries) that *i* spells /ē/ in al*i*as, bacter*i*a, cop*i*ous, v*i*sa, etc. (There were 440 words in the computer study which were misspelled in the "phonetic" respelling.)

3. The letter *o* spelling /ə/, not /ō/. You may be inclined to believe the information found in the Sixth and say we do pronounce the sound spelled by the letter *o* as /ō/ in hist*o*ry. But that would be because you would pronounce the word in isolation, giving each letter an unnatural value and making the sounds artificial and stilted. No good current dictionary shows such a pronunciation. *Merriam-Webster* in the Sixth showed /hĭs′ tō rĭ/, but the Seventh gives /hĭs′ t(ə) rē/, indicating that we pronounce the word in two or three syllables, the middle vowel sound being so weakened that if it is pronounced at all, it is a schwa. Here are more samples of words in which the correction was made: dec*o*rate, fel*o*ny, mel*o*dy, pr*o*found, pr*o*nounce, and pr*o*vide.

4. The spelling of the schwa sound. Apparently it was once believed that hearers could tell the difference in the sounds spelled by the various letters. The Sixth used italicized letters to indicate a somewhat weakened sound. So it must have been assumed speakers distinguished between *a* and *o* and *u* in *a*pprove, *o*ppose, and *u*pon; between *e* and *i* in Franc*e*s and Franc*i*s; and between *a* and *o* in can*o*e and c*o*nnect and capit*a*l and capit*o*l.

In any event, the programmers had the unfair advantage of knowing in the "phonetic" respellings how the schwa sound was spelled in thousands of words. Presumably, the basic assumption was that words were originally to be spelled phonetically, that is, as they are actually pronounced in ordinary discourse, and rules for conventional spelling were to be established from genuinely phonetic spellings. Thus, the programmers should have started with /dī′ nəs tē/, /ō′ vəl/ and /vī′ təl/ for *dynasty, oval,* and *vital.* Instead, they began with /dī′ năs tĭ/, /ō′ văl/ and /vī′ tăl/.

Or to take one final example, *elegant.* We pronounced it in 1940 as we do today, /ĕl′ə gənt/, and that is what we find in the Seventh. In the Sixth, however, we find /ĕl′ ē gănt/. (The middle letter was to be pronounced as the first *e* in *event* was thought to be pronounced, semi-long.) If the programmers had begun with phonetic spelling, the machine probably would not have been able to spell the word correctly, as it did, but might have come up with *eligont* or even *elagount*. (The letters *ou* spell /ə/ in huge numbers of words, e.g., fam*ou*s, lim*ou*sine, and superflu*ou*s.) Beginning with the unfair advantage, the computer spelled these words correctly: cons*e*crate, des*e*crate, int*e*grate.

The investigators who conducted the computer study expected criticism of the dictionary they selected and its so-called phonetic respellings. They anticipated this criticism when they wrote, "No other aspect of this investigation is likely to generate so much discussion, perhaps controversy, as the dictionary chosen by the research team. . . . It is readily admitted that this (dictionary's) pronunciation key has several critical weaknesses." (p. 13)

Why, then, was it chosen?

The goal of this chapter was to illustrate how badly our sounds (words) are spelled. The computer study did that for us. When I used the word "wretched" at the beginning of the chapter to describe the spelling of English words, I employed the same adjective as Professor Albert M. Marckwardt did to characterize the spelling system of English. He gave this reason: "(There is a) lack of relationship between the spoken and the written form of the language." (*American English,* pp. 171, 172) Surely the computer study, even with its unfair advantages, confirmed his statement.

If the following quotation had appeared in the first chapter of this book, you might have dismissed it forthwith. Perhaps now you will consider it seriously. In *The Treasure of Our Tongue* Professor Lincoln Barnett describes the English system of spelling sounds as "antiquated, irrational, exasperating, obsolete, indefensible, crazy, and mixed up." (p. 36) Unwillingly, slowly, and very gradually I have come to accept Barnett's strong statement. If you do, you know why Johnny can't read.

CHAPTER 5

Three Handicaps—Sometimes Three Strikes

HANDICAP #1

Even before they begin school many children from deprived homes have one strike on them when they are confronted with the task of attempting to learn to read. These are the children who have never been read to, who never see a book—often not even a newspaper—in the home, and seldom, if ever, see a parent read, and who sometimes lack all motivation. A whole lot of these children fear the great unknown and are quite apprehensive about trying to learn to read. The printed symbols frighten them. They start off with one strike against them.

In addition, there are, of course, slower learners who come from middle-class homes, but those children often have some kind of block, either emotional or mental. It could be overcome more easily and more surely if they had been born in another country, perhaps Hungary, and didn't have two other handicaps, or obstacles, to contend with.

HANDICAP #2

The irrational spelling of a majority of English words makes the process of learning to read our language considerably more difficult for all children than would be the case if all, or even most, of our words were spelled phonetically. Thus, many children have a second strike on them.

HANDICAP #3

Our indefensible spelling "system" imposes severe limitations on the choice of words which writers of first-year and even second-year readers may use. What they write results perforce in distressingly dull reading matter, and the silly material fails to motivate many children, especially boys, to further reading, even to further learning. Little realizing the rigid limitations which our meager stock of phonetically spelled words imposes on the writers, many a parent has been exceedingly bitter to think the authors write such dry and uninteresting stuff—"drivel" is what one parent called it. But those parents should try to write ten or twenty pages of gripping reading matter—within the range of phonetically spelled words and the capabilities of most six-year-old children.

In the realm of teaching reading the gap between supposition and reality is gigantic. Most adults assume our written symbols stand for sounds as they are supposed to represent them. Once we have learned to read and spell thousands of words, we apparently become almost oblivious to the role individual letters play in spelling sounds. Thus, it seems logical to most people that teachers need only tell their pupils the sound each letter spells and they'll be able to read. As a matter of fact, Flesch based his *Why Johnny Can't Read* book on that misconception. He wrote, "Teach the child what each letter stands for and he can read." (p. 3) When he amended the statement later, he revealed the implication was that most letters represent a single sound, for he added, "Finally, tell him (the child) that some letters do not spell one sound but two." (p. 27)

Most parents would probably approve the following approach:

Let's suppose you pick up a beginning elementary reader and open it to the first page. Suppose you see there the following information:

A is for apple   (a picture of an apple)
E is for elephant   (a picture of an elephant)
I is for Indian   (a picture of an Indian)

The apple looks appetizing, the elephant looks massive, and the Indian looks imposing, for he is a proud chief.

Surely if the pictures are in color, children's interest will be whetted. But the children will be extremely confused and bewildered:

First of all, in the three words the *a* does not once stand for the sound /ā/ as the name of the letter indicates. One time it stands for /ă/, and twice it represents /ə/.

Secondly, the *e* does not stand for /ē/, as it should if it were logical. Once it represents /ĕ/ and once /ə/; and once it spells nothing at all (in appl*e*).

Finally, the *i* does not stand for /ī/, as children have a right to expect. We see it twice in I*n*d*i*an; once it spells /ĭ/ and once /ē/!

How about that? Why don't we start where the learners are? And do we have to confuse them? No wonder some give up in despair.

You say that no writer of a first elementary text would ever begin a book that way? Well, if you'll open up *Why Johnny Can't Read* to the second part, which was intended to be a "primer," that is, a beginning reader, you'll find the letters, the words, and the pictures!

Three Handicaps—Sometimes Three Strikes

Of course my point is that all authors of elementary readers in English have to restrict rigidly their choice of words so they fit into easy spelling patterns. Educators have known ever since universal education was introduced that most children simply do not have the requisite linguistic ability to handle many spellings if they are thrown at them all at once in the beginning. Limited by an extremely small supply of regularly spelled words, authors have given children inane, insipid, and uninspired reading material which, quite naturally, has bored millions of children, especially boys. As everyone should know, interest is an indispensable factor in learning. So all of our children have these two handicaps: (a) They have to struggle with unreliable symbols; and (b) At the same time the reading material does not motivate many of them to want to learn.

We'll return to Handicap #2, which is the reason for Handicap #3. If you hadn't picked up this book and hadn't read the two preceding chapters, how many sounds would you have imagined the letter *a* spells? Ask around and you'll hear answers ranging from two or three to four or five. Then ask how many ways *a* combines with other letters to spell sounds. Finally, ask how many sounds the combinations spell and how many ways the combinations spell sounds. By the time you have finished, you may be locked up; but if you aren't, you'll find disgust or contempt on the faces of those you put the questions to. The facial expressions will indicate that your questions are unimportant. What difference do all the questions make?

To our learners the answers to the questions make a huge difference. We'll see if *a* spells just one or two or even three or four sounds. More than fifty years ago Anna D. Cordts, for her doctoral dissertation, made a study of the sounds which the letter *a* spells. She limited her study to thirty elementary readers, ten each for the first, second, and third grades. She searched out the letter-sound relationships of the letter *a* and letters which combined with it to spell sounds, and she went through page after page in the thirty readers, placing each occurrence into its proper category.

This is what she found: In those elementary readers the letter *a* alone and in combinations spelled fifteen (of our nineteen) vowel sounds! The dissertation was not published, but you may find a report of it, which was made by Dr. Cordts' adviser, Professor Ernest Horn, in the *Journal of Educational Psychology* in March, 1929. The article bears the title, "The Child's Experience with the Letter *A* in Grades I to III."

Dr. Cordts' study led me to make a more complete investigation; I decided to see how many letter-sound relationships there are in adult material. It was a major undertaking, but I believe the results prove that it was worthwhile. I found that the letter *a* alone spells twelve different sounds and, with the help of other letters, spells ten of the same sounds all over again and four additional sounds besides. This means the letter *a* is involved in the spelling of sixteen of our nineteen vowel sounds. Furthermore, the worst part of this highly unfortunate condition is that I found the letter *a* and its helpers spell the sixteen sounds in 114 ways!

In Table 2 you will see seventy of the spellings. You will find no erudite words in the list. Indeed, I suggest that you take a pencil and cross out any words which you consider too hard for children of average ability upon completion of the eighth grade. Please judge on the basis of reading recognition only, not on the basis of the ability to spell correctly.

Table 2

The Letter *a* Alone and in Combinations with Other Letters Spells 16 Sounds in These 70 Ways

SOUNDS	LETTERS	WORDS	SOUNDS	LETTERS	WORDS
/ā/	a	*A*pril	/ă/	a	*a*t
	a-e	*ate*		a-e	h*ave*
	ai	f*ai*l		ai	pl*ai*d
	aigh	str*aigh*t		al	h*al*f
	ai-e	r*aise*		au	l*au*gh
	au-e	g*auge*		ua	g*ua*rantee
	a-ue	v*ague*	/ä/	a	*a*rm
	ay	d*ay*		a-e	*are*
	ea	gr*ea*t		ah	*ah*, hurr*ah*
/â/	a	p*a*rent		au	h*au*nt
	a-e	d*are*		ea	h*ea*rt
	ai	h*ai*r		ua	g*ua*rd
	ai-e	million*aire*	/ô/	a	c*a*ll
	ay	pr*ay*er		a-e	f*alse*
	ea	b*ea*r		al	t*al*k
/ə/	a	*a*gainst		ao	extr*ao*rdinary
	ae	Mich*ae*l		as	Arkans*as*
	a-e	pir*ate*		au	f*au*lt
	ai	mount*ai*n		au-e	bec*ause*
	au	*au*thority		augh	d*augh*ter
	ea	El*ea*nor		aw	s*aw*
	ia	Georg*ia*		oa	br*oa*d

Three Handicaps—Sometimes Three Strikes

Sounds	Letters	Words	Sounds	Letters	Words
/ər/	ar	beggar	/ē/	a	Israel
	oa	cupboard		ae	sundae
				ay	Sunday
/ĕ/	a	any		ea	eat
	ai	said		ea-e	please
	ay	says	/ī/	ai	kaiser
	ea	bread		ai-e	aisle
	ea-e	cleanse		ia	diamond
/ĭ/	a	spinach	/ō/	eau	bureau
	a-e	postage		oa	board
	ai	chaplain		oa-e	coarse
	ea	hear	/û/	ea	learn
	ea-e	mileage		ea-e	hearse
/ŏ/	a	wallet	/yo͞o/	eau	beauty
/ou/	au	sauerkraut	/ŭ/	a	what (unstressed)

As you read through the list, you may have questioned three or four of the spellings of sounds. However, these spellings are based on a consensus of eight good, recent dictionaries; all phonetic respellings are given in at least five of them as I have shown them. Let me offer one example. If you will look up the respellings of the days of the week, you will find the first choice in your dictionary will show that -*ay* represents /ē/, not /ā/, as in *Sunday*, /sŭn′ dē/.

I know how little importance the average good reader will attach to the list of seventy spellings. Isn't that the way it is in all languages? Indeed not! We should do as Mencius suggests, make a comparison. Using German again as our basis of comparison, I have made a study of material in different places in the two languages.

First, I took two lists of words of highest frequency, one in each language. Fortunately, frequency lists based on more than four million running words have been made in both English (Thorndike's *The Teacher's Word Book*) and German *(A Minimum Standard German Vocabulary)*. Here are my findings for the first thousand words in each list:

Letter *a* (and Combinations)	English	German
Number of sounds spelled:	14	2 (plus two diphthongs)
Ways sounds are spelled:	44	5 (including diphthongs)

Children speaking both languages know the sound of the letter *a*, which is its name. Thereafter, German children have to learn one other sound the letter *a* spells and the spelling of two diphthongs; but our children have to learn the other thirteen sounds which the letter *a* spells, or helps to spell, in words on the Thorndike list, and most of them are illogical spellings. Thus, an incomparably greater load is placed on our learners. Moreover, in the words of highest frequency (greatest use) German children need to learn only five spellings with the letter *a*, but our children must learn forty-four, almost nine times as many!

Second, it seemed logical and necessary to compare adult reading matter, connected reading, not just isolated words. This I did, counting the number of sounds the letter *a* alone and in combinations spells, as follows:

For English I read seventeen pages of *The Innocents Abroad* (Chapters 1 and 28) and the front page of the *San Francisco Chronicle*, December 30, 1978.

For German I counted spellings in all of Goethe's *Novelle* and ten pages each in two novels by Heinrich Böll, a widely read contemporary author. Here are the results:

LETTER *a* (AND COMBINATIONS)	ENGLISH	GERMAN
Number of sounds spelled:	16	2 (plus two diphthongs)
Ways sounds are spelled:	69	6 (including diphthongs)

The letter *a* is not unique. I have made a careful study of the letter-sound relationships of the letter *e* and have found that it alone and in combinations outdoes the letter *a* with its helpers by spelling 17 (rather than 16) of our 19 vowel sounds! To date I have found the letter and combinations spell the sounds 105 ways. There are probably a few more, just as there are quite likely more than 114 sound-letter relationships with the letter *a*, some of which I may have missed. Here are one-fifth of the spellings:

ie:

ch*ie*f /ē/; misch*ie*f /ĭ/; fr*ie*nd /ĕ/; sold*ie*r /ə/; p*ie* /ī/; l*ie*u /o͞o/; v*ie*w /yo͞o/; linger*ie* /ā/

ei:

r*ei*n /ā/; f*ei*gn /ā/; n*ei*ghbor /ā/; dec*ei*t /ē/; w*ei*rd /ĭ/; h*ei*r /â/; nonpar*ei*l /ĕ/; fahrenh*ei*t /ĭ/

Three Handicaps—Sometimes Three Strikes 47

eu:

neutral /ōō/; neurotic /ōō/; Europe /yōō/; feud /yōō/; grandeur /ə/

Table 3 shows how English and German compare when using the letter *e* alone and in combinations. Section I is a count of the same first thousand words from the frequency lists used in the letter *a* count. Section II is a count of nine pages of *The Innocents Abroad,* Chapter 28, and Goethe's entire *Novelle* (22 pages). Section III is a count of the same front page of the *San Francisco Chronicle* as used in the letter *a* count and, for German, the same 20 pages as I used in the letter *a* count in two novels by Heinrich Böll.

Table 3

Comparison of the Letter *e*

LETTERS AND COMBINATIONS	ENGLISH	GERMAN
I		
Number of sounds spelled:	17	4 (and two diphthongs)
Ways sounds are spelled:	64	7 (including diphthongs)
II		
Number of sounds spelled:	17	4 (and one diphthong)
Ways sounds are spelled:	71	7 (including diphthongs)
III		
Number of sounds spelled:	14	4 (and two diphthongs)
Ways sounds are spelled:	38	8 (including diphthongs)

These tables do not take into consideration an important factor in English, the so-called "silent" *e*. Nearly everybody assumes it was devised as a method to tell readers that the preceding vowel, with an intervening consonant, is "long." That is not true. Besides, many English experts say the "rule" should not be taught, and there are two reasons.

First, usually it is not true in *un*stressed syllables, e.g., in definit*e*, feminin*e*, futur*e*, imaginativ*e*, minut*e*, volum*e*, etc. Second, too often it is not true even in stressed syllables, e.g., in becom*e*, giv*e*, gon*e*, mov*e*, shov*e*, ther*e*, wer*e*, etc.

A count of the words containing an unsounded final *e* in the first 2,000 words on the list in Thorndike's *The Teacher's Word Book* supports the experts. In only 55 percent of the words does a vowel letter represent a "long" vowel sound when the letter *e* follows in the same syllable. In the other 45 percent of the words the preceding vowel spells other sounds, as in car*e*, dar*e*, loos*e*, measur*e*, mov*e*, pictur*e*, and circl*e*, doubl*e*, hous*e*, nois*e*, piec*e*, etc.

If a great majority of the thousand or two thousand most frequently used words of English were spelled phonetically, learning to read those words would be immeasurably easier. We would then have a nucleus of words which even slower learners could master and be able to read in a reasonable length of time. And then it would be considerably easier to learn dozens, even scores, of irrational spellings because there would be a base on which to build. In theory the best elementary reading books would start with those of our words which are spelled phonetically and in the beginning would be restricted to just those words. Surely the plan seems logical.

As a matter of fact, some linguists have followed that procedure. For example, the late Professor Leonard Bloomfield, one of the most highly regarded linguists, and Professor Clarence L. Barnhart, also a linguist and a well-known lexicographer, wrote *Let's Read—A Linguistic Approach*. Initially, it uses only phonetically spelled words (if we may assume that our one-syllable words with the "short" vowel sound are spelled phonetically). The authors started of necessity with that type of word. They did not even attempt to tell stories or write interesting and absorbing information, as the following samples, taken as they are from the book, illustrate:

> "A big, fat pig sat in a pigpen. A wet hen sat in a tub. Ben, get us a net. Len had a pet hen." (p. 88) "Chuck let Al quiz him but did not tell. Nick got a cod, and Cliff got a squid. A duck quacks. Ducks quack. Jess, let's stop and rest." (p. 162)

Ichabod and Johnny would find page after page of these meaningless and irrelevant sentences boring beyond belief. The writers overlooked the element of greatest importance, THE LEARNERS! The authors assume children wouldn't be interested in what they were reading, but only in the written symbols and the sounds they represent. These are Professor Bloomfield's words: "The child is too busy with the mechanics of reading to get anything out of the context.... During the actual process of

Three Handicaps—Sometimes Three Strikes 49

learning to read the words, he does not concern himself with the content." (p. 34) Involuntary interest, of which there would not be any here, certainly not in poorer learners, is perhaps the most important element needed in learning. Nearly all children have at best a short attention span. In the authors' minds language is paramount and children's interest and motivation are completely disregarded.

Most writers of elementary readers, however, attempt to make the reading matter interesting, but then they run into the need to use irregularly spelled words. Or they simply use a few words with an "Oh, just that?" attitude. I'm convinced that many authors have had too little knowledge of phonetics and linguistics. In several series I have found words whose spellings have not been introduced. Unsuspecting adult readers, probably even teachers, will see nothing wrong with words they have read literally hundreds or thousands of times. I have seen elementary readers in which *ear, fear,* and *near* had been introduced, and then *bear* puts in an appearance and supposedly fits into the same pattern. *Ball* was used repeatedly and then *balloon* is injected; but the *a* in *balloon* spells a schwa. Nobody says /bô lōōn′/. Or the word *now* is taught and used, and then *know* slips in. How are children supposed to work out the sounds of the new word? I have seen *color* in two series and no attention was paid to the fact that neither *o* spells /ō/ or /ŏ/. Compare /kŭl′ ər/. And if Ichabod and Johnny have been taught that the final "silent" *e* makes the preceding vowel letter spell a "long" sound, they will be confused and frustrated when they see such all-important words as *are, have, some,* and *to live.*

This is what Professor Bloomfield wrote in his book: "When it comes to teaching irregular and special words, each word will demand a separate effort and special practice." (p. 206) Well, more than half of the words in that sentence would require separate practice. I very much doubt if Bloomfield ever tried to make a count of our unphonetically spelled words because he was writing about a great majority of our words. Thus, many thousands of words "demand a separate effort and separate practice." In the Bloomfield-Barnhart program there are five thousand carefully selected words, as many of them spelled phonetically as possible. But even so, not half of them are spelled phonetically. I counted the first 500 words listed alphabetically and only 31 percent are spelled phonetically.

First-year German primers offer a decided contrast. I have inspected a large number of them and have carefully examined one first-year series. I listed and alphabetized every word in the last book and found a relatively high total of words, 472 different words. Of that number only ten are spelled unphonetically. There are many American readers with only a fifth as many total words, and more than ten of the total will certainly be spelled unphonetically.

The much broader vocabulary enabled the German writers to put their characters into lively actions: They ride on their scooters, their bikes, their sleds, in a car, on a bus, and on a merry-go-round. They fly kites, balloons, and toy airplanes. They blow soap bubbles, buy things in a store and in a bakery. They climb trees, paint doors and fences, play and run with their animals, make a snowman, and eat apples, oranges, bananas, cake, bread, and candy. They have fun at a playground, go down the slide, and play on a "jungle gym." They celebrate Christmas and birthdays and receive and open packages and are pleased with what they find. What is there left to do?

This type of reading is infinitely more enjoyable, more interesting, and more motivating than our Dick and Jane's "Run, run, run! Let us run." There are a few artificial sentences, to be sure, but in comparison with our readers they are few in number; and in the last book they vanish.

It is superfluous to repeat that the reason so many words could be used in the German series is that a whole lot more of them are spelled phonetically. I didn't know why I took the time to list the words in the big German primer and then to translate each one, but when I had completed the undertaking and made a careful analysis of each English word, one fact stood out: Not even a fourth of the translated words are spelled phonetically. The major reasons are provided in Chapter 3 of this book. For example, a fifth of the English words found in my list of translated words contain digraphs. (As you remember, a digraph is a combination of letters to represent one sound.) Of course we can and do accept *ee* in *see* and *three,* but we cannot accept the others. If we go back to the statement that teachers only need to tell the sound each letter spells and the children will be able to read, we ask ourselves what the letter *u* represents in these digraphs, all taken from the translated words:

ua: g*ua*rd;   *ue*: bl*ue*;   *ui*: b*ui*lding;   *uy*: b*uy*s;
ou: s*ou*p, enorm*ou*s;   *eau*: b*eau*tiful
au: l*au*ghs, *au*tomatic;   *ough*: thr*ough,* d*ough*

There are ninety English words with digraphs on the list; they contain twenty-five different digraphs, which spell sounds thirty-nine ways.

We'll carry coals to Newcastle: In the final analysis, German is so much easier for German children to learn to read, because German spellings of sounds are far easier to learn and obviously much more reliable. American educators who visit elementary classrooms in Germany are astonished when they hear how well children read aloud in lower grades, even when the material is completely new to them. Horace Mann visited German classes nearly 150 years ago, and he was greatly impressed.

Three Handicaps—Sometimes Three Strikes 51

I myself have observed German classes, and I, too, found what Mann reported and what Professor Ralph C. Preston (University of Pennsylvania), who spent five months in Germany studying the elementary school system, observed. He had the opportunity to listen to the 5 poorest and 5 best readers in each of 12 classrooms read unknown material aloud. Of the 120 readers only 11 had low word-recognition skills, 8 in the first grade, 2 in the second, and 1 in the fifth grade.

After the experience, Preston was better able to understand and believe "the generally expressed opinion of German teachers that by the end of Grade II almost any child can read orally (without regard to the degree of comprehension) almost anything in print." ("Comparison of Word-Recognition Skill in German and American Children" *The Elementary School Journal,* 1953, p. 443) He attributed the success of German children to a considerable extent to the "nature of the German language," that is, to the sounds being spelled phonetically and consistently.

A good many authorities have clearly stated what every English-speaking individual who reads experiences, namely, as Professor Jespersen said, we cannot tell how a word is pronounced just by seeing its spelling. Thomas Pyles also expressed the same thought; in his *The Origin and Development of the English Language* he quoted the renowned etymologist and eminent Cambridge scholar, W. W. Skeat, who said, "I hold firmly to the belief . . . that no one can tell how to pronounce an English word unless he has at sometime or other heard it." (p. 48)

Two friends of mine told me about their experiences. One, who was taking his oral examination for the Ph.D degree at the University of Cologne, had a minor in English. He was asked how the word "awry" is pronounced. He fell into the trap. By chance he knew the word "outlawry," which is pronounced /out′ lô rē/. So he answered, "/ô′rē/." By asking the question the professor revealed that he didn't know what many authorities have said about the pronunciation of English words. We know that "awry" is pronounced /ə rī′/, *but only because we have heard it.* Another good friend had associated "ascertain" with "certain." So he pronounced it as /ə sûr′tən/ and felt embarrassed when he was asked why he mispronounced /ăs′ ər tān′/. It is as Professors Jespersen and Skeat and also Professor Albert C. Baugh have written, "One cannot tell how to spell an English word by its pronunciation or how to pronounce it by its spelling." (*A History of the English Language,* p. 13)

Implied in the quotations is that someone reading new words in another language can know how they (or almost all of them) are pronounced. The reason we can't be sure how unknown words are pronounced is found in this statement: "English spelling is the most confusing alphabetic writing in use." These are the words of Samuel Noory in his *Dictionary of Pronunciation,* p. ix. Professor Noory is traveling in distinguished company. One of the most widely read authors on language is the late Professor Mario Pei. In *The Story of the English Language* he wrote, "It (our spelling system) places the English language at the very bottom of the scale among languages using a phonetic or semi-phonetic system of writing." (p. 305)

If we adults can't be sure how to pronounce new words we read in our weekly newsmagazines or in *Sports Illustrated,* then it stands to reason that our children face a gigantic task when they embark on a program of learning to read. All words are new to them, and too many don't fit into easy patterns. They need all the help they can get. If we are compassionate human beings, we should make every effort to help every single individual to become functionally literate, to see to it that as few strike out as possible. You will find this matter is the subject of the last chapters in this book.

CHAPTER 6

Authorities Agree

In the university community where I live few people believe—or want to believe—that there are many millions of adults in our country who cannot read. Fewer still believe that written English is as difficult as I describe it to be.

Scores of scholars, however, have recognized how unsystematic and irrational our spelling is. I have quoted ten eminent authorities; and to give further evidence that my message is true and that it has been told before—but to the wrong people—I offer the following eighteen quotations, most of them made by professors of English, several of whom are teaching or have taught at major universities. The authors are listed in alphabetical order:

1. Margaret Bryant: "The study of the consonant sounds of English is obscured by an unphonetic alphabet and spelling." *Modern English and Its Heritage,* p. 132

2. Bergen Evans: "The chief obstacle to the adoption of English as a world language is probably its spelling, that fantastic lack of correspondence between our written symbols and our sounds." In Professor Evans' chapter in Henry Bradley's *The Making of English,* p. 201

3. Norman Foerster, J. M. Steadman, Jr., and James B. McMillan: "English words are spelled inconsistently and unphonetically . . . Every word must be remembered visually." *Writing and Thinking,* p. 272

4. Robert M. Gorrell and Charlton Laird: "Whimsical spelling constitutes one of the great weaknesses of the English language. . . . (It) is highly confusing to the beginner." *Modern English Handbook,* p. 507

5. Robert A. Hall, Jr.: "If the spelling of English were wholly or nearly phonetic, like the spelling of Finnish or Hungarian or even that of standard Italian, there would be no problem." *Leave Your Language Alone,* p. 133

6. Arthur Garfield Kennedy: "English spelling is unsystematic . . . inadequate . . . wasteful . . . illogical . . . sometimes absurd (p. 121) (and) . . . misleading (p. 261)" *Current English*

7. John M. Kierzek: "The utter lack of correlation between English spelling and English pronunciation is well known to all. The two are often not on speaking terms with each other." *The Macmillan Handbook of English,* p. 391

8. Charlton Laird: "We have the most erratic spelling of any of the great languages." *The Miracle of Language,* p. 228

9. Donald J. Lloyd and Harry R. Warfel: "We don't pronounce the way we spell, and we don't spell the way we pronounce." *American English in Its Cultural Setting,* p. 65

10. The same professors, Lloyd and Warfel: "In English, if we hear a strange (new) word, we cannot tell for sure how to write it; if we see a strange word, we cannot tell how to say it." *American English in Its Cultural Setting,* p. 364

11. Thomas R. Lounsbury: "English orthography (spelling) is nothing but a mass of inconsistencies." *English Spelling and Spelling Reform,* p. xii

12. John Nist: "The spelling practices of Modern English are the worst of any major language in the world." *A Structural History of English,* p. 16

13. Samuel Noory: "The germ of Johnny's predicament lies not in any particular teaching procedure, but in the very structure of English spelling itself." *Dictionary of Pronunciation,* p. vi

14. Mario Pei: "English has a divergence between speech and writing which is far greater than in any other western tongue." *The Story of the English Language,* p. 331

15. Axel Wijk: "It has been widely recognized for hundreds of years that the spelling of the English language is extremely antiquated and confused, far more so than is the case with any other living language." *Regularized English,* p. 17

16. Axel Wijk: "It has been estimated that it takes an English-speaking child from one to two years longer to learn to read and write his language than it takes children of other nations to achieve similar results in their languages." *Rules of Pronunciation for the English Language,* p. 143 (Incidentally, Professor Wijk says English has so many common words which are spelled irregularly that his book "is intended only for advanced students." p. 11)

Authorities Agree 55

17. Richard M. Wilson: ". . . by the time the printers (in the sixteenth century) had managed to fix the orthography (spelling—of English), it was already completely unphonetic." *Encyclopaedia Britannica* (Under "The English Language," Vol. 8, p. 567B, 1957 printing)

18. Robert Eugen Zachrisson: "Of all languages of culture English has the most antiquated, inconsistent, and illogical spelling." *Anglic* (p. 10)

In the context of this book perhaps the thirteenth quotation has the most significance: "The germ of Johnny's predicament lies . . . in the structure of English spelling itself." I think two analogies are in order:

On the wall in our mountain cabin hangs a cartoon which is particularly appropriate to our family. We are obliged to take supplies across a lake, and very often we come close to overloading our boat. The cartoon consists of a series of pictures in which we see a man loading his boat with supplies he plans to take across a lake to his cabin. In the first picture, the boat is riding high in the water, but in each succeeding picture, as the man continues to pile cartons and shopping bags into the craft, it sinks lower and lower. In the final picture the boat has gone under; the load was just too great.

Now if we assume the boat represents the capacity, or ability, of individuals and the supply of words represents the load to be carried, we see how those individuals with great native ability are like 25- or 30-foot boats, which can comfortably handle large loads; they can learn to read large numbers of words. Similar loads simply cannot be handled by individuals who have the capacity of 10-foot boats; and because millions of individuals have limited capacity (ability) and are like 8- and 10-foot boats, they cannot manage large loads, that is, learn to read large numbers of difficult words.

This analogy is helpful when we think of natives of other countries learning to read their languages. They have the same varying capacities, i.e., potential reading ability, as we, and their varying supplies of words are their loads. However, there is a significant difference in the composition of the material to be loaded, that is, learned. With weight, a pound is a pound, but with words, as we know, some are much easier and some are much harder to learn. Two definitions of two of our words are apt in this analogy. In *Webster's New World Dictionary* we find these two meanings for *light:* (1) "in weight"; and (7) "easy to do; not difficult." The two pertinent definitions for *heavy* are these: (1) "in weight"; and (7) "hard to do; difficult." When our slower learners try to load their boats, a great deal of the material is too heavy, and when they try to learn to read, much of the material is too hard.

When Continental European children load their boats, that is, start to learn to read, far more of their material, their supply of phonetically spelled words, is light and easy. In other words, given the same limited capacity, Dutch- or German-speaking children with the same effort are able to learn to read several times as many words as our children are.

It goes without saying that in all countries where other Germanic languages are spoken there are the same ranges of linguistic ability as here. But inasmuch as illiteracy is virtually unknown among natives in Scandinavia, Holland, and the German-speaking countries, the reason has to be found in the type of words "on the dock" in those countries. In five years of living on the Continent I have come into contact with a number of individuals whose language ability was quite limited. We might compare their capacity with 8- or 10-foot boats. They could not easily handle their spoken and written languages; they made mistakes, even glaring ones in their grammar. Yet they could read; they were not illiterate, not even what we would call functionally illiterate.

The second analogy is found in the pieces of music which follow. Just as the first piece is relatively very easy to learn to read, so are the languages which Finnish and Hungarian children learn to read. The second piece, which is somewhat harder, represents the degree of difficulty children speaking Germanic languages have to master. The last piece is difficult to learn to read and play. It represents our language.

CHAPTER 7

Try Again!

The illustrations you will find in this chapter could well be for some readers even more eloquent than the statements made by authorities and quoted in the preceding chapter.

It is often said that the best teacher is the one who does the least teaching. That may be true when learners are dealing with orderly, regular, and logical subject matter and when children can discover for themselves relationships and develop general and dependable rules. In Finland, children can infer and draw reliable conclusions when they learn to read, and that is the reason why such a high percentage of them learn to read at home before ever spending a day in school. However, a great majority of our children need all the help they can get because their inferences have to be false very, very often. Most educators know this. I found it expressed clearly and succinctly by a British educator, Vera Southgate:

> Written English does not constitute a regular spelling system. If the written form of our language represented a one-to-one relationship between written symbols and spoken sound, we might have a reasonable basis for hoping that by heuristic methods (stimulating pupils to learn by themselves) children could be encouraged to discover these relationships and to form generalizations. But our poor spelling system actually prevents children from making generalizations. . . . Such a situation not only discourages the child from trying to discover things for himself, but makes it practically impossible for him to do so.

You may find this statement in a 1970 book with the title, *Reading Skills*. (p. 72) It consists of a number of essays by reading specialists and was published by the United Kingdom Reading Association.

In a very large sense we find the theme of this book in that quotation: "Our spelling system prevents children from making generalizations . . . (It) not only discourages the child from trying to discover things for himself, but makes it practically impossible for him to do so."

Now I wish to illustrate what Professor Southgate and the other authorities say and what I have been writing about. I'll divide my efforts into four main sections.

1. Children must hear words of two or more syllables before they can know the values of the vowels. If we had reliable rules, that would not be necessary. In Chapter 3 under Reason 4 you saw a number of examples. Here are a few new ones to refresh your memory. Read along:

"Short"	"Long"	"Short"	"Long"
Latin	latex	gradual	gradient
talent	latent	radical	radial
stamina	stamen	valid	valence
register	region	venom	venal
meditate	medium	senate	senior
hinder	binder	blink	blind
novice	notice	bionic	tonal
globular	global	solace	solar

2. Now you will get more clear-cut evidence that many associations children might form would be faulty. English has a large number of "eye" rhymes, that is, pairs of words in which the last portions of the words appear to rhyme because their spelling is similar. However, their pronunciation differs. You can get a better idea of the problems facing our learners if you will read aloud both words and in the second word in each pair try to read it as if it rhymed with the word above. Here are sixty-three pairs representing large numbers:

has	that	dash
was	what	squash
later	lager	farce
water	wager	scarce
hanger	female	baked
ranger	morale	naked
days	maintain	daughter
says	mountain	laughter
ether	fete	flea
tether	complete	yea
been	break	hew
seen	creak	sew

Try Again! 59

weight	five	office
height	give	suffice
fiend	indict	uranium
friend	predict	nasturtium
lone	above	along
none	drove	among
no	both	golf
to	moth	wolf
horse	cook	couch
worse	spook	touch
bury	Jesuit	but
jury	recruit	put

In the following group we have the same principle, but note that words are within words. Again, try to make the second word rhyme with the first:

chase	ant	have
purchase	giant	behave
age	late	are
savage	palate	care
male	east	earth
tamale	breast	hearth
pear	river	rice
appear	driver	caprice
dine	vice	finite
sardine	service	infinite
lice	site	hose
malice	opposite	whose
now	done	own
snow	condone	down
promise	how	poise
compromise	throw	porpoise
try	union	liar
artistry	bunion	peculiar

In English there are at least fifty groups of "triplets," meaning groups of three words, in which like spelling represents dissimilar sounds. Here are fifteen of them:

bather	finale	forage	
father	pale	mirage	
gather	rationale	outrage	
plaid	here	great	
raid	there	heat	
said	were	threat	
brine	chemise	feline	
marine	demise	masculine	
margarine	premise	Vaseline	
bomb	cover	does	/dŭz/
comb	mover	goes	
tomb	over	shoes	
flood	cough	four	
mood	dough	hour	
good	rough	tour	
	through		

Please forgive this sample of my doggerel:

The Tail (Sorry, Tale) of a Dog

What has my master d*o*ne?	/ŭ/
I think he must have g*o*ne.	/ô/
And left me without a b*o*ne.	/ō/
I believe I saw one on the st*o*ve.	/ō/
But that would now be hard to pr*o*ve.	/o͞o/
Oh, Master, please show me your l*o*ve.	/ŭ/
I'll give you a big welc*o*me	/ə/
If you'll return to our h*o*me.	/ō/
Of fidelity I am the epit*o*me.	/ə/, /ē/

* * *

3. The reverse situation is found in some 1,250 words in which the sound is the same as in 1,250 other words, but the spelling varies.

Try Again!

These words are called homophones (homonyms). Here are eight pairs as samples:

aught, ought	cache, cash	colonel, kernel	him, hymn
/ôt/	/kăsh/	/kûr′nəl/	/hĭm/
fair, fare	knight, night	lean, lien	marshal, martial
/fâr/	/nīt/	/lēn/	/mär′ shəl/

In English we have more than a hundred (I have collected 115) groups of words in which three words rhyme, but all are spelled differently. Here are twenty sample groups:

buy, by, bye	cere, sear, seer	crews, cruise, cruse
dew, do, due	earn, Ern, urn	ewe, yew, you
gnu, knew, new	holey, holy, wholly	meat, meet, mete
oar, or, ore	pair, pare, pear	peak, peek, pique
praise, prays, preys	rain, reign, rein	rapped, rapt, wrapped
road, rode, rowed	seas, sees, seize	sew, so, sow
	their, there, they're	to, too, two

We even have a few sets of four-word homophones:

air, e'er, ere, heir   aisle, eye'll, I'll, isle

FALSE STARTS

4. There is even more convincing evidence in this chapter to demonstrate that with many thousands of words children cannot generalize, but must memorize. You probably remember how impossible it is for children to sound out words beginning with the letter *a* without having to back up and try another sound. As I stated earlier, almost half of all those words begin with the schwa sound. And even after children have learned to read words with three or four or even five letters, they cannot be at all sure what those letters, especially the vowels, stand for in longer words. For instance, *a* represents /ă/ in *man*. If children could count on the *a* to spell /ă/ in all words beginning with *m-a-n*, they wouldn't flounder as they do now in other words. They are safe with:

/ă/ in m*a*nic, m*a*nicure, and m*a*ndolin, but note these words:
/ā/ in m*a*nia, m*a*ngy, and m*a*niac
/ə/ in m*a*neuver, m*a*nipulate, m*a*nure
/ĕ/ in m*a*ny

Similarly, *a* spells /ă/ in c*a*n and

/ă/ in c*a*ncel, c*a*nteen, c*a*nton, but note
/ā/ in c*a*nine
/ə/ in c*a*nal, c*a*nary, c*a*nasta

The *a* spells /ā/ in *came,* but see these spellings:

/ă/ in c*a*mel, c*a*meo, c*a*mera
/ə/ in c*a*mellia

Children learn the word "cat" /kăt/. But in "cater" the *a* spells /ā/. Now put "cater" into "caterpillar" and again the *a* spells /ă/. Why?

Or children learn "lemon" and the *e* spells /ĕ/, although it spells /ē/ in "demon." But put "demon" into "demonstrate," and now *e* spells /ĕ/.

The point, of course, is that when the same letter spells different sounds in the same language environment, children cannot know which sound it spells in a new word. To expect them to guess, to try various sounds, especially when their chances of getting the correct answers are so poor, is antithetical to good teaching. And because English letters are unreliable, that unreliability places a burden on all learners, but on slower learners it is a monstrous burden. I am offering a plethora of examples.

We assume *a* spells /ä/ in *mar,* /mär/, as it does, and in quite a few other words. But it spells /ă/ in m*a*rathon, m*a*rijuana, and m*a*rionette. And it spells /ə/ in m*a*rauder, M*a*rie, and m*a*roon. It even spells /â/ in a well-known name, M*a*ry.

Surely, we say to ourselves, *par* spells /pär/ in most words in which these are the first three letters. Well, in 101 words it does, as in p*a*rdon, p*a*rsley, and p*a*rty. But in 147 other words the *a* spells three other sounds:

/ă/ in 102, as in p*a*radox, p*a*ragon, p*a*ragraph, p*a*ramount
/ə/ in 38, as in p*a*rade, p*a*rameter, p*a*rental, p*a*renthesis
/â/ in 7, as in p*a*re and p*a*rent.

The main obstacle to our being able to get down to Ichabod's level, excluding the fact that he doesn't have our native ability, is that we have lived all our adult lives with the knowledge of the ways words used as examples in this book are spelled. To us, the first *a* in these words is the only possible spelling: fanatic, fatigue, madonna. We are conditioned to think in terms of the visual. Ichabod, on the other hand, must start from the aural, from what he *hears* (/hĭrz/), and when he sees *madonna,*

Try Again! 63

he sees /măd′ŏn ă/; and when he sees *fatigue,* he sees /făt′ĭg yōō ē/ or something similar.

So how can I help you to get down to Ichabod's level? Perhaps this scheme will help. I'll write a word and then confuse you, as Ichabod is confused, by using capital letters when incorporating it in a longer word. It will be confusing because the vowel sound in the second word is not the same as it is in the first. But even this fact must be noted: The first spelling in most words is not phonetic either. I'm showing that even after Ichabod has memorized one spelling he cannot count on it; indeed, he MUST NOT count on it. So if Ichabod follows the instructions of phonics teachers, he will wind up horribly mixed up. I am sure the effect will be heightened if you will read all words, especially the words within words aloud. By the way, I planned to restrict the number of "false start" words here to 100, but stopped eliminating examples which I had gathered when I reached 120.

SINGLE SAMPLES

all, ALLergy	bear, BEARd	breath, BREATHing
broth, BROTHer	cafe, CAFEteria	circuit, CIRCUITous
close, CLOSEt	cloth, CLOTHing	coal, COALition
come, COMEt	count, COUNTry	coup, COUPle
court, COURTeous	cove, COVEr	coy, COYote
crow, CROWd	cur, CURious	cut, CUTicle
deal, DEALt	dear, DEARth	do, DOn't
doze, DOZEn	drive, DRIVEn	dub, DUBious
edit, EDITh	flour, FLOURish	flow, FLOWer
fun, FUNeral	go, GOwn	grave, GRAVEl
grow, GROWl	hat, HATred	heal, HEALth
hide, HIDEous	hum, HUMiliate	idol, IDOLatry
Jane, JANEt	know, KNOWledge	line, LINEn
lot, LOTus	map, MAPle	mean, MEANt
mime, MIMEograph	miner, MINERal	minus, MINUScule
miser, MISERy	nut, NUTrition	place, PLACEbo
plea, PLEAsant	post, POSTure	pun, PUNy
ran, RANge	real, REALity	rise, RISEn
rod, RODent	rout, ROUTine	scour, SCOURge
she, SHEllac	should, SHOULDer	show, SHOWer
sold, SOLDer	sour, SOURce	south, SOUTHern
spur, SPURious	stall, STALLion	steal, STEALth
tape, TAPEstry	tea, TEAr /â/, /ĭ/	though, THOUGHt
ton, TONic	trip, TRIPod	us, USual
vicar, VICARious	was, WASte	we, WEre
wear, WEARy	who, WHOle	yea, YEAst

Three Words, Three Possibilities

all, ALLay /ə/, ALLey /ă/
ball, BALLot /ă/, BALLoon /ə/
bar, BARrage /ə/, BARrier /ă/
cad, CADence /ā/, CADet /ə/
call, CALLigraphy /ə/, CALLous /ă/
colon, COLONial /ə/, COLONy /ŏ/
cap, CAPable /ā/, CAPacity /ə/
car, CARavan /ă/, CAReer /ə/
face, FACEt /ă/, FACEtious /ə/
hear, HEARd /û/, HEARty /ä/
hone, HONEst /ŏ/, HONEy /ŭ/
labor, LABORatory /ă/, LABORious /ə/
leg, LEGion /ē/, LEGitimate /ə/
not, NOTable /ō/, NOThing /ŭ/
pal, PALatial /ə/, PALtry /ô/
past, PASTrami /ə/, PASTry /ā/
pat, PATernal /ə/, PATience /ā/
path, PATHetic /ə/, PATHos /ā/
pot, POTable /ō/, POTato /ə/
tow, TOWard /ô/, TOWer /ou/

Authorities have said English spelling is chaotic. These word comparisons demonstrate how right they are. In conclusion, I offer you a few more samples of words in words; here we have fourteen more "false starts":

(a) pea /ē/, PEAr /â/, PEARl /û/
(b) tab /ă/, TABle /ā/, TABLEt /ă/
(c) ma /ä/, MAt /ă/, MATe /ā/, MATErial /ə/
(d) Leo /ē/, /ō/, LEOn /ē/, /ŏ/, LEONard /ĕ/,
     LEONora /ē/, /ə/
(e) he /ē/, HEr /û/, HERe /ĭ/,* HEREtic /ĕ/, HERETICal /ə/

In the first chapter I quoted from a series of articles commissioned and supervised by the Associated Press. I think it is in order now to repeat a quotation because it shows how little most people know about written English: "In English there are very few irregular words for which the rules don't apply."

If we change "In English" to "In certain languages," the statement is then more nearly correct. It definitely is NOT true in English, as about 500 (of the 584) sample words in this chapter alone attest.

Poor Ichabod and Johnny.

*As previously noted, five dictionaries show that *e* spells /ĭ/ in here.)

CHAPTER 8

How Our Irrational Spelling Developed (I)

> The traditional way of writing English is far from being so consistent that it is possible, if we know the sounds of a word, to know how it is to be spelled, or inversely, from the spelling to draw any conclusions as to its pronunciation. . . . However chaotic this may seem it is possible to a great extent to explain the rise of all these discrepancies between sound and spelling, and thus to give, if not rational, at any rate historical reasons for them.
> Otto Jespersen, *Essentials of English Grammar*, p. 61

In this and the following chapter you will read some of the historical reasons for the discrepancies between spelling and sound. There are at least ten major reasons, of varying importance, why there are so many flaws in our written language. But before we consider them, let me give a bit of historical background.

When the Angles, Saxons, and Jutes left the area between Denmark and Holland, which is now known as Schleswig-Holstein, they landed in England, speaking closely related dialects of a major language group, known variously as Germanic and Teutonic. The dialects closest to theirs were Frisian, Dutch, and Low (referring to low altitude) German, the dialect spoken in parts of Northern Germany. It is assumed the members of the three tribes did almost no writing, and what they did was in runic letters, the alphabet at that time also of the other Germanic tribes. From Ireland came Christian missionaries who spoke Latin. They used the Roman alphabet when they wrote Old English (Anglo-Saxon), and the Roman alphabet gradually displaced the runic one as settlers in England became Christianized.

REASON #1. Our writing got off on the wrong foot when a one-to-one relationship between each sound and each symbol was not established at the outset. Latin letters were introduced, but the ideal beginning would have been for the missionaries to develop an alphabetic system tailored to fit the sounds of Old English. For instance, they might have used doubled vowel letters to indicate "long" vowel sounds (as in d*ee*p, k*ee*p, and s*ee*n, to use a Modern English example), and single vowel letters to represent "short" vowel sounds. They could have spelled each sound just one way, and made each letter or combination of letters spell a single sound. Indeed, they did use the *æ* to represent /ă/, a sound which was unknown to the missionaries, and they used three runic symbols to spell three other sounds new to them, and, as a result, those four sounds were spelled phonetically. But in spelling many of the other sounds of an entirely different language family, Germanic, the missionaries, using their Roman alphabet, made a good many compromises, so many, in fact, that a whole lot of words were not spelled phonetically because there was not a one-to-one fit. Sadly, I must also report that the four sounds which were once spelled phonetically, in the course of time lost their special symbols and very often were no longer spelled phonetically.

What could one expect? The Latin alphabet at the time consisted of just twenty-three letters (*j, u,* and *w* were added later) and could not possibly be ideal for Old English, which had more than forty sounds and, therefore, needed more than forty letters.

REASON #2. The Norman Conquest (1066) not only changed the course of English history, but resulted in vast and significant changes in the vocabulary and spelling of English. Possibly this would not have been true if the Normans had given up their Norman-French language right away and had gone about learning and using English, the language of the people they had conquered. As a matter of fact, the forebears of the Norman Conquerors had originally come from Scandinavia in the tenth century and had settled in Normandy, an area in northern France. It was there that they had abandoned their Germanic dialect(s) and had adopted a dialect of the French tongue—because they had no intention of returning to Scandinavia. They assumed they were in Normandy for good. They were, of course, reigning in Normandy when they made their Conquest in 1066, and they made other conquests in southern Italy and Sicily. They did not learn Italian either, but continued to speak their French dialect. They made no attempt whatever to learn Old (and then Middle) English. In England they used French exclusively. By decree French was the official language, and it was used in government, in the law courts, and in the Church. Only a few of those who were subjugated could write at all.

Meanwhile, our spoken language was changing rapidly. Without the restraining forces that writers and writing would undoubtedly have exerted on English to hold back the revolutionary changes, which, incidentally, had already begun before the coming of the invaders, great changes came relatively rapidly. The language underwent sweeping modifications in grammar. First and foremost, the nouns lost their grammatical gender; and nouns, adjectives, and verbs gradually lost almost all of their endings.

As a consequence, a very large number of two-syllable words became monosyllables, and longer words lost the last syllable, which had previously helped to indicate genders, cases, and numbers of the words used. What Middle English lost, present-day German still has, and that is what makes German grammar so difficult to master; nouns still have grammatical gender, and adjectives and verbs still maintain endings. In Middle English the endings were almost entirely lost before Shakespeare. When written endings remained, they first became schwas and then "silent."

For some time the Norman rulers reigned over Normandy, much of Great Britain and a part of Italy, as well. But in Normandy their fortunes went downhill, and in 1204 King John was defeated and was obliged to withdraw to his English holdings. The kings of England did not recognize the French conquest of Normandy until the Treaty of Paris (1259). It was not until then, almost two centuries after their Conquest, that the rulers decided it was time to learn English! The result was a significant, sometimes momentous, development. The transfer from speaking French to English was doubly difficult because the Normans had used almost exclusively their own French-speaking cohorts in government, in the law courts, and in the Church. Indeed, the French language held sway in the law courts for centuries; it took an act of Parliament in 1731 to abolish the use of French and to establish the use of English! The English-speaking people held almost no good positions; they were largely unlettered men and women, working as peasants and artisans at all the menial tasks.

The Anglo-Normans did not systematically set up schools for themselves, possibly because there were extremely few qualified teachers, and they couldn't use books, since books didn't exist. Manuscripts were scarce and expensive. Naturally, they could not consult dictionaries, for no English dictionary had ever been written and none was to be attempted for four more centuries. When the descendants of the Normans were stumped for an English word, they simply threw in a French word—and that happened much too often. When those who could write were writing English and didn't know how to spell a word, they sometimes wrote it using French ways to symbolize English sounds. This was a haphazard, hodge-podge situation. Professor Mario Pei, in his *Story of the English Language,* expressed what transpired aptly and concisely when he wrote, "Our spelling troubles are due to the original sin of the mingling of two languages and two systems of writing." (p. 294)

If you have difficulty imagining how there could be any problem when words are transferred from another language, let me use an analogy. What would develop if we were to make a car and were to use a mixture of parts, some based on the metric system of measurement with meters and centimeters and others on yards and inches? Of course that is somewhat exaggerated, but the principle is sound. The symbols used in our written language are much more deficient and inefficient than they would have been without the foreign intrusion.

So the Normans mixed up a curious concoction consisting of two basically quite different spelling systems. They wrote what looked good to their eyes, not realizing that for many hundreds (thousands?) of years people would pay a heavy penalty for their changing what was at best only a moderately satisfactory system into something that was neither fish nor fowl, partly Germanic and partly Romanic. The samples which I am about to offer seem to me to be representative, and certainly not exaggerated.

(a) In Middle English, words spelled *ou* were sounded /ou/ (as in o*u*r and gr*ou*nd); in French, words spelled *ou* were sounded /o͞o/. When the Anglo-Normans imposed words containing the /o͞o/ sound on the English language, they did not use English spelling, but continued to use what looked right to them. Thus, every word with the *ou* spelling for the /o͞o/ sound was immediately an unphonetic spelling, since, as we know, *ou* in English represented the diphthong /ou/, as in *bounsen (bounce)* and *pownen (pound)*. Thus, these words are not spelled phonetically:

    coupon   group   roulette   routine   soup

Since *ou* in none of these words spells /ou/, each one must be learned separately. This could have been avoided if the spelling had been changed or if the Anglo-Normans had given the value of /ou/ to the *ou* spelling. They did neither; if they had changed the spelling, these words would have looked as normal as cr*u*sade, dr*u*id, fl*u*id and tr*u*th do to us now:

    kupon   grup   rulett   ruteen   sup

Here are additional words every single learner must master:

    bo*u*doir   co*u*p   do*u*che   Lo*u*is   Lo*u*ise
    n*ou*gat   r*ou*ge   r*ou*te   s*ou*venir   tr*ou*pe

Of course the fifteen samples are not confusing to you now, but you were obliged to learn and memorize them. Incidentally, do you pronounce *route* as /ro͞ot/ or /rout/? A highway, say *Route* 66? A newspaper *route*?

(b) When we see *trousseau*, we can know it came from French,

How Our Irrational Spelling Developed (I)

not only because *ou* spells /o͞o/, but also because *eau* spells /ō/, which is another unfortunate burden for poorer learners:

beau   bureau   chateau   plateau   tableau

(c) The Anglo-Normans even tampered with good and logical spelling of native English words. A good example is the word *guard* (and *guardian, bodyguard, color guard, honor guard,* etc.). The word was spelled logically as *gard* and was pronounced as it is now. The Anglo-Normans wanted to make sure that the *g* would be hard, as it already was, and inserted the *u, guard*. How in the world are children supposed to sound out the word now?

(d) The insertion of *u* was relatively innocuous; I used that example because it can be readily seen and understood. But what the Anglo-Normans did with the letter *c* represented a fundamental and wholly unnecessary change. Up to that time, the /k/ sound was spelled by *c,* as in *cat, comb,* and *catacomb,* as it still is in those words and as it is in *can, cup, picnic* and *tonic.* But the interlopers thought *c* should spell /s/, as it did (and does) in French. So when they replaced a perfectly good word, *gesiht,* meaning *face,* with their French word, *face,* they used their own spelling, using a *c* instead of an *s.* English now has thirteen ways to spell /s/, and the Anglo-Normans were responsible for introducing more than one of them. We are speaking here of one, *c.* If they had spelled *face* as *fase,* you would have accepted it, just as you accept *s* in *base* and *case.* It is possible we would have survived if we spelled *lace, pace,* and *race* with *s* instead of *c: lase, pase, rase.*

Many more examples are available, but three more should suffice. The descendants of the invaders decided *cwic* and *cwen* (and other words) didn't look right. (To the native English eye they did.) So they arbitrarily changed the spelling to *quick* and *queen* and created not only more headaches, but more unphonetic spellings. They allowed *c* to spell /k/ when followed by *a, o, u,* or a consonant, as in *cap, cot, cut, clash,* and *crash,* but when *c* was followed by *e, i,* or *y,* it had to represent /s/. Thus, we have another burden for our children. We are all obliged to learn and then memorize.

Here is an excellent example where reasoning, using analogies, lets our learners down. Words like *barricade, brigade,* and *brocade* were borrowed by French from Italian, and these words, ending in *-ade,* found their way into English, along with native French words, such as *arcade, escapade,* and *persuade.* These words English borrowed or had forced into its supply by the Anglo-Normans. And so we learn them. We see another word ending in *-ade, facade.* It is pronounced /fə säd'/, but it is often mispronounced because people put their minds to work to reason out the pronunciation, using analogies. So it comes out /făk'ād/

or /făk ād′/. And what happens? People laugh at those who have used their brains and reasoned logically and intelligently.

You see what happens when two systems of writing are mingled. The next example is a rather extended one, and therefore I am calling it number three.

REASON #3. We have about 300 words, many of them of very high frequency, in which the vowel sound /ŭ/ is spelled by *o* (m*o*ther, l*o*ve) or *ou* (en*ou*gh, t*ou*gh). The Anglo-Normans were to blame. In cursive writing certain letters were difficult for them to decipher. Again they arbitrarily changed phonetic to unphonetic spelling; but their changes resulted in 300 words that have to be learned individually. Here are eleven words to illustrate how the words looked in early Middle English (minus case and verb endings):

```
cum     becum              duf   luf    sum         sun
tun     tung    cuntree    ruh  (rugh  h, gh = /f/)  trubl
```

If you will read the words aloud, you'll probably recognize all of them. The Anglo-Normans changed the *u* to *o*, for example, in *come, become, dove, love, some, son, ton,* and *tongue;* and to *ou,* for example, in *country, rough,* and *trouble.*

Where is the logic? It is just chance that we don't spell *come* as *coume, love* as *louve, son* as *soun, trouble* as *troble,* etc.

Why were these illogical changes made? When common people wrote English, they used a sharp vertical stroke or strokes to write letters like *m, n, u* (which also served for *v*), *w (uu)* and *i* (which writers didn't dot then). So when the Anglo-Normans had difficulty deciphering those letters (the printing press hadn't been invented), they arbitrarily changed the spelling of the *u* to *o* or *ou*. Thus, the modern word *son,* which with its *u* ending was then spelled *sunu* and looked like 𝓼𝓾𝓷𝓾 , became *sonu* (and later lost the *-u* ending).

We are puzzled and wonder how it is possible that *o* and *ou* represent the /ŭ/ sound until we learn what transpired many centuries ago. So, with tongue in cheek, let me tell you what happened: One day in the thirteenth or fourteenth century bees were making *hunig* (*hunig*— the ending *-ig* was later changed to *ey*). When the bees weren't looking, the written form of the end product became *honig*. But people still called the substance /hŭn′ ĭg/. Since the bees couldn't read, they didn't have much to say about spelling and simply continued to "do their thing." The meddlers, who counted most those days when it came to writing, made the changes; and these changes did not look wrong to them. In addition, English borrowed or had thrust upon it other words in which *o* and *ou* spell /ŭ/, e.g., *color, cover, dozen, cousin,* and *touch.* Today this illogical

How Our Irrational Spelling Developed (I)   71

spelling helps nobody and hinders—penalizes, if you will—many. Perhaps you can remember how hard it was for you to learn to spell (and probably to read) *tongue*. Wouldn't the earlier form, *tung,* which, ironically, looks strange to you today, be considerably easier for everybody to learn?

These samples give you an idea of the havoc the ruling class wrought on our language many years ago.

REASON #4. The proliferation of schwas spelled by various vowel letters and combinations began in earnest with the gigantic flood of Norman-French words which swept across the land. The schwa had entered the language when the noun and adjective endings were gradually changed from various vowel sounds and then began to receive less force and emphasis. During this period, the schwa began to appear in weakened syllables of the alien words and was spelled by the letters the words had in the original French. This is still another illustration of what Pei meant when he said our spelling troubles resulted from the merging of two dissimilar languages. Naturally he was speaking of spelling in the broader sense, the spelling or symbolizing of sounds. French words were only lightly stressed, if at all, and certainly *not* on the first syllable, but only lightly toward the end. English words, on the contrary, were heavily stressed, usually on the first syllable. When French words were used in English, there was a tug-of-war, a push-pull situation. The unlettered English natives naturally wanted to pronounce the words their way. The new words with a light stress toward the end sounded wrong in a Germanic language, since *all* Germanic languages stress the root, ordinarily the first, syllable. And since English has the heaviest stress of all Germanic languages, the weakened syllables were truly weak, and the schwa sound was the inevitable result.

The transfer of the accent did not take place immediately; indeed, many words were stressed for centuries in more or less the French manner, and the shifting of the stress occurred quite gradually. Even now we have great numbers of words taken from Romance languages where the stress may be found on varying syllables. (The word *romance* is an example; it may be stressed on either the first or the second syllable.) Only chance has determined what has taken place and our present location of stress. And so borrowed words of two, three, and more syllables have been and are stressed on various syllables. Actually, in the earliest borrowings the stress was transferred in vast numbers of words to the first or the root syllable, and many of these alien words, even the longer ones, became naturalized and sound like native words.

But in many, many words the stress ended up on other syllables, and in them we hear a primary stress and often one or even two secondary stresses. It is in the unstressed syllables, as we have seen, where we find the schwa sound with its many spellings. And it is precisely here where learners have so much trouble.

Although not all Norman-French (and Parisian-French) words which came into our language were long, a high proportion of our borrowed or loan words are longer than our native Anglo-Saxon words. The shorter words which intruded and too often pushed aside completely satisfactory words sometimes look as if they had come down from Old English. Here are a few samples: *age, blue, cost, cream, dress, gay, hour, joy, price, taste,* and *use.*

Here are samples of longer words which entered our language from French. You may wish to note the number of *un*stressed syllables, which are indicated by italicized letters:

1. Stress on the first syllable: govern*o*r, parl*i*am*e*nt, counc*i*l; trin*i*ty, min*i*ster, sav*iou*r; reven*ue*, ten*a*nt, pris*o*ner, judgm*e*nt, pan*e*l, fel*o*n; fash*io*n*a*ble, lux*u*ry, butt*o*n; reg*u*lar, saus*a*ge, lett*u*ce

2. Stress on the second syllable: *a*ssembly, *a*llegi*a*nce; r*e*ligi*o*n, the*o*logy, r*e*demption; c*o*mpress (vb.), *a*ward, *a*pparel; *a*cquit, d*e*fend*a*nt, *a*rrest; m*e*dalli*o*n

3. Stress on the third, fourth, or fifth syllable: un*i*vers*a*l, contr*i*bution, retr*i*bution, s*u*perior*i*ty, rec*a*pit*u*lation, rec*o*nciliation

You will have noted fifty-six instances of weakened vowel sounds in thirty-six words; those fifty-six weakened sounds are spelled in ten (!) different ways.

It would be a grievous oversight on my part if I failed to remind you that the location of stress is something all beginners have to learn. This is the case not only in hundreds, but in thousands of words. Perhaps this fact is best illustrated by using pairs where the stress shifts and adds another burden on our learners. This time the italicized letters will indicate the stressed syllable: am*e*liorate, ameli*o*ration; cont*i*nue, continu*i*ty; c*o*nverse, convers*a*tion; r*u*in, ruin*a*tion; s*a*crifice, sacrif*i*cial; s*a*crilege, sacril*e*gious.

In our consideration of the loan words from French we are talking about an enormous number of words. The net result of the borrowings of both necessary and unnecessary French words, as Charlton Laird wrote in *The Miracle of Language,* was that "More than a quarter of our vocabulary comes from French." (p. 131)

REASON #5. In late Old English and early Middle English there was no unifying force, no power which gave primacy to the spelling of sounds in large numbers of words. The result was confusion, bordering on chaos. In France, what was spoken and written in Paris was regarded as correct, as *comme il faut.* Italy, Spain, and Denmark, to name three other countries, had dominant dialects that set the standard for their respective languages. Not knowing otherwise, we would assume that

London had exerted a similar influence on English, but during the crucial centuries this was not true. There were a great many minor and four major dialects: Northumbrian, Mercian, West Saxon, and Kentish.

In the western part of the United States many readers will not appreciate what I am talking about, but British readers will know. You can best understand about dialects if you have studied a foreign language in school or college and then have gone abroad to use your hard-acquired skill. You have discovered that the inhabitants of the country whose language you studied are bilingual; they can speak and understand the language you learned, but in the home and with friends they speak quite a different language, a dialect. If you go to German-speaking Switzerland or to Austria or to many of the West or East German states, e.g., Franconia or Mecklenburg, you will hear strange sounds that don't seem to come close to those you learned in your German class. If you speak well, your listeners will be able to understand you; and if they make the effort to speak standard German, you will be able to understand them. One time when my wife and I went for a long walk in German-speaking Switzerland we got lost. We came to a hamlet, where I asked a boy of ten or eleven how we could find our way back to the city. Instead of answering my question, he burst out laughing and said in barely understandable German, "You talk the way our minister talks."

What I am emphasizing is that on the Continent and in the British Isles even today there are strong regional dialects, and many people can tell by the speech of other people who live fifty or perhaps even twenty miles away where they come from. This is difficult for us to believe, where residents in Denver would probably not be able to detect by their speech whether speakers came from Los Angeles, Seattle, or even Denver. Of course American English has its regional differences, e.g., New England, Bostonian, Brooklyn, and Southern. But European, including British, dialects are far greater in number and much stronger and more pronounced.

Now all of this explanation is definitely essential because the lack of a unifying force resulted in large numbers of varied spellings of sounds and in varied pronunciations of letters or combinations of letters. This is a complicated subject, but one example stands out very clearly, and it will be enough to explain a phenomenon which perplexes many. Please remember, however, that it is only one illustration and represents great numbers of anomalies. Think of the *-ough* words. Had there been a unifying force whose absence we have been considering and deploring, the diverse pronunciations might easily have become just one sound (or a diphthong) to represent the vowel combination. But *-ough* words were pronounced one way in one dialect, a second way in another dialect, and a third in still another. What we have today is the result of one dialect winning out in some words, another winning out in others, and a third in still others. Consequently we have:

(a) /ou/ bough, drought   (b) /ō/ dough, though
(c) /o͞o/ through   (d) /ô/ fought, thought
(e) /ŭ/ rough, tough   (f) /ə/ thoroughfare
  (*Slough* has three pronunciation: /slŭf/, /slou/, and /slo͞o/)

Now look at the *-gh,* not the vowel combination. The consonant combination may represent nothing (be "silent") or /f/. If there had been a central authority that could have made final decisions, and if the decision had been made to pronounce the guttural sound which was pronounced a thousand years ago in Old English and was represented by *h* or *gh,* then we'd probably have forty-five sounds instead of forty-four and (a) *gh* would not stand for /f/ or be litter in our language, and (b) we'd still have the same guttural sound in our language which German still has and pronounces in words after the vowels *a, o,* and *u,* as is true in *Bach, Koch,* and *Bruch.*

Incidentally, the London and East Mercian dialects eventually, but relatively very late in the development of our language, exerted the greatest influence.

We'll reserve for the next chapter a discussion of the five other major reasons for our faulty spelling system.

CHAPTER 9

How Our Irrational Spelling Developed (II)

There is an element of truth in this tale. The Losen (rhymes with chosen) family slept much longer than Rip van Winkle did. You may recall the story by Washington Irving. He had Rip sleep twenty years; and when Rip woke up, he found that everything had changed. Well, our fictional family, the Losens, living in England, slept much longer, say from the year in which Chaucer died (1400) until the year Alexander Pope died (1744). After the long sleep, the Losens felt well rested, but they weren't prepared for what had happened to their names: the spelling had remained the same, but all the vowel sounds had changed! The mother was Ida, and the father was Peter. Their children were David and Irene.

When the mayor of the small village asked them their names, they couldn't understand him because they had never heard the word /nāmz/ in all their long lives. They had heard the word /näm'ə/ (as in f*a*ther). But when they finally understood, they said their names as they had always heard and spoken them: Ida said /ē'dä/, Peter said /pā'tär/, David said /dä'vēd/, and Irene said /ē rä nä/. A cluster of villagers had formed around the mayor and the family, and all were staring in disbelief; nobody had ever heard any one of those names. They sounded strange and quaint. Then the mayor asked Mr. Losen if he would write the names. Of course he was unable to do that because he couldn't write. However, he remembered that the priest had written all their names on a piece of linen. And when he found it, he handed it to the mayor. The lattter, who was one of the few villagers who could read, was astonished when he saw the writing; he could read all the names, and he triumphantly read them, /ī'də/, /pē'tər/, /dā'vĭd/, /ī rēn'/.

Unfortunately, the priest had written the *n* in the family name to look like an *r*. So the mayor read the name as *Loser* /loō'zər/. Thus, the Losens (chosens) became the Losers.

REASON #6. Although the episode is fictional, it is really true that during the period covering roughly from around 1400 to about 1750 a major change took place in the pronunciation of our "long" vowel sounds without consistent changes in spelling to follow the changes in the sounds. Most spellings remained constant! The vowels in the five names illustrate what actually happened.

This is such a bizarre historical happening that you might wonder if I dreamed it up. No, you will find it described in all books dealing with the history of the English language. The phenomenon is called the "Great Vowel Shift." It occurred not only in proper names, but in many thousands of words. The mystery to me, in addition to the fact that it could take place at all, is that today very few people have ever heard of the Great Vowel Shift. We learn about many other historical events which transpired between the fifteenth and the eighteenth centuries, and I am sure many of them are not as important to us as is something which affected so profoundly our language and greatly disrupted its vowel spelling, something every educated English-speaking person should know about. Why has it been kept secret from us? A good friend, who is a distinguished historian and prolific writer, slyly suggested that the Great Vowel Shift would be better known if it were called "The Great Vowel Movement."

To be sure, it is difficult to believe it occurred and just as difficult to explain, but it is of overwhelming importance because it is one of the major reasons why enormous numbers of spellings of our sounds became unphonetic and thus, why our written language is so hard to learn to read and to spell.

This is what took place. In the fourteenth century, Chaucer pronounced "long" vowels as they had been pronounced in Old English and in early Middle English and as they had been pronounced in Latin, and as they were and still are pronounced today in *all* Romance languages and in *all* Germanic languages except English.

Here are the differences between the ways Chaucer and Shakespeare (1564–1616) wrote and pronounced sample words:

CHAUCER WROTE AND PRONOUNCED:	SHAKESPEARE WROTE AND PRONOUNCED:
macian /mä′kē än/	make /māk/
David /dä′vēd/	David /dā′vĭd/
ded— /dā′d—/	deed /dēd/
Peter /pā′tār/	Peter /pē′tər/
tima /tē ′mä/	time /tīm/
Ida /ē′dä/	Ida /ī′də/
col /kōl/	cool /ko͞ol/
Losen /lōz—/	losen /lo͞o′zən/
hus— /ho͞os/	house /hous/

How Our Irrational Spelling Developed (II)

(All three vowel sounds in Irene changed, /ē/ to /ī/, /ä/ to /ē/ and /ā/ to /ə/ or "silent" *e*.)

In general the vowel sounds shifted as you see here:

/ä/ to /ā/   /ā/ to /ē/   /ē/ to /ī/
/ō/ to /o͞o/   /o͞o/ to /ou/

What happened was that the vowel sound which was pronounced lowest in the mouth moved toward a higher position of articulation; the next lowest one also moved upward; and so on until the highest, /o͞o/, could not move any higher and became the diphthong /ou/; and that is the reason Old English *hus-*, pronounced /ho͞os/, became Modern English *house* and *suth* became *south*.

Nobody can explain why people started giving the "long" vowel sounds different values; nobody gave the movement direction; and nobody consciously stopped the shifting. Since the changes were so gradual, probably most people were quite unaware of what was happening. Of course very few people could read, and the great majority wouldn't have and couldn't have known that spelling changes were not accompanying sound changes. A somewhat related occurrence had taken place in the seventh century in Old High German, when there was a consonant shift. However, as the sounds shifted, spelling changes were made to correspond to the different sounds. Consequently, no spelling (or reading) problems developed.

During our Great Vowel Shift the spelling did change when *u* (/o͞o/) became the diphthong /ou/. And so we quite properly spell the Old and Middle English words *mut* and *ut* as *mouth* and *out*. But otherwise when the sounds shifted upward, writers did not ordinarily use the letters which represented the new sounds. They usually continued to use the old and familiar spellings, which, obviously, were no longer appropriate for the new pronunciations. I'll give a few examples. Our Modern English words *soon, spool,* and *spoon* were once spelled and pronounced *sona* /sō'nä/, *spole* /spō lā/, and *spon* /spōn/, respectively. When the vowel sound shifted to the higher sound, the proper spelling would have been to use the letter *u*, as the words *hus, mut, suth,* and *ut* had been written. That wasn't done, and the spelling *oo* was used; and so we now often indicate the sound with those two letters to spell /o͞o/. We are conditioned to it and think there must be something sacred about it, sanctified by usage. But note that we also show the same pronunciation with the use of the letter *u*. Compare the words cr*u*el, J*u*ne, r*u*de, R*u*th, tr*u*th, and t*u*na. As you remember (from Chapter 3), we have more than a dozen common ways to spell /o͞o/, and the Great Vowel Shift made its confusing contributions.

Unfortunately, the digraph *oo* did not wind up spelling only /o͞o/, as you will see in eight more words, all of which had the /ō/ sound and the *o* spelling in Old and early Middle English. In these samples you will see how inconsistent many of the spellings became. In the eight words, four different sounds are spelled by *oo,* including /ō/(!), since the sound did not invariably change. Here the spelling did! So we have /ō/, /o͞o/, /o͝o/ and /ŭ/:

Old English	Modern English	Modern English	Modern English	Modern English
all/ō/	/ō/, /ô/	/o͞o/	/o͝o/	/ŭ/
dor, fod, boc, blod	door	food	book	blood
flor, gos, fot, flod	floor	goose	foot	flood

Do you now understand why several experts and authorities have said English spelling is irrational? Incidentally, you may have wondered why some speakers say /ro͞of/ and some say /ro͝of/, and some say /ro͞om/ and others says /ro͝om/. The same two pronunciations are used with a few other words, such as *groom, hoof,* and *root.* This is an indication that the Great Vowel Shift even now has not come to a complete halt. Of course both pronunciations are correct. In some dictionaries you will even find three pronunciations for the *oo* spelling in the word *soot:* /so͞ot/, /so͝ot/, and /sŭt/. How do you say *room* and *poolroom?* Note /fo͝otsto͞ol/. Does a person put one's /fo͝ot/ in one's /bo͞ot/? There has to be something wrong with such a spelling system.

My reason for choosing the name "Losen" in the bit of fiction is to show how illogical the spelling is of *lose, prove, approve, move, remove,* etc. Of course *lose* should rhyme with *rose* and *prove* with *stove.* And *do, to,* and *who* should rhyme with *go, no,* and *so.* Now it is clear why they do not; the Shift is to blame.

Incidentally, both *shoe* and *toe* had the same spelling, *o,* and vowel sound, /ō/, in early Middle English; the sound in *shoe* shifted; in *toe* it didn't! Of course the spelling of both vowel sounds by *oe* in Modern English doesn't help either word—or learners, whether they are learning to read or to spell.

Another important matter must be mentioned. By my choice of examples I have given the impression it was only native words whose vowel sounds underwent change. That is by no means correct. The vowel sounds in words borrowed from Norman- and Parisian-French (and Latin) were not spared; they were shifted in large numbers of these words also. A good example is the word *face.* When it was borrowed, the vowel was pronounced /ä/. It became /ā/ as a result of the Great Vowel Shift.

How Our Irrational Spelling Developed (II)

Reason #7. Before the huge wave of French words that crashed over the English language between 1250 and 1400 fully subsided, another gigantic wave containing many more thousands of new foreign words began to inundate English. These words, largely from Latin, but also from Greek and again from French, were brought in by Renaissance (Revival of Learning) scholars beginning in the fourteenth and continuing into the seventeenth century. The learned men consciously added multitudes of words to our language, wishing to enrich it. We get an idea of the number of words involved in our borrowing when we read Professors J. B. Greenough and G. L. Kittredge's statement that "English has appropriated a full quarter of the Latin vocabulary"! (*Words and Their Ways,* p. 106)

We'll consider the borrowing of so many words from Latin, Greek, and French from three aspects:

A. If the two waves of borrowing had come from a related language, that is, from another Germanic language, we surely wouldn't have half as many illiterates as we do, and certainly not more than a fifth as many functional illiterates. What Pei said about our borrowing from French holds true—possibly to an even greater degree—for our borrowing from Latin. Here are seven thoughts we should bear in mind:

1. Latin was the mother of the Romance languages and is quite unlike English in many respects.

2. The words borrowed in the second wave were, for the most part, more scholarly and learned, and for that reason fewer became naturalized.

3. The Latin words were borrowed more recently, most of them during the sixteenth century, and so they had less chance of becoming naturalized.

4. Many people seldom hear a good many of the borrowed words and are uncertain how they should be pronounced, mainly because they don't know where the stress or stresses fall.

5. Slow learners have no idea how such words sound or what they mean.

6. The tendency to shift the stress to the first syllable in the Latin loan words has been even less successful than in the earlier French borrowings.

7. In general, the words from Latin were longer than native words, and partly for that reason do not lend themselves to be used in conversation as readily as shorter native words do.

Going from the abstract to the concrete, we'll examine thirteen loan words from Latin, together with nineteen words which are related to them. You will find that two-thirds of all the words are not stressed on the first syllable. The stress is on the syllables as shown in the following list:

First	Second	Third	Fourth	Fifth
syllable				syllabification
	appropriate		appropriation	
educate		education		
	subordinate		subordination	
implicate		implication		
		superficial		superficiality
	superior		superiority	
illustrate	illustrate	illustration		
	illustrative			
intellect	intelligent	intellectual		intellectuality
		individual		individuality
mechanize	mechanic		mechanization	
idiot		idiotic	idiosyncracy	idiosyncratic
paradise			paradisiacal	

If we examine the words critically for the location of the stress, we realize that with such words as these we cannot generalize. It is apparent, therefore, that each word has to be learned individually. We do not find this deplorable situation in other Western languages. Although scholars in other countries where Germanic languages are spoken—for example, in Germany and Holland—borrowed from Latin, they did it on a relatively minor scale. In general, they translated the ideas expressed in the foreign words into their own languages, using native elements. As a result, it is much less difficult to learn the meaning and pronunciation of these words in Dutch or German than it is in English. In my opinion, the fact that the classical scholars failed to do what was done elsewhere brought about a condition with which millions have been unable to cope; and here we have a basic reason for so much functional illiteracy in the English-speaking world.

B. The new wave of loan words brought along more spelling problems. One type will serve as an illustration. Since the Great Vowel Shift, the letter *i*, as we have seen, now spells /ī/ (and /ĭ/), but it still spells /ē/ in other European languages, as it did in Latin. The later loan words in which the letter spelled /ē/ in Latin should have undergone a change in spelling and allowed the letter *e* to represent the /ē/ sound. But logic did not prevail. Surely the last two letters in ster*eo* are easily learned, both the reading and the spelling. But now we have thousands of words in which *i* spells /ē/, and not a single one of them is spelled phonetically, and each one has to be learned separately. These few samples came from Latin: affil*i*ate, associ*a*te, aud*i*o, man*i*ac, med*i*ate, rad*i*ate, rad*i*us, stad*i*um; and these words also came from Latin but by way of French: champ*i*on, id*i*om, obv*i*ous, patr*i*ot. The following four words from Latin will show you what I mean when I say we must learn each word individually: med*i*cation, med*i*eval, med*i*tate, med*i*um. In each word the value of the first *e* has to be learned, and in two words the first *i* spells a schwa and in the other two it represents /ē/. See how learned you are to know these things.

C. Seeking to improve our language, the classical scholars tried to make it possible for readers to know the source of as many loan words as possible. It goes without saying that Ichabod and Johnny (and most learners) couldn't care less. The scholars paid little or no heed to "correct" pronunciation, and they made a number of words less phonetic, more illogical, and, hence, harder to learn to read and spell.

Nearly all writers on the history of the English language emphasize this movement and devote many pages to it, but in all honesty, even though I deplore the changes, I think they are of relatively minor importance. Some of the changes are interesting. Here are examples of what the scholars did. English received the word *isle* from French after French had dropped the *s* from the word. So in English it was spelled *ile*. But the scholars inserted an *s* because the French word had once had it! The next example is even worse (or better). The word *island* came from Old English and was not borrowed from French. It had become *iland* in Middle English. But the scholars stupidly inserted an *s* and so today we write the word as *island!* And *aisle* also had to take on a worthless *s*, again for no reason.

There are a few words English borrowed from French that had no letter *b* in either French or English. Scholars later burdened the words with the superfluous *b* because the original Latin words had a *b*. Since then, we have written dou*b*t, de*b*t, and su*b*tle and have assumed that somewhere in the history of the language the *b* had become "silent." Actually, however, even after the *b* was added people did not pronounce it in any of the words. Here are more samples with other inserted letters: the *c* in indi*c*t and vi*c*tual, the *g* in rei*g*n and sovere*g*n, the *l* in sa*l*mon, and the *p* in recei*p*t. These letters were added gratuitously, and promptly became garbage letters.

Rhinoceros, rhubarb, rhyme, rhetoric, and a few other words beginning with *rh* had slipped into our language surreptitiously without the *h,* but the scholars made the "corrections." They did worse: They inserted an *l* in *coude,* to become *coulde* because *should (scholde)* and *would (wolde)* had the letter and it was sounded in both words. Isn't it too bad they didn't knock the *l* out of *should* and *would* (and from *could,* also) when it no longer was sounded in these words?

Three other words should surely be mentioned. In *all* words except three, when you see the worthless combination *gh* (or *gh* = /f/), you can be certain they came from Old English. The three exceptions were borrowed from French, and for no reason at all scholars added those letters. What was their thinking? Where was their logic? The three words are *haughty, sprightly* and *delight.* I think Middle English and Modern English would have been able to muddle through without the "improvements." *Delight* was *deliten.*

REASON #8. At the three most critical periods in the history of our language, rank amateurs played crucial, major roles. You will recall how the first persons to write English in the Roman alphabet were foreigners, Latin-speaking missionaries. You remember also how those who did most of the writing when English was revived as a written language were French-speaking and English-learning Anglo-Normans. Finally, in 1476, when Caxton brought the printing press to England, he brought along foreign (Dutch and Flemish) printers who had learned their trade in their native provinces and knew little English.

Imagine for a moment what might have been. This was a crucial, a pivotal, moment in the history of the written language. The invention of the printing press was the greatest boon to universal education. (It also helped to fix or set the spelling of words.) If Caxton had taken linguistically gifted, educated men with him to the Continent and had had them learn the printing trade and then had brought them back to England to print English books, think of the possibilities. Written English, the spelling of our sounds, was badly in need of repair. If those men had established rules and had followed them, countless billions of hours would have been saved up to now. Countless trillions of hours will be lost in the future because this was not done. Instead, the printers Caxton brought to England had considerably less education than the writers for whom they set up type. How could they have made improvements? They set up letters, not words, and were fortunate if the letters were the same as those in the manuscripts.

However, all the information I have been able to garner indicates that the printers at least didn't do great harm to the language. We must keep in mind that all over Europe Latin was the language of learning, and professors at Oxford, Cambridge, Prague, Heidelberg, Paris, and so forth, lectured in Latin. So English professors wrote their scholarly treatises in Latin also. Consequently, by 1500 not even a third of the books printed in England were in English. The printers became (in)famous for inserting the *h* in a few words; and present-day writers usually say they did so because the equivalent words in Dutch had an *h* after the *g*. They should get the facts. In Flemish, *ghost* was written with an *h, gheest,* but the Dutch word was then and is today *geest,* and the Dutch word for *ghastly* never did resemble our word. Actually, Dr. Samuel

How Our Irrational Spelling Developed (II)

Johnson added the ridiculous, worthless *h* there! At least we got rid of the *h* in *ghess, ghest, ghospel,* and *ghossip.* Residual Anglo-Norman influence controlled the first two, the Church must have taken care of the *ghospel,* and I suppose a whole lot of people participated in *ghossip.*

REASON #9. One of the most important reasons why our spelling has become unphonetic is the litter in our language—the innumerable, useless, unsounded, purposeless, empty letters that pollute our language. As I have said before, I am not about to set out on a crusade for the reformation of our spelling. If I were to do so, I would be doing a disservice to the cause which I have taken up. An effort to start a spelling reform would be doomed to fail, just as the many attempts in the past have failed. My concern is for and with our learners, their parents and teachers, our illiterates, and our poor spellers.

You have long since come to accept our wasted and worthless "silent" letters, and you rarely give them a thought. English has more of those wasteful letters than any other major language or, for that matter, more than a combination of several languages. Finnish has none, and you can be sure English has far more "waste" letters than German and Dutch combined, and I say this from a careful and intimate study of the three languages.

This chapter is concerned with the "how" as well as the "why." I think there are five chief reasons for our having so many unsounded letters. Briefly, they are as follows:

(a) Certain letters that used to represent sounds no longer do, but we still write them. We'll take an instance in which this is *not* true. In Old English the words for *loaf* and *roof* were *hlaf* /hläf/ and *hrof* /hrōf/. We have good reason to believe the English-speaking people in the ninth and tenth centuries pronounced both beginning letters, *h* and *l* and *h* and *r,* when they spoke those words and words like them. We must assume they did not choke, at least not to death. In the course of time, some speakers started to drop the *h,* and eventually everybody followed suit. Writers had the good sense to stop writing the letter *h* in those words when it was no longer spoken. And so we have *loaf* and *roof.*

But when English-speaking people stopped pronouncing the *b* in cli*mb* and la*mb,* the *k* in *k*nee and *k*not, and *w* in *w*rite and *w*rong, writers did NOT have the good sense to stop writing the letters which no longer performed any phonetic function. You know without my telling you that my six words are simply examples and represent other letters and hosts of other words. German also had the *b* in *klimban* and later in *klimben;* but when the *b* was lost in speech, a second *m* was added to show the *i* spelled a "short" sound; thus, Germans still write the word phonetically, *klimmen.* The consonant was also lost in speech in the German word for *lamb,* but again a second *m* informs the reader that the vowel is "short," *Lamm.* Since Germans still pronounce as well as write the *k* in the *kn* combination, there is no worthless letter in *Knie (knee)* or *Knoten (knot),* and German children don't have to learn that *k* plus *n* can represent just *n,* as our children do.

This is something to ponder: If the sound /r/ should be dropped universally when final, then our total number of unsounded letters will shoot up disturbingly, and children will be confronted with an even greater problem. It is not in ou*r* poo*r* powe*r* to dete*r* or even slow down such a movement. If enough of the right (wrong?) people make the dropping of the /r/ the thing to do, teachers and all others will be powerless.

(b) We have borrowed many words which have "silent" and quite worthless letters, as in Chabli*s, depot, physique, r*hododendron, *p*neumonia, and *p*sychology. We sometimes assume *p* and *s* cannot be blended, but we pronounce both letters in *caps, lips,* and *stops*. Germans and French do pronounce them in their equivalents for *psychology,* but the Italians and Spanish-speaking people don't spell the word with a *p* since they don't speak it!

(c) We have thousands of words in which letters serve no phonetic function. Because of lay people's protests, I am not including the *e* following a consonant to indicate the preceding vowel is "long," or that a preceding *c* or *g* is soft. What phonetic role does the final *e* play, for instance, in such words as curv*e*, delv*e*, glov*e*, improv*e*, valv*e*, intensiv*e*, doctrin*e*, famin*e*, intestin*e*, quarantin*e*, cultur*e*, featur*e*, fixtur*e*, pastur*e*, composit*e*, consulat*e*, legat*e*, obstinat*e*, comrad*e*, lonesom*e*? We must remember that very large group of words ending in *-le:* legibl*e*, profitabl*e*, ampl*e*, appl*e*, bottl*e*, saddl*e*, and muffl*e*. (Aren't there two nonfunctional letters in each of the last four words?)

For that matter, the letter *e* is not truly necessary in such words as barl*ey*, Cockn*ey*, chimn*ey*, and voll*ey*. Of course you rightly say that such words without the *e* would not look right. But the following words (and a whole lot of other words) get along without the *e:* silky, sticky, and Nancy. See how they look with the *e:* silk*ey*, stick*ey*, Nanc*ey*.

(d) Reason "c" overlaps reason "d" somewhat. We have embedded in our words a great many fossils which you will find if you but look for them. Of course we have such letters as the *t* in rus*t*le and whis*t*le. We used to think we uttered a /d/ sound in he*d*ge and ri*d*ge. We do not think so today. Did we ever utter the /t/ sound in di*t*ch (compare rich)? But we have known for a long time we don't sound the /t/ in ha*t*ch, Sco*t*ch, and wre*t*ch.

It is habit, convention, that dictates how many words are written in English. Convention requires a *w* on lo*w*, shado*w*, slo*w*, sorro*w*, and

How Our Irrational Spelling Developed (II)

swallow. Convention dictates no *w* on other words, such as echo, ego, photo, tomato, and zero. They look queer with a *w:* echow, egow, photow, tomatow, and zerow, but "go slow" would look ridiculous to us if *slow* had been spelled *slo* for the past three or four centuries. *Go slo* makes more sense than *go slow*. English just "growed."

We have made a good beginning. There are countless "silent" vowel letters. If bead is correct (beed would be better!) then head has an unsounded vowel, the *a,* and so do many other words, such as dead, deaf, dread, spread, sweat, and thread, and so do jealous, weapon, and weather, among others. And if the *e* in her spells /û/, then the *a* is superfluous and "silent" in such words as early, learn, pearl, search, and yearn. In a similar manner if *art* is /ärt/, then the *e* is wasted in heart.

The combination *ou* provides us with a great many more examples of wasted letters. It should spell /ou/, as it does, in a large number of words. But (1) If *u* spells /o͞o/ in prudent, ruby, and stupid, then we don't need the *o* in youth, acoustics, Vancouver, etc.; (2) If *o* spells /ô/ in for, nor, and or, we don't need the *u* in course, mourn, pour, etc.; (3) If *u* spells /ŭ/ in cut, lumber, and tumble, we don't need the *o* in couple, double, young, Douglas, etc.; (4) If *u* spells /û/ in curt, purr, and slur, we don't need the *o* in encourage, nourish, sojourn, etc.; (5) If *o* spells /ō/ in bolt, colt, and fold, we don't need the *u* in cantaloupe, poultice, poultry, etc.; and (6) If *u* spells the schwa in many words, why do we need the unnecessary *o* in a tremendous number of words, e.g., heinous, miscellaneous, ruinous, stupendous, vigorous, vociferous, etc.? Compare cactus, citrus, impetus, stylus, versus, etc.

(e) For almost a thousand years there has been a tendency to shorten English words. As a consequence, English has more short words than any other Western language. I have previously described two processes: (1) English dropped grammatical endings and thereby lost the final syllable on most nouns, adjectives, and verbs; and (2) A syllable was lost and words were shortened when the consonant sounds spelled by *c, s, ss,* and *t* merged with the following vowel sounds spelled by *i* or *e* to form the /sh/, /ch/, and /zh/ sounds, as in ocean, bastion, and vision. We have also lost another syllable which I have not mentioned; it is in hundreds of verbs in the past tense form, where the *e* represents no sound, e.g., rubbed, jogged, nailed, filled, dreamed, strummed, mined, pinned, roared, played, weighed, ploughed, plowed, mowed, coached, bluffed, coughed, cooked, gasped, collapsed, pressed, wished, unearthed, mixed.

The strong stress of English with the attendant understressed syllables lends itself to a further dropping of sounds and leaving worthless letters (as far as the spelling of sounds is concerned). This tendency prevails over the entire English-speaking world, but it is strongest in Britain. When you see the following examples of words in which we are losing a vowel sound, please remember how difficult it is for us to pronounce words as we usually do in normal conversation when we examine isolated words. At least two of my dictionaries show the loss of a syllable in all of the following examples. Most often it is given as an alternate, but acceptable, pronunciation:

asp*i*rin	average	cath*o*lic	choc*o*late
com*fo*rtable	desp*e*rate	diff*e*rence	element*a*ry
ev*e*ry	fact*o*ry	fam*i*ly	fav*o*rite
gen*e*ral	int*e*rest	myst*e*ry	priv*i*lege
rest*au*rant	sep*a*rate	tet*a*nus	veg*e*table
Barb*a*ra	Cath*e*rine	Dor*o*thy	Marg*a*ret

You may hear how the syllable represented by *a* is often, probably almost always, dropped in several hundred words ending in *-ally,* usually in *-ically*. Dictionaries don't often show the pronunciation—they can't show everything because of the extra space, weight, and cost—but I have found shortened respellings for these words: accident*a*lly, incident*a*lly, specific*a*lly, basic*a*lly, practic*a*lly, and diametric*a*lly. With the spelling of the schwa by *a* in the first three words there are five syllables; in the next two there are four, and in the last one there are six. Many Romance language words have five and six syllables, but each vowel gets treated well; in fact, the beauty of the spoken languages, for instance Italian, especially when it is sung, is due in large part to the full, round vowel sounds. English speakers are in a hurry.

If you remember the reasons for our many "silent" letters, you will be partially prepared for this astounding statement by Professor Rolf Johnson, the man who rightly said that 80 percent of our words are not spelled phonetically. He wrote as follows:

> In all, English contains hundreds of thousands of silent letters. Of the 604,000 words in the *Merriam-Webster* unabridged dictionary, over 400,000 have at least one silent letter; and many, of course, have more than one.
> (*The American Mercury,* September, 1948)

REASON #10. Our final reason for the enormous number of flaws in the spelling of English sounds is that virtually nothing has been done to correct them. We must not point proudly to those superficial changes Noah Webster made; there are so few of them and they are, after all,

How Our Irrational Spelling Developed (II)

so trifling that they hardly deserve mention. Besides, they were not universally accepted. When I complain that so little has been done to make corrections, you may well ask if it would have been possible. Certainly it would be a mountainous undertaking today, immeasurably more difficult than in Caxton's day, in part because so many more can read now. Above all, very few people even want any improvements. The *Chicago Tribune* once adopted the phonetic spelling of fewer than one hundred words, and the uproar and the anger which resulted were unbelievable. When *Time* magazine reported on the *Tribune's* abandonment of the project, a *Time* writer expressed warmest approval. The general attitude in the entire English-speaking world is expressed in these words: Leave our spelling alone!

Shall we consider what might have been? Since Caxton, several languages have improved their spelling, especially Turkish, Russian, and French. When Kemal Attaturk held the reins of government in Turkey (1923–1938), he adopted the Roman alphabet; and because scholars made the letters follow the sounds, Modern Turkish is spelled phonetically. Earlier, when the Cyrillic alphabet was modified and simplified to spell Russian words, great numbers of phonetic adaptations were made. In addition, the spelling reform of 1918 aided in making the spelling of most Russian words phonetic.

About 400 years ago Cardinal Richelieu and the French Academy decided that some 5,000 words needed to be spelled phonetically and the changes were made accordingly. The decree went out that the new spelling was to be used, and it was. Since that time, French children have easily and quickly learned those 5,000 words. Thousands of German words are spelled phonetically because of the great influence of the largest state in the German Empire, Prussia. In 1880 it issued a small book containing rules for the reform of German spelling, which made a great many spellings follow sounds. Other states fell into line, and German spelling was considerably improved. Moreover, further improvements were made in a conference in 1901, and they were approved by the governments of the German Empire, Austria, and Switzerland. The changes are in universal use today wherever German is written. Further minor improvements are in the offing and very likely will be accepted in this century, especially since many people are already using some of them. In the last century improvements in Dutch spelling have been made twice; the most recent ones went into effect in 1946.

Other languages in which important changes have been made in the writing of sounds—all in the past hundred years—include, among others, Danish, Norwegian, and Portuguese. As I have previously indicated, it would be quite impossible to make sweeping changes to improve either Finnish or Hungarian. The learners know where the stress falls and even in unstressed syllables the letters represent essentially the same values as in the stressed ones.

Imagine how much easier it would be to learn to read English if the spelling of the 5,000 most frequently used, unphonetically spelled words had been corrected and written phonetically four hundred years ago. It was John Geenleaf Whittier who wrote in *Maud Muller* these words:

> For of all sad words of tongue or pen,
> The saddest are these: "It might have been"!
>
> (Stanza 53)

CHAPTER 10

Fifty-Five Common Ways to Spell Six Consonant Sounds

Even though you have seen many hundreds of examples of words which are not spelled phonetically and have read how bizarrely the spelling "system" of English evolved, unless you are a most unusual individual, you may still fail to see how most of the words you read are not spelled phonetically. The consonant spellings give us that impression. And their spelling, as I have said, is more regular than that of the vowel sounds. But it behooves us to devote two chapters to survey what Ichabod and Johnny have to learn if they are to succeed. In this chapter we'll proceed primarily from sounds to spelling and in the next from spelling to sounds.

Again, we find an unfortunate situation; we have more consonant sounds than symbols, twenty-five sounds and only eighteen symbols in our alphabet with which to spell them. That means we have to use combinations of letters to spell some of the sounds, as with *c* plus *h, ch,* to spell /ch/ and *s* plus *h, sh,* to spell /sh/.

But again we find that English couldn't leave well enough alone: several sounds are spelled by various letters and combinations of letters. In short, there isn't just one way to spell each consonant sound. For example, in the word "congratulations," even though three vowels spell three schwas, the other letters appear to be doing what they should do. But the letter *t,* which occurs twice, does not in either instance spell the /t/ sound: /kən grăch'ə lā shənz/; the first *t* spells /ch/, and the second, with the help of *i,* spells /sh/.

Let's look into the spelling of six consonant sounds:

THE SPELLING OF THE /S/ SOUND

When we read, our minds are, of course, where they should be, on content, that is, on meaning. Even when working on the manuscript for this book, I have had to force my mind to look for spelling symbols rather than for meaning, and I have often not seen what was in plain sight before my eyes. For instance, I passed a church hundreds of times and, more often than not, read a sign: SCIENCE OF MIND—CENTER FOR SELF-AWARENESS. It didn't occur to me for a long time to analyze the spelling of the sounds, but one day it struck me: Here the /s/ sound is spoken five times in three words and is spelled five different ways, namely, by *sc, ce, c, s,* and *ss*. The two logical ways, *s* and *ss*, came to us in a perfectly natural way, from Old English. As you have seen, the Anglo-Normans forced onto English the spelling of *c* to represent /s/, as in *c*enter, *c*entipede, and *c*ertain; and once *c* spelled that sound, English took in words directly from Latin and gave *c* the same pronunciation, as in *c*ensus, *c*entury, and *c*eremony. It is no wonder that even we who get along rather well spelling English words are obliged to reach for a dictionary when we wish to spell such words as "consensus" and "concession" because we spell an /s/ sound one way in con*s*ensus and *s*ession and another in *c*ensus and con*c*ession.

The Anglo-Normans did the language a similar "favor" when they introduced *sc* to represent /s/. As a result, we have *sc*ience, mu*sc*le, and ob*sc*ene. It follows, then, that we also accepted the *sc* spelling in words we took directly from Latin, as in *sc*intillate, mi*sc*ellaneous, and mi*sc*ible.

If Ichabod ever learns to read well, he'll have to learn even more ways to spell the sound.

TWELVE FAIRLY COMMON WAYS TO SPELL /s/:

1) *s:*	sits u*s*	2) *c:*	*c*ent do*c*ile	3) *ss:*	ble*ss*ing bo*ss*
4) *sc:*	*sc*ent a*sc*end	5) *se:*	suspen*se* mou*se*	6) *st:*	moi*st*en hu*st*le
7) *x:*	wa*x* si*x*	8) *ps:*	*ps*ycho- *ps*uedo-	9) *ce:*	oun*ce* fen*ce*
10) *sce:*	coale*sce* convale*sce*	11) *sse:*	fine*sse* impa*sse*	12) *z:*	quart*z* walt*z*

It is disquieting and dismaying to find how seven(!) letters are used in those twelve spellings of the /s/ sound: *s, c, e, t, x, p,* and *z*. It seems strange that we spell /s/ by *ps*. When we say such words as *ps*alm and *ps*ychotic, we pretend the letter *p* is not there; at least we ignore it when we pronounce such words. Other European languages also borrowed these and other words like them from Greek. But in German the *p* represents /p/ and is sounded, as it usually is in French. As a matter of fact, when Germans say the word *"Psalm,"* they speak five sounds, whereas most of us speak only three, /säm/.

It is also illogical that we spell /s/ by *st*, but we sometimes do. We say *cast, fast,* and *list,* and sound both the /s/ and the /t/. But in *castle, fasten,* and *listen* children are taught in school to ignore the letter *t* and that is more difficult for some than for others.

Of course there are less common spellings of the /s/ sound, but most of them are rare. The one exception may be the spelling *sw*, but I have found it in only four words, of which an*sw*er and *sw*ord are two. Perhaps that spelling should be included among the "fairly common spellings" because the word "answer" is one of our more frequently used words.

If you have ever wondered how good your memory is, here is proof that it is mighty good if you can spell all or even most of these sixteen words:

farce	hence	commence	coincidence
parse	dense	intense	recompense
sauce	silence	essence	residence
sparse	nonsense	dispense	incense

THE SPELLING OF THE /K/ SOUND

We have a perfectly good letter, *k*, to spell the /k/ sound, but the letter *c* (unfortunately pronounced /sē/) spells it in at least twice as many words as *k* does! Investigation shows that we spell the sound eighteen ways, but we'll concern ourselves only with the nine variations our children might be expected to learn in the early grades:

1) *c*:	*c*art	2) *k*:	*k*ing	3) *ck*:	lo*ck*
	*v*i*c*tory		*k*ey		sa*ck*
4) *ch*:	*ch*orus	5) *cc*:	a*cc*omplish	6) *q*:	li*q*uid
	s*ch*eme		o*cc*ur		*q*uarter
7) *lk*:	cha*lk*	8) *que*:	pictures*que*	9) *cq*:	a*cq*uaintance
	ba*lk*		brus*que*		a*cq*uittal

It is interesting to note how once again seven(!) letters are involved in the spelling of another sound, the /k/ sound: *c, k, q, l, u, e,* and *h*.

THE SPELLING OF THE /J/ SOUND

You can win bets on the spelling of the /j/ sound. Everybody will tell you there are two ways to spell it, by the letter *j* and by the letter *g* when either *e* or *i* follows the *g*. Well, to begin with, if you will count the words in a dictionary in which *i* follows *g,* you will find that *g* spells /g/ ("hard" *g*) in more words than it spells /j/! Moreover, there are a dozen ways to spell the sound.

Here are two groups of words to illustrate how confusing the spelling of the sound is:

I

It is not *g*ewel and *j*em;	it is *j*ewel and *g*em
It is not *g*ester and *j*esture;	it is *j*ester and *g*esture
It is not *G*ean and *J*ene;	it is *J*ean and *G*ene

II

/g/	/j/	/g/	/j/
*g*et	*j*et	*g*ive	*j*ive
*g*imlet	*g*iblet	be*g*in	*g*in
*g*ift	*g*ibe	*g*ill	*g*ill
*g*ird	*g*iraffe	(fish)	(liquid measure)

Here you have samples of words in which the /j/ sound is spelled eight ways:

1. *g:* *g*entle, *g*ypsy, le*g*end, or*g*y
2. *j:* *j*ack, *j*oke, *j*oy, pa*j*amas
3. *ge:* banda*ge,* Geor*ge,* gou*ge,* lar*ge*
4. *gi:* conta*gi*on, egre*gi*ous, le*gi*on, neural*gi*a
5. *d:* a*d*ulate, gra*d*ual, indivi*d*ual, proce*d*ure
6. *dge:* do*dge,* e*dge,* fu*dge,* lo*dge*
7. *dg:* ba*dg*er, cu*dg*el, fi*dg*et, ju*dg*ment
8. *dj:* a*dj*acent, a*dj*oin, a*dj*ourn, a*dj*ust

It has been known for more than fifty years that we do not pronounce the /d/ sound in such words as ba*dg*er, bri*dge*, and a*dj*acent. Yet even now if some people attempt to pronounce the words in isolation, they will make a great effort to include that sound.

The pronunciation of /j/ spelled by *d* is a language phenomenon which has been developing in the present century. Speakers who are tied to printed letters try to give the *d* in "e*d*ucate" the value of /d/, but four of my college dictionaries give only the sound of /j/, and the fifth gives both /j/ and /d/. A word in which the sound is swinging back and forth between /j/ and /d/ is the word "pen*d*ulum." All five dictionaries

Fifty-Five Common Ways to Spell Six Consonant Sounds

now give both sounds in the respellings. If the development continues in the same direction it has been taking, by the year 2000 (or 2020) all good dictionaries will show only the sound /j/ spelled by *d* in both words. In the following words the process seems to have been completed, and the italicized *d* is supposed to represent /j/: ar*d*uous, deci*d*uous, gra*d*uate, un*d*ulate, and ver*d*ure.

The strength of such language movements may be found in a situation where we might expect the development to have been held back. In glan*d* the *d* spells /d/, but in glan*d*ular the *d* spells /j/. This is also true in these examples: aci*d* /d/, aci*d*ulous /j/; resi*d*ue /d/, resi*d*ual /j/; and both cre*d*ible and cre*d*ulity /d/, as opposed to cre*d*ulous /j/.

In stressing common spellings, I am again being unfair to poorer learners. The rarer spellings are probably much harder to learn because they aren't seen often enough, and sometimes they are quite illogical. Here are four samples in which we find rarer spellings of /j/:

di: cor*di*al, sol*di*er   *de*: gran*de*ur
gg: exa*gg*erate   *gio*: presti*gio*us, reli*gio*us

Six letters play a role in spelling our /j/ sound, *d, e, g, i, j,* and *o.*

THE SPELLING OF THE /ZH/ SOUND

The /zh/ sound was the last one to come into English, having been heard first in the Middle Ages. And it is heard in fewer words than any other of our other sounds. We have not yet developed a single standard symbol to represent it, neither a letter nor a combination of letters. Dictionaries use the digraph "zh" to spell it phonetically. When I was young, I was mistakenly taught that only the letter *z* spells it, as in "azure." It is quite easy to find individuals who are unaware of its existence, even though they and all of us use it. We have to when we say such words as "u*s*ual" and "televi*s*ion." A good many people don't hear the /zh/ sound in such words as "corsa*g*e" and "gara*g*e," etc. They have learned that *ge* spells /j/, as in wa*ge* and lun*ge*, and they assume the sound is /j/ not /zh/, not /kôr säzh′/, but /kôr säj′/, and not /gə räzh′/, but /gə räj′/. Most of the words in which *g* and *ge* spell /zh/ are not seen very often by a good many readers and are heard even less frequently, e.g., badina*ge,* corte*ge,* decoupa*ge,* entoura*ge,* *g*endarme, melan*ge,* etc. Here are some common spellings of the /zh/ sound:

s: compo*s*ure, mea*s*ure   *si*: confu*si*on, delu*si*on
ge: bei*ge,* massa*ge*   *g*: ne*g*ligee, re*g*ime

Other spellings are *z*: a*z*ure, sei*z*ure; *zi*: bra*zi*er, gla*zi*er; *j*: bi*j*ou; *ti*: equa*ti*on; *sh*: ca*sh*mere, Mo*sh*er.

Of course, children in the lower grades will not be expected to learn more than two or three spellings, but functionally literate readers surely have to be able to read four to six.

THE SPELLING OF THE /CH/ SOUND

When we think of the sound /ch/, we think automatically of the spelling *ch*. It is spelled by *ch* in hundreds of words. However, there are problems. A retired elementary school teacher told me that if she were still teaching, she would teach her charges that at the end of a word the /ch/ sound is spelled -*tch*. She said her pupils had spelled pa*tch*, pi*tch*, scra*tch*, etc., without the *t*. But if she were to teach her new way, they would be likely to misspell even more words, including these important ones: Mar*ch*, lun*ch*, mu*ch*, ri*ch*, and su*ch*. And how would these spellings look to her: bea*tch*, ben*tch*, sandwi*tch*, spee*tch*, and tou*tch*? There are many more words ending in /ch/ which are spelled by *ch* than by *tch*. For that matter, there are more words in which *t* alone spells /ch/ than there are words in which *tch* spells /ch/! The words "infa*t*uation," "punc*t*uation," and "si*t*uation" (and a half dozen other words) are like the word "congra*t*ula*t*ions"; there are two *t*'s, but neither spells /t/; again, the first one spells /ch/ and the second one, with *i*, spells /sh/.

In descending order, we have these common ways to spell /ch/:

1. *ch:* ben*ch*, chur*ch*, par*ch*, pin*ch*
2. *t:* ac*t*ual, bo*t*ulism, crea*t*ure, fa*t*uous
3. *tch:* bu*tch*er, i*tch*, ki*tch*en, ma*tch*
4. *ti:* celes*ti*al, combus*ti*on, conges*ti*on, sugges*ti*on

Although we have a number of additional ways, they are to be found in probably not many more than a score of words:

5. *c:* con*c*erto, du*c*e
6. *cc:* cappu*cc*ino, capri*cc*ioso
7. *che:* avalan*che*, ni*che*
8. *cz:* *Cz*echoslovakia, *Cz*erny
9. *te:* ama*te*ur
10. *teo:* righ*teo*us
11. *th:* pos*th*umous
12. *ts:* ca*ts*up

Fifty-Five Common Ways to Spell Six Consonant Sounds

THE SPELLING OF THE /SH/ SOUND

Wouldn't you think the most frequent spelling of the /sh/ sound is the combination *s* plus *h, sh?* And, offhand, how many ways would you have supposed English has to represent the /sh/ sound if you had not read the third chapter of this book? And how many ways do you imagine there are? Our language has more ways to spell that one sound than there are consonant sounds in English! Now that I have given you advance notice, try to find all the ways used in this bit of nonsense:

HORATIO AT THE RAIL

On the luxury liner *Vespucius,* handsome Horatio Jones from Cheyenne asked a girl from Kalamazoo, Michigan, Theodosia Schubert, a luscious, curvaceous blonde with a heavenly complexion, if she would dance the schottische with him that evening. Now Theodosia felt the young man had panache and replied, "Surely, I'd be happy to." He appreciated her answer so much that he invited her to enjoy a bottle of champagne before the dance. His conscience bothered him a bit, for he was presumably on the wagon. But because the young lady was something special and had accepted so graciously, he went to the bar and bought a bottle, paying for it with five Polish groszy and the Austrian schillings he had left.

Horatio was not really chivalrous, for he somewhat incautiously drank his champagne too fast, and he also drank too much. But he said to himself, "Pshaw, I have never known nausea." So, reassured, and twirling his mustache, he escorted Miss Schubert to the dance. After the schottische, the young couple continued to dance, going round and round, in one graceful waltz after another. Meanwhile, the ocean had become exceedingly rough, and when the band reached a crescendo, Horatio became anxious and felt the compulsion to go out on deck. "This situation is nauseous," he thought, and he said hastily, "With your permission, I must excuse myself." In the foyer he could not negotiate well, and he tripped over a lovely fuchsia and then ran to the rail.

Moral: Under certain crucial conditions, anti-seasick pills are more efficacious and beneficial than champagne.

You were aware, of course, that the episode was written for the sole purpose of showcasing all the ways the /sh/ sound is spelled in English. Perhaps you underlined, circled, or numbered them. If you found twenty-eight different ways, you caught them all and should go to the head of the class. (Duplicates do not count.) Admittedly, several, say, five or six of the ways, are rarely ever seen, but even so, we have between fourteen and eighteen fairly common ways to spell the one sound. Before I list them, I'd like once more to point out that I did not develop the method of showing the various ways the sound is spelled. I simply used the method language experts have employed.

EIGHTEEN FAIRLY COMMON WAYS TO SPELL THE /SH/ SOUND

1. *c:* offi*c*iate
2. *ce:* licori*ce*
3. *ceo:* herba*ceo*us
4. *ch:* *ch*auvinist
5. *che:* dou*che*
6. *ci:* an*ci*ent
7. *cio:* pre*cio*us
8. *s:* *s*ure
9. *sch:* *sch*wa
10. *scio:* con*scio*us
11. *sh:* *sh*ip
12. *si:* expul*si*on
13. *ss:* i*ss*ue
14. *ssi:* admi*ssi*on
15. *t:* ini*t*iate
16. *ti:* ini*ti*al
17. *tio:* ficti*tio*us
18. *xio:* obno*xio*us

We use eight different letters, *c, e, h, i, o, s, t,* and *x,* in various combinations to stand for the one sound. We have become so enamored of, and conditioned to, our various spellings of the /sh/ sound that a single logical spelling, which obviously would be incomparably easier to master, looks like the writing of an illiterate person. I'll give a dozen examples and, to be somewhat consistent, I'll use the letter *e* to spell the schwa sound, as is done in German:

ambitious	ambishes	delicious	dilishes
dilution	dilushen	fictitious	fiktishes
licorice	likerish	mustache	mustash
passion	pashen	pension	penshen
sufficient	sefishent	insure	inshoor
tissue	tishoo	viscious	vishes

English has about as many ways to spell /sh/ as a magician has tricks. In contrast, German has only three common ways to spell it. We ask, therefore, how some of our ways developed. I do not wish to oversimplify, but one explanation covers several of the spellings. As you saw in the previous chapter, when some of our present two-syllable words came into English, they were pronounced in three syllables. The words *nation, ocean, pension,* and *special* are good examples. In the course of time, the consonant sounds spelled by *t, c,* and *s* merged with the following vowel sounds spelled by *i* or *e,* and the two sounds became a different single consonant sound, /sh/. This same merging occurred, of course, in longer words as well, four-syllable words shortening to three syllables, and five-syllable words becoming four syllables, as in our present word *variation*. I purposely used as examples words which have very similar German equivalents, words which German also borrowed. But in that language the merging did not take place, and the German words still have one more syllable than their English counterparts.

If you are interested in this phenomenon, you might listen carefully whenever you hear the word "controversial," and you may well be able to hear how the merging is developing. Some speakers give a five-syllable pronunciation, as we all might if we were trying to speak very "correctly." Thus, you will often hear /kŏn′ trə vûr′ sē əl/. But sometimes you will hear the shortened form, /kŏn′ trə vûr′ shəl/. Over the past ten years, or so, I have been intrigued, particularly so because I am quite sure I have heard on TV, on the radio, from the lectern and the pulpit, and in daily conversation the longer form more often than I have heard the short, four-syllable one. This is the interesting feature: Four of my recent college edition (and two other good) dictionaries offer only the shortened pronunciation in phonetic respelling, and the seventh edition of the *Collegiate* shows both. Should the longer form eventually win out, that will run counter to the general movement in our language. In the past thousand years huge numbers of words have been shortened, and large numbers are now in the process of acquiring shorter pronunciations. Evidently lexicographers assume the word "controversial" will follow the pattern. The result will not be known for many years; at present it is controversial.

One unanswered question remains: What is the most frequent spelling of the /sh/ sound? No, it is not *sh*, it is *ti*! At the beginning of words we usually spell the sound by *sh-*; at the end we almost always spell it by *-sh*. But it is spelled by *-ti-* in twice as many words as by *sh*. Usually we find it in the suffix *-tion*, as in abbrevia*ti*on, ac*ti*on, affec*ti*on, applica*ti*on, etc. (and also in *-tial*, as in essen*ti*al, impar*ti*al, ini*ti*al, etc.).

You should note that there are a few words in which the sound occurring medially is spelled *-sh-*, e.g., bu*sh*el, ca*sh*ier, u*sh*er, wor*sh*ip, etc. Naturally, these instances do not include: compounds (fla*sh*light, over*sh*adow, war*sh*ip), words with suffixes (hard*sh*ips, puni*sh*ment, wa*sh*able), and inflected forms (di*sh*es, ru*sh*ing, she spla*sh*es).

As you might expect, you have read about the sounds with the most spellings, but even if a sound has only three or four spellings, it should not have that many. I think you will now be prepared for the words of two professors who have written about our spelling of our consonant sounds. Robert Lado made a comparison study of Spanish and English. With reference to English, he wrote, "The relation between sounds and letters is quite complex. Representation of consonants is only slightly less complex than that of the vowels." (*Linguistics across Cultures,* p. 100) John Nist in his *Structural History of English* agrees. After describing a few of the illogical spellings of our vowel letters, he states, "To complicate this phonetic disorder, the consonants of Modern English are a welter of confusion." (p. 16)

The linguistic load is simply too much for many of our learners. That is why they cannot handle it.

CHAPTER 11

Knotty Naughty Consonant Letters

THE LETTER C

"*C* is for *c*at." How many times do you suppose that expression has been spoken in the past hundred years? Surely we have all heard it any number of times. Why do people say such a thing? Carefully considered, it doesn't make sense, at least not to children who do not know how to read or are just learning. The letter *c* is pronounced /sē/, and those two sounds are the last ones in the word "illiteracy." They are not the first two sounds in the word "cat." Of course we adults know that the symbol *c* represents both /s/ and /k/, but we don't count when it comes to learning to read English. In German and Dutch, children do not hear such nonsense because *k* stands for *Katze* (female) and *Kater* (male) in German and for *kat* in Dutch. It must be bewildering to many children, particularly those who are not linguistically gifted, to hear that "*c* is for *c*at."

Knowing that *ch* spells /ch/, as in *ch*air, *ch*eek, and *ch*oke, we wouldn't say "*ch* is for *Ch*ristmas" or "*ch* is for *Ch*icago." I see no basic difference; it is equally illogical to confuse children by saying "*c* is for *c*at."

You recall, no doubt, how the Anglo-Normans were responsible for making *c* represent /s/. But *c* also spells three other sounds; and then, combined with other letters, it spells the same four sounds eighteen additional ways. When you see Table 4, which contains twenty-five items, I hope you will bear in mind that all children who learn to read have to learn most of the patterns and must be able to recognize them in the large number of words which half the samples represent.

Smaller hurdles, but still obstacles on the path leading to reading mastery, are found in words where the *c* is superfluous. Indeed, scholars added the *c* gratuitously in some of our words. Professor Lounsbury, whom I have previously quoted, said, "There is not the slightest justification for the unnecessary *c* in such words as *scent, scythe, scion, scimitar,* and *scissors*." He added, "Some of these words have had a wide variety of spellings. English orthography has exhibited, as is not unusual, a perverse preference for the spellings which depart furthest from the pronunciation." (p. 175)

This is a fact: *scent* came into English from Latin by way of Old French without a *c*. It was spelled *sent* until the seventeeth century! And "scythe" in Old English was spelled *sithe!*

Table 4

Sounds Which *c* and Its Assistants Spell:

Letters	Sound /k/	Sound /s/	Sound /ch/	Sound /sh/	Sounds /ks/	"Silent" No Sound
c	cap	cell	cello	depreciate		Tucson
cc	accrue				accept	
cch	saccharine					
ce		choice		ocean		
ceo				cretaceous		
ch	school		chill	machine		drachm
che	ache		Blanche	pastiche		
ci				facial		
cio				spacious		
ck	sick					
cq	acquaint					
cu	biscuit					
cz			Czech			czar

THE LETTER *H*

The all-purpose utility consonant is the letter *h*. It serves more functions than any other consonant letter, as you will see in this list.

1. With *a* it helps to spell /ä/, as in hurr*ah*, sh*ah*
2. With *a* it helps to spell /ə/, as in Delil*ah*, Tirz*ah*
3. With *c* it helps to spell /ch/, as in *ch*ance, *ch*oose
4. With *c* it helps to spell /k/, as in *ch*emist, *ch*romium
5. With *c* it helps to spell /sh/, as in *ch*alet, *ch*iffon
6. With *c* it helps to spell silence, as in s*ch*ist, ya*ch*t
7. With *e* it helps to spell /ā/, as in *eh*, h*eh*
8. With *g* it helps to spell /f/, as in laug*h*ter, coug*h*

Knotty Naughty Consonant Letters

9. With *g* it helps to spell silence, as in ei*gh*t, ni*gh*t
10. Alone it spells /h/, as in *h*eaven, *h*ell
11. Alone it spells silence, as in *h*onor, ex*h*ibit, ag*h*ast
12. With *k* it helps to spell /k/, as in *kh*aki, *kh*an
13. With *o* it helps to spell /ō/, as in o*h*, o*h*m
14. With *p* it helps to spell /f/, as in *ph*ase, *ph*iloso*ph*y
15. With *p* it helps to spell /v/, as in Ste*ph*en, ne*ph*ew (Brit.)
(16. With *ps* it helps to spell /sh/, as in *psh*aw)
17. With *r* it helps to spell /r/, as in *rh*apsody, *rh*eostat
18. With *s* it helps to spell /sh/, as in *sh*ape, *sh*eep
19. With *t* it helps to spell /th/, as in *th*in, *th*ree
20. With *t* it helps to spell /*th*/, as in *th*an, *th*em
21. With *t* it helps to spell /t/, as in *Th*ames, *th*yme, *Th*eresa
22. With *t* it helps to spell /ch/, as in pos*th*umous(ly)
23. With *tc* it helps to spell /ch/, as in no*tch*, stre*tch*
24. With *w* it helps to spell /hw/, as in *wh*ale, *wh*ile
25. With *w* it helps to spell /h/, as in *wh*o, *wh*ole
(26. With *w* it helps to spell /w/, as in *wh*oa)

If anybody should protest and say some of the spellings are a bit far-fetched, for example *ah* spelling /ə/, we should remember Jehov*ah* and Messi*ah* and many prophets of the Old Testament, e.g., Jeremi*ah* and No*ah*. Please note that I did not include *eh*, as in Ninev*eh* or *iah*, as in Isa*iah*, or *bh*ang, *bh*eesty, *dh*arma, *mh*o, and *phth*isis, etc., because they are indeed rare spellings.

Although *h* with its helpers cannot hold a candle to *a* and its cooperative companions, which—as I wish to remind you—spell 16 of our 19 vowel sounds (114 ways), the spellings of *h* with its friends are amazing; they spell ten of our consonant sounds.

In considering the letters *c* and *h* separately, there was, of course, overlapping in the spellings of the digraph *ch*. But here is a point which is particularly revealing and convincing. Children cannot sound out words beginning with that combination of letters with any greater degree of success than they can words which begin with the letter *a*. In order to check on the validity of this claim, I made a count in a college dictionary of the sounds spelled by the digraph *ch* in the initial position in all 693 words. I found that in 48 percent of the words (337) it spells /ch/, in 39 percent (271) it spells /k/, and in 13 percent (85) it spells /sh/. Again, we must not begin after the fact, knowing how a great many of the words are pronounced. We must remember Ichabod, who is going through the learning process with every single word beginning with the digraph *ch*- that he acquires. These six words may help you recognize Ichabod's plight: *chaetopod, chalaza, chalcedony, chalcocite, chalcography,* and *chalone.* How can children—how can we—know that the *ch-* spells /k/ in all six words? If children guess /ch/, they'll be wrong with all six words. And yes, all of them came from a college dictionary.

Here are additional samples of words containing the digraph *ch*:

/ch/	/k/	/sh/
chamber	chameleon	champagne
charity	charisma	charlatan
chart	Charon	chartreuse
Charles	Christina	Charlene
chaste	chasm	chaise
orchard	orchestra	brochure
archbishop	archangel	ricochet
starch	monarch	————
avalanche	headache	gauche

Note the additional *e* at the end of the last three words. Obviously, we have learned all these words the hard way because the spelling doesn't tell how they are pronounced, as it should—AND WOULD—*if* our spelling of the words were phonetic. Many an Ichabod has been unable to learn them.

THE LETTER *G*

The greatest problem children have learning this letter is the spelling of the /g/ and /j/ sounds. I'll not repeat what I wrote in the preceding chapter, but I will add that I have good reason to believe the letter *g* spells /g/ in about two-thirds and /j/ in roughly one-third of the words in which the letter occurs. Table 5 shows the different sounds the letter *g* spells.

Table 5

The Sounds Which *g* and Its Assistants Spell:

LETTERS	SOUND /g/	SOUND /j/	SOUND /zh/	SOUND /f/	SOUNDS /gj/	SOUNDS /ny/	No SOUND "Silent"
g	get	generous	genre				gnash
gg	egg	exaggerate			suggest		
ge		charge		prestige			
gh				rough			thigh

Knotty Naughty Consonant Letters

Letters	Sound /g/	Sound /j/	Sound /zh/	Sound /f/	Sounds /gj/	Sounds /ny/	No Sound "Silent"
gi		nostalgia	adagio				
		adagio					
gio		prodigious					
gm							apothegm
gn						cognac	resign
(gue	intrigue						)

When children are learning to read, the letters in the "No Sound" column are just as important as the letters in the other columns. Children don't come by silence naturally; and they have to learn that the letter has no phonetic value. And there are more than a hundred fairly common words in which g represents silence. Unfortunately, there is another complication and extra work for learners. In some words the letter stands for no sound, and in related words it represents /g/. Here are samples: design, designate; gnostic, agnostic; phlegm, phlegmatic; sign, signature (and signify and signal).

THE LETTER N

This is an easy letter to master, and there are not large numbers of words in which the *n* does not spell a sound. But just as the letter *g* is not sounded in certain forms and is sounded in related forms, so does the *n* represent silence in some words and a sound in related words. Compare autumn and autumnal; column and columnist; condemn and condemnation; damn and damnation; hymn and hymnal, etc.

The combination of *n* and *g, ng,* is confusing to learners. As a child I was taught that the combination always spelled /ng/, as in ring, and that there was no other way to spell the sound. A bright boy named Gordon asked if "ink" should be spelled "ingk," since the sound was spelled by *ng*. Our teacher called him a "smart aleck" and let the matter drop. Gordon, however, was tenacious (as well as smart), and the following day he asked if the "ng" in "blancmange" (/blə mänzh′/) spelled the /ng/ sound. When my classmates (and I) snickered, he was sent to the principal. I don't remember the outcome of his trip to see Mr. Bradford, but as I recall, our teacher said the word "blancmange" was a French word and we weren't going to waste our time learning French words! (Incidentally, in less affluent days blancmange pudding was a fairly regular dessert because it was cheap to make, and I now surmise that, by chance, Gordy had had pudding for dinner the evening after he had asked about "ingk.")

Well, I have since learned that the letter *n* alone spells /ng/ without the help of the *g* when *n* precedes a letter or letters that spell the /k/ sound, no matter how it is spelled; and this is true in almost all words in which we find the situation. (Examples will follow.)

We also find that *ng* does not always spell /ng/; in many words the combination spells /nj/, as in cha*ng*e, cri*ng*ing, messe*ng*er, plu*ng*er, spo*ng*e, etc.

Sometimes the *g* following *n* does double duty, spelling /ngg/: a*ng*le, hu*ng*er, la*ng*uage, lo*ng*er, si*ng*le, etc.

Here are nine samples showing why children are sometimes bewildered and become frustrated. Please read across:

/ng/	/ngg/	/nj/
ha*ng*er	a*ng*er	ra*ng*er
si*ng*er	fi*ng*er	gi*ng*er
stri*ng*er	stro*ng*er	stra*ng*er

Table 6 shows the various sounds spelled by the letter *n*.

Table 6

The Sounds Which the Letter *n* Spells:

Letters	Sound /n/	Sound(s) /ng(k)/	Sounds /nj/	Sounds /ngg/	No Sound "Silent"
n	ru*n*				sole*mn*
nc		u*nc*le			
nch		a*nch*or			
nd	ha*nd*some				
ng		si*ng*	scave*ng*er	li*ng*er	
nk		ba*nk*			
nn	ru*nn*er				
nq		ba*nq*uet			
nx		a*nx*ious			

THE LETTER *S*

The thirty-seven (!) samples you will find in Table 7 attest to the fact that our busiest consonant letter is the letter *s*. More than ten percent of our words begin with it. In addition, plural forms of most nouns end in *s* (/s/ or /z/), and third-person singular verb forms in the present tense, with few exceptions, end in *s* (/s/ or /z/). The various uses to which *s* and its partners are put to work are a major source of difficulty for our learners.

There are relatively few words in which *s* represents no sound, and about half of them come from French, as in apropo*s*, bourgeoi*s*, chassi*s*, preci*s*, etc. The French (and Indian) influence is found in several geographical names, as in Arkansa*s*, Illinoi*s*, De*s* Moine*s*, and Loui*s*ville.

You will note, I assume, that in the thirty-three different words in the table *s* spells /s/ in only eight words! Would you care to cross out the words that are not spelled phonetically?

Table 7

Spellings of the Letter *s* and Its Assistants:

LETTERS	SOUND /s/	SOUND /z/	SOUND /k/	SOUND /sh/	SOUND /zh/	NO SOUND "Silent"
s	cat*s*	dog*s*		*s*ugar	enclo*s*ure	debri*s*
sc	di*sc*ern	di*sc*ern	vi*sc*ount	fa*sc*ism		
sch	*sch*ism			*sch*nitzel		
sci				fa*sci*a		
scio				con*scio*us		
se	u*se*	u*se*		nau*se*a*	nau*se*a	
seo				nau*seo*us	nau*seo*us	
sh				*sh*ell	ca*sh*mere	
si		bu*si*ness		expan*si*on	occa*si*on	
sl						i*sl*and
sne						deme*sne*
sp		ra*sp*berry				
ss	stre*ss*	de*ss*ert		a*ss*ure		
ssi				Pru*ssi*a	sci*ssi*on	
st		gli*st*en				
sth	i*sth*mus	a*sth*ma				
sw		*sw*ord				
sz				gro*sz*		

*Other pronunciations given in dictionaries for "nausea" are /nṓ sē ə / and /nṓ zē ə /; it has almost as many pronunciations as "banal."

Also take note of these samples of inconsistencies in the sounds /s/ or /z/:

/s/	/z/	/s/	/z/	/s/	/z/
serve	preserve	morsel	damsel	transom	crimson
sign	resign	beside	reside	reset	resent
bison	prison	research	result	desolate	designate
basin	partisan	isolate	hesitate	assess	possess

THE LETTER *T*

This letter would be much easier for learners to master if it, sometimes joined by vowels, didn't spell /ch/ and /sh/ so often, and if it weren't for the wasted use in many words of high frequency, very often in the two combinations, -*stle* and -*tch*. I have previously pointed out that *rich* and *pitch* rhyme because the *t* is not sounded in "pitch." In addition, the *t* does not represent a sound in several loan words from the French, as in balle*t*, cabare*t*, croche*t*, debu*t*, etc. (Pronunciation of the *t* fluctuates in parts of Britain, as in bere*t*, cabare*t*, and vale*t*.) See Table 8.

Table 8

Spellings of the Letter *t* and Its Helpers:

LETTERS	SOUND /t/	SOUND /ch/	SOUND /sh/	SOUND /zh/	SOUND /th/	SOUND /th/	NO SOUND "Silent"
t	hi*t*	ri*t*ual	nego*t*iate				sof*t*en
tch							la*tch*
te		ama*te*ur					
teo		righ*teo*us					
tg							mor*t*gage
th	Es*th*er				*th*ing	*th*at	clo*th*es
ti		bes*ti*al	par*ti*al	equa*ti*on			
tio			cau*tio*us				
tt	be*tt*er						

These are samples of inconsistencies. Read along.

/th/	/th/	/th/	/th/	/th/	/th/
a*th*eist	fa*th*er	ca*th*edral	hea*th*en	epi*th*et	lea*th*er
A*th*ens	ra*th*er	e*th*ics	ei*th*er	bro*th*	bro*th*er

Knotty Naughty Consonant Letters

Now let me call your attention to some interesting features in at least 526 pairs of words, all of which English borrowed from French or Latin. Half of them are verbs, and the other half are nouns. Because they do not follow English patterns in the transfer from verbs to nouns, the result is that spelling and sounds change unpredictably; and for that reason the words require more time, effort, and language skill to acquire. I planned to stop collecting when I had 300 pairs, but the other pairs came to me without any searching. (A great majority of the verbs end in *-ate,* as in "illumin*ate*.") I will illustrate what I mean by using twenty-seven pairs. I have divided the words into three groups.

A. VERBS ENDING IN -D (-DE):

VERBS	NOUNS	
conce*de*	conce*ss*ion	*d* becomes *ss,* and *ssi* spells /sh/
defen*d*	defen*se*	*d* becomes *se,* /s/
descen*d*	descen*t*	*d* becomes *t*
ero*de*	ero*s*ion	*d* becomes *s,* and *si* spells /zh/
inten*d*	inten*t*ion	*d* becomes *t,* and *ti* spells /sh/
succee*d*	succe*ss*	*d* becomes *ss,* /s/
suspen*d*	suspen*s*ion	*d* becomes *s,* and *si* spells /sh/

The verb "pretend" and the noun belong to this group; the noun corresponding to the verb has two spellings, one used here and the other in Britain; is it spelled with *-ce* as in sequen*ce,* pretence, or *-se,* as in inten*se,* preten*se*? In Britain you'll be wrong if you get it right in the United States. And is /prĭ tĕn′ shən/ spelled with a *c* as in suspi*c*ion (preten*c*ion), with an *s,* as in man*s*ion (preten*s*ion), or with a *t,* as in atten*t*ion (preten*t*ion)?

B. VERBS ENDING IN -*T* (-*TE*):

celebra*te*	celebra*t*ion	*t* is still *t,* but *ti* spells /sh/
collec*t*	collec*t*ion	*t* is still *t,* but *ti* spells /sh/
commi*t*	commi*ss*ion	*t* becomes *ss,* but *ssi* spells /sh/
conver*t*	conver*s*ion	*t* becomes *s,* and *si* spells /zh/
dicta*te*	dicta*t*ion	*t* is still *t,* but *ti* spells /sh/
dissen*t*	dissen*s*ion	*t* becomes *s,* and *si* spells /sh/
equa*te*	equa*t*ion	*t* is still *t,* but *ti* spells /zh/
remi*t*	remi*ss*ion	*t* becomes *ss,* but *ssi* spells /sh/

If you are shaking your head in surprise and dismay, I remind you there are historical reasons for the changes, but historical reasons do not help poorer learners one bit.

C. VERBS AND NOUNS WITH VARIOUS ENDINGS:

advi*se* /z/	advi*c*e	*s* becomes *c*, which spells /s/
analy*z*e	analy*s*is	*z* becomes *s;* /z/ is now /s/
critici*z*e	critici*s*m	*z* becomes *s*, but the sound is still /z/
expo*se* /z/	expo*s*ure	*s* is still *s*, but now it spells /zh/
expre*ss*	expre*ss*ion	*ss* is still *ss*, but *ssi* spells /sh/
provo*k*e	provo*c*ation	*k* becomes *c*, but /k/ remains /k/
reciproc*a*te	reciproc*i*ty	*c* is still *c*, but *c* now spells /s/
recogni*z*e	recogni*t*ion	*z* becomes *t; ti* spells /sh/
redu*c*e	redu*c*tion	*c* is still *c*, but *c* now spells /k/
acqui*r*e	acqui*s*ition	*r* becomes *s*, which spells /z/
aboli*sh*	aboli*t*ion	*sh* becomes *t*, and *ti* spells /sh/
demoli*sh*	demoli*t*ion	*sh* becomes *t*, and *ti* spells /sh/

There are enough anomalies here to discourage those who are blessed with even average gifts of language. Please note especially the final two pairs on the last list. Two vowel sounds change in each pair of words, but the strangest phenomenon is that in both nouns the very symbol which is assumed to be *the* proper spelling of /sh/, *sh,* is replaced by *ti.*

It is discouraging, isn't it?

CHAPTER 12

The Eyes Have It—Wrong!

If you completed your formal education in the fifties or before, it is probable that you won't believe, at least won't want to believe, what I am about to say. (Even if you finished school in the sixties, chances are good that you won't want to believe either. You may have used an old dictionary; and many teachers haven't yet made the discovery.)

I. The first *e* in each of the following words does *not* stand for the /ē/ sound:

b*e*low	b*e*neath	d*e*ceive	d*e*ny
*e*lastic	*e*liminate	r*e*member	r*e*noun

Most dictionaries printed before the fifties offered what you would prefer to believe.

II. The *e* in the second syllable of the following words does not stand for /ĕ/ or even /ə/, the schwa sound:

earn*e*st	harv*e*st	goodn*e*ss	kindn*e*ss
helpl*e*ss	hopel*e*ss	nugg*e*t	targ*e*t

In the forties, dictionaries began to show alternative pronunciations, giving first the /ĕ/ sound and then the /ĭ/ sound. Now the eight good and current dictionaries with which I am acquainted no longer offer alternative forms; in all sixteen words the italicized *e* spells /ĭ/!

Who believes this right away? Well, if you'll consult a good recent dictionary, you'll find the phonetic respellings of r*e*tard*e*d and d*e*ment*e*d to be /rĭ tär′ dĭd/ and /dĭ mĕn′ tĭd/, and it appears that some people to whom I give this information think I am /rĭ tär′ dĭd/, if not downright /dĭ mĕn′ tĭd/.

We are thinking here of the spelling by *e* in a few thousand unstressed syllables. You'll be able to hear it in this oldie: "In the third century A.D. the Colosseum went broke because the lions ate up all the

/prŏf′ ĭts/." (It tells better orally than in writing.) If you will look up the phonetic respellings of *profit* and *prophet,* you will find that the words have identical pronunciations and, therefore, are true homophones.

My introduction to this subject came about in 1947, during the semester when I taught my first group of very poor readers. One exceedingly serious and eager young man asked me what /ĭ fĕm′ ər əl/ means and why he couldn't find it in the dictionary. We looked it up and found the word *ephemeral.* Then he asked me if I hadn't pronounced the first *e* as if it were an *i,* as /ĭ/. I wasn't sure, but feared he was right.

By a happy coincidence, the following weekend I chanced to read a book that I had been intending to read for years, *Essentials of English Grammar,* which was written by the eminent Danish philologist and authority in the English language, Otto Jespersen. There, before my eyes was the information which I needed: In many unstressed syllables in English the letter *e* stands for the sound /ĭ/. (p. 44)

Jespersen explained that the strong stress in English "has had far-reaching consequences on the whole sound system of the language." (p. 43) He gave examples of weakened syllables which had ultimately completely disappeared in our sound system, e.g., the second syllable in king*es*, erl*es*, duk*es*, and bold*e*. The sound in the second syllable in princ*es* did not go away, but it changed from /ə/ to /ĭ/. Then, far ahead of the dictionaries of his time, Jespersen gave these examples of words in which the letter *e* spells /ĭ/:

nos*e*s	bridg*e*s	fetch*e*s	end*e*d	hand*e*d
lat*e*st	weak*e*st	twenti*e*th	coll*e*ge	knowl*e*dge
haml*e*t	badn*e*ss	car*e*less	car*e*lessn*e*ss	fitt*e*d

(He also gave other spellings which represent /ĭ/, e.g., *a* and *u* as in "cour*a*ge" and "min*u*te.") Thereafter, he gave samples of prefixes in which the letter *e* also spells /ĭ/: b*e*fore, pr*e*fer, r*e*ject, r*e*form, r*e*move, r*e*cover.

So if I pronounced *ephemeral* as /ĭ fĕm′ ər əl/, I was pronouncing it as most people were at the time, and I simply wasn't aware of it.

Wishing to know the extent to which this aberrant spelling occurs, I counted it in all the words of a dictionary in those areas where I thought it most likely to be. I used a copy of *Webster's New World Dictionary,* Second College Edition. When I had finished my count, I discovered I had worked my way through one-tenth of the book and had come up with 4,285 words in which *e* spells /ĭ/ at least once. My count did not include many hundreds of words whose inflected forms, that is, grammatical endings, contain the spelling of the sound, as in these samples: (a) The plane land*e*d; they doubt*e*d; (b) the girl is gift*e*d;

The Eyes Have It—Wrong! 111

the book is appreciated; (c) save the ashes; he wears glasses; (d) Ken pitches and Charley catches; they care who loses; (e) this rope is longest; they are the shortest.

If you haven't been conscious of hearing the /ĭ/ sound when spelled by *e* in unstressed syllables, you will probably hear it more and more frequently now if you will listen for it. It seems to be heard quite distinctly in "excited" /ĭk sī′ tĭd/, not /ĕk sī′ tĕd/. You may also hear it rather clearly in the following four sentences if you will read them aloud as you normally would and try not to give eye pronunciations:

> The rose's wilted. The roses wilted.
> The colleges closed. The college's closed.

The sound, which, of course, is not spoken with the same force as vowel sounds in stressed syllables are, can usually be picked up in some of these words:

basket	blanket	bracelet	carpet	cricket
Everest	Everett	Frances	Mildred	Moses
mattress	molasses	princess	waitress	weakness

We sometimes hear the sound we are discussing in middle syllables, as in these words:

imprecise	majesty	markedly	misdemeanor
modesty	pedestal	represent	travesty

Having discussed this spelling with large numbers of people, I recognize how difficult it is for most individuals to accept it. Even though the phonetic respelling of *eleven* is /ĭ lĕv′ ən/, when we say it slowly in isolation, we pronounce the first sound as /ē/. This is to be expected; it is explained by Professors Donald J. Lloyd and Henry Warfel in their *American English in Its Cultural Setting:* "Spelling is more closely related to words spoken in isolation than to words integrated into running speech. When we pronounce a word by itself, we give it a word stress rather than stresses built into the overall stress-patterns of the utterance, and we give each sound its fuller treatment. We consciously pronounce it as we think it ought to be pronounced, often saying it syllable by syllable." (p. 354)

So when we think of the first sound in the isolated word "enough," we imagine an angry parent (tsk! tsk!) saying, "That will be enough!" and stressing each word and syllable, so that "enough" comes out /ē′ nŭf′/. But dictionaries now offer what we hear when words are used in normal discourse, as, for instance, in "We don't have enough time to eat." In such discourse we are likely to pronounce the word as we find it exclusively, that is, with no choice, in six of seven dictionaries. We are thinking of Ichabod, who does not have the benefit of your spelling learning and experience, only what he has heard in his six, seven, or eight years.

The subject we are discussing supports Socrates' claim as reported by Plato in *Phaedo,* namely, that we cannot believe even what our two most reliable senses, sight and hearing, tell us. We assume we hear /ē/ and /ĕ/ when we see "departed," but actually we ordinarily hear (and say) /dĭ pär′ tĭd/.

Now that we are discussing the spelling of the /ĭ/ sound, it is logical that we look for other ways it is spelled, in addition to *i,* of course. We have seen how *a* spells it in *-age* and *-ace,* as in garb*a*ge and furn*a*ce. In unstressed syllables it is also spelled by *a* in *-ate,* as in sen*a*te. Curiously, if there is a secondary stress on that syllable, it spells /ā/. But since we don't use accent or stress marks in English, children get no warning and they can get it wrong as easily as right. Thus, if we *appropriate* money, we /ə prō′ prē āt′/ it, but if a gift is *appropriate,* it is /ə prō′ prē ĭt/. Here are more examples:

Word	As Verb	As Adjective or Noun
alternate	/ôl′ tər- nāt′/	-nĭt/
deliberate	/dĭ lĭb′ə- rāt′/	-ər ĭt/
duplicate	/doo′ plə- kāt′/	-kĭt/
elaborate	/ĭ lăb′ə- rāt′/	-ər ĭt/

In Chapter 5 there was brief mention of the "silent" *e* that presumably makes the preceding vowel sound "long." There are vast numbers of words with *un*stressed syllables in which that "rule" is completely wrong. For instance, I collected more than 300 words ending in *-tive* alone (like crea*tive,* destruc*tive,* rela*tive,* etc.) in which the letter *i* clearly spells /ĭ/, and such spellings make a mockery of the "rule." Here we have more samples, and they represent great numbers of words in which the letters *a* and *i* (with following *e*) spell the /ĭ/ sound:

Base Word:	Unstressed Syllable:		Base Word:	Unstressed Syllable:	
lace	pal*a*ce	/ĭ/	late	pal*a*te	/ĭ/
late	chocol*a*te	/ĭ/	rice	dentifr*i*ce	/ĭ/
line	anil*i*ne	/ĭ/	alive	ol*i*ve	/ĭ/
mice	pum*i*ce	/ĭ/	mine	determ*i*ne	/ĭ/
nice	corn*i*ce	/ĭ/	(ig)nite	gran*i*te	/ĭ/
rate	corpor*a*te	/ĭ/	site	appos*i*te	/ĭ/
tine	dest*i*ne	/ĭ/	dice	prejud*i*ce	/ĭ/

The Eyes Have It—Wrong!

Now if we leave unstressed syllables and turn momentarily to the spelling of /ĭ/ in monosyllabic words, we find five different spellings in a single sentence: Sitting in the upper t*ie*r, our friends ch*ee*red the h*e*ro so loudly that we could h*ear* them even down h*ere*. Four of my college dictionaries (and two others) agree that those words all have the /ĭ/ sound, and that means there are five ways to spell it in similar words. I had a very hard time getting people in my audiences to believe that the *ea* digraph in *ear* stands for /ĭ/ until I hit upon a scheme. I had them repeat after me the words *irritable, irritant, irritate*. Then I asked the audiences to say just the first two sounds in *irr-*; finally, I would say, "Now please say those two sounds and touch your 'ear.'" At this point everybody has agreed, and I brought out a dictionary which supported them and me; "ear" respelled is /ĭr/. So we spell the vowel sound in *hear* and *here* three ways, those two and /hĭr/, the phonetic respelling.

A summary of the many ways the /ĭ/ sound is spelled in English is in order. It is also quite revealing, for in Table 9 you will see that all six of our vowel letters spell it, and they are supplemented by twelve digraphs. In keeping with earlier statements, I wish to point out that children who succeed in learning to read have to learn many of the less common spellings. For instance, don't they have to learn these twelve words taken from the samples in the table of less common spellings: w*o*men, b*u*siness, b*u*sy, b*ui*ld, mil*ea*ge, char*a*cter, sp*i*nach, forf*ei*t, marr*ia*ge, lett*u*ce, min*u*te, and for*ei*gn?

Table 9

Nine Common and Fourteen Other Ways to
Spell the /ĭ/ Sound

	STRESSED SYLLABLES	UNSTRESSED SYLLABLES	
i:	*i*n, aux*i*liary, beg*i*n	*i*nane, am*i*cable, att*i*c	
e:	*E*nglish, sup*e*rior, adj*e*ctive	Qu*e*bec, sacr*e*d, budg*e*t	
i-e:	g*ive*, forg*ive*, outl*ive*	bod*ice*, exam*ine*, dec*isive*	
ie:	b*ie*r, cash*ie*r, p*ie*r	kerch*ie*f, misch*ie*f	
e-e:	h*ere*, m*ere*, sinc*ere*	coll*ege*, privil*ege*	
y:	sympath*y*, polygam*y*, ab*y*ss	s*y*nopsis, pol*y*gon, pol*y*p	
ea:	cl*ea*r, g*ea*r, sm*ea*r	*a-e:*	popul*ace*, surf*ace*; ad*age*, pass*age*; accur*ate*, commensur*ate*
ee:	b*ee*n, d*ee*r, j*ee*r		
ie-e:	s*ieve*		
o:	w*o*men	*ea-e:*	acr*eage*, mil*eage*
u:	b*u*siness, b*u*sy	*a:*	char*a*cter, sp*i*nach
ui:	g*ui*ld, g*ui*lt	*ai:*	chamberl*ai*n, portr*ai*t
		ei:	forf*ei*t, surf*ei*t

Here are some additional spellings in unstressed syllables: *ia-e*: carr*ia*ge, marr*ia*ge; *u-e*: lett*u*ce, min*u*te; *ae*: *A*egean, C*a*esarian; *eig*: for*eig*n; *oe*: Ph*o*enician; *ue*: tourniq*ue*t; *y-e*: apocal*ypse*; (and *ehea*: for*ehea*d; *i-ue*: odal*isque*).

It is necessary to discuss additional spellings in unstressed syllables in the next chapter. There you will find a summary statement.

CHAPTER 13

Those Insidious Schwa Spellings

Not long ago, an hour before I was to speak to a service club on the quirks of English spelling, the chairman of the day, a doctor and a good friend of mine, was at a loss for a way to collect fines painlessly from the membership. He was assigned the job of collecting a minimum of twenty-five dollars. He asked me for suggestions. I said, "Ask all who can tell what a 'schwa' is to stand up. Those who remain seated are to give fifty cents each for not knowing what might well be the greatest single reason for our having so many illiterates in our country. Those who stand up had better be able to define the word because each one who fails will be fined five dollars." My friend cleared his throat, scratched his head, and said to me, "Stan, what the hell is a schwa?" I told him and gave him a number of examples. He used the scheme, and the club's kitty was enriched by about forty dollars. There were just a few more than eighty men present.

Two of the features which distinguish Germanic from Romance languages are the degree and the location of the stress. Whereas the Romance languages, e.g., French, Italian, Portuguese, and Spanish, have only a very light stress, and it tends to fall on a syllable at or near the end of a word, Germanic languages, e.g., Danish, Dutch, German, and Icelandic, all have a relatively heavy stress, and it usually falls on the root (stem), which is the first or second syllable. English has the strongest stress of all. As Stuart Robertson in *The Development of Modern English* wrote, "In most cases we have come to overemphasize, as compared even with German, the accented syllable and to underemphasize the unaccented (syllable)." (p. 28)

For borrowed words, some Germanic languages applied a basic rule and transferred the stress to the first (or second) syllable, but German left or transferred the stress to the last syllable, thereby identifying the alien source of the words. But in English, which has by far the most borrowed words, no such rule was applied; our stress wound up now here and now there. And, worst of all, those underemphasized unaccented syllables have become schwas or have the /ĭ/ sound and are spelled in many ways. In the following four words note both the location of the stresses and the eleven schwas:

reh*a*bil*i*tate	/rē′ hə bĭl′ ə tāt′/
anthr*o*pol*o*gic*a*l	/ăn′ thrə pə lŏj′ ĭ kəl/
*co*mmun*i*c*a*ti*o*n	/kə myōō′ nə kā′ shən/
*o*n*o*mat*o*poe*ia*	/ōn′ ə măt′ ə pē′ ə/

When we say those four or similar words aloud, we recognize the role stress plays in English. If we include the absence of stress, we have roughly five degrees of stress:

1. The primary stress, as on the first syllable in *sentiment:* /sĕn′ tə mənt/
2. The secondary stress, as on the first syllable of *sentimental:* /sĕn′ tə mĕn′ t′l/
3. An intermediate stage, as in the third and sixth syllables of *sentimentality:* /sĕn′ tə mĕn tăl′ ə tē/
4. No stress in a weakened syllable, as in the second and third syllables of *sentiment:* /sĕn′ tə mənt/
5. An even weaker syllable, in which the vowel sound is barely perceptible, as in the fourth syllable of *sentimental.* (See #2 above.)

Three college dictionaries use the apostrophe to spell the extremely weak schwa sound; two use a diminutive schwa symbol.

Since there are hundreds of thousands of weakened syllables in our language, resulting in the most frequently heard sound in English, the schwa deserves more than just the few pages it received early in the third chapter. Dictionaries were incredibly slow in beginning to use the /ə/ symbol that represents it. This may have been true in part because lexicographers knew that nearly everybody prefers to believe eye pronunciations, which the dictionaries gave until relatively recently. But when the *American College Dictionary, Webster's New World Dictionary,* the *Thorndike Century* and the *Thorndike-Barnhardt* dictionaries started to use the schwa symbol, other dictionaries were forced to accept reality and fall in line.

You can find evidence even today that a whole lot of people still like to be fooled and prefer eye pronunciations, for that is the kind of pronunciation "help" the *Reader's Digest* offers its readers in "Word Power," a section which appears in every issue. Either the schwa doesn't exist and all recent dictionaries are wrong or the *Digest* is. For the benefit of those readers who have never seen "Word Power," I should say it is a

Those Insidious Schwa Spellings

list of twenty words which are followed first by supposedly correct pronunciations (in parentheses) and then by four words or phrases, one of which is a synonym or near synonym. The other three items are not related to the key word. In short, it is a kind of multiple-choice test for readers to see how many of the words they know.

We are concerned here only with the pronunciation, the "correct" respellings in parentheses. In the past ten years I have noted many hundreds of eye pronunciations, in some issues in half the words, pronunciations which conflict with dictionary phonetic respellings. The whole point is that it would be easier for Ichabod and Johnny to learn to read if in actual connected discourse words were really pronounced as the *Digest* shows them. I will restrict my examples solely to the spellings of the schwa sounds as given in all good dictionaries.

The vowel sound in the middle syllable of the following words is unquestionably /ə/, not as shown in "Word Power": alk*a*li (-kă-), cit*a*del (-tă-), ev*a*nescent (-ă-); alch*e*my (-kĕ-); fum*i*gate (-mĭ-), profl*i*gate (-lĭ-), man*i*fest (-ĭ-); acc*o*lade (-kō-), chlor*o*phyll (-ŏ-).

Surely the first vowel sound in the following words is /ə/ and not /ă/, as in the *Digest: a*ppendage, *a*vuncular, c*a*rafe, *a*gog, *a*ghast, *a*rray.

Here are six other examples:

WORD:	anathema	component	homogenize
Dictionaries:	/ə năth′ə mə/	/kəm pō′ nənt/	/hə mŏj′ ə nīz/
Digest:	/ă nath′ĕ muh/	/com pō′ nent/	/hō moj′ ĕ nīz/
WORD:	irreparable	monogamous	solicitous
Dictionaries:	/ĭ rĕp′ər ə bəl/	/mə nŏg′ ə məs/	/sə lĭs′ ə təs/
Digest:	/ĭ rep′ ă ră b'l/	/mŏ nog′ ă mus/	/so lĭs′ ĭ tus/

There are thirty-four schwa sounds in the twenty-three words in the above samples; and if pronunciation respellings are given, they should be correct. Using just one of the words as a sample, I maintain that if the following sentence is spoken normally, the word "anathema" will have three schwa sounds: "Even the mention of his name is anathema in our group." The first vowel sound will not be /ă/, and the third will not be /ĕ/.

The respellings in the *Digest* resemble those in dictionaries of fifty years ago, inadequate, misleading, often incorrect, and frequently confusing. Perhaps the editor of "Word Power" assumes that readers will automatically fill in the schwa sounds, which, to put it charitably, is unreasonable; or he thinks we truly do pronounce words as he shows them, and that strains our faith in dictionaries. If his readers already know the correct pronunciation, the respellings are superfluous; and if they don't, the respellings really ought to help. As you have seen, too often they do not because they are wrong.

Leaving the *Digest,* we'll pursue other schwa problems. Many people are extremely reluctant to believe that the schwa sound spelled by one letter, say, *a,* is the same sound as spelled by another, perhaps *o, u,* or *ou.* We'll use eight(!) approaches which, combined, should make the acceptance of dictionary respellings easier. In most of the sample words in the groups the vowel sound will be in similar language environments.

1. The schwa sound is spelled four ways in these words:

/ə/:	at*la*s	asbest*o*s	camp*u*s
/ə/:	friv*olo*us	moment*ous*	pomp*ous*

2a. We find that the three sounds /-təl/ can be spelled nine ways; the schwa is spelled in seven:

a) -*tal:*	ren*tal*	b) -*tel:*	man*tel*	c) -*til:*	len*til*
d) -*tile:*	fu*tile*	e) -*tol:*	pis*tol*	f) -*tyl:*	bu*tyl*
g) -*btle:*	sub*tle*	h) -*tle:*	ti*tle*	i) -*ttle:*	ca*ttle*

2b. In this next group the schwa is spelled ten ways, but /-səl/ is spelled in the incredible number of twenty ways:

a) -*cel:*	par*cel*	b) -*cil:*	pen*cil*	c) -*cile:*	do*cile*
d) -*sal:*	rever*sal*	e) -*scle:*	corpu*scle*	f) -*sel:*	tin*sel*
g) -*sil:*	ton*sil*	h) -*ssail:*	wa*ssail*	i) -*ssal:*	dismi*ssal*
j) -*ssel:*	ve*ssel*	k) -*ssil:*	fo*ssil*	l) -*ssile:*	mi*ssile*
m) -*ssle:*	tu*ssle*	n) -*stle:*	bri*stle*	o) -*sul:*	con*sul*
p) -*xel:*	A*xel*	q) -*xil:*	a*xil*	r) -*xle:*	a*xle*
s) -*s'll:* This*'ll* be good				t) -*ss'll:* Our cla*ss'll* win	

(Although the last two entries were included for fun, the schwa sound is definitely spelled by the apostrophe there.)

3. In this group we have words in which no vowel letter at all spells the sound, and yet it is heard in hundreds of words, such as ample /ăm′ pəl/, angle /ăng′ gəl/ ankle /ăng′ kəl/, Bible /bī′ bəl/, etc. In the words in the second and fourth columns no vowel letter spells the sound. I have selected five homophone pairs to illustrate the point that the schwa sound is the same, no matter how it is spelled:

Those Insidious Schwa Spellings 119

brid*a*l	bridle	lab*e*l	sable
med*a*l	meddle	Ab*e*l	able
gamb*o*l	gamble	nick*e*l	pickle
symb*o*l	simple	usef*u*l	trifle
id*o*l	idle	id*y*ll	sidle

4. Here are eighteen additional samples of homophone pairs whose phonetic respellings are identical. (Read down.)

alt*a*r	aug*e*r	bar*o*n	bett*e*r	carr*o*t	cell*a*r
alt*e*r	aug*u*r	barr*e*n	bett*o*r	kar*a*t	sell*e*r
chol*e*r	counc*i*l	cous*i*n	curr*a*nt	cymb*a*l	divis*e*r
coll*a*r	couns*e*l	coz*e*n	curr*e*nt	symb*o*l	divis*o*r
du*a*l	Eth*e*l	fish*e*r	gall*o*p	less*e*n	min*e*r
du*e*l	eth*y*l	fiss*u*re	Gall*u*p	less*o*n	min*o*r

5. Obviously the same sound is spelled by *a* and *i* in words ending in the suffixes *-able* and *-ible* or we wouldn't have to consult our dictionaries so often to find the conventional spelling. Note in particular how the preceding sounds are alike in each pair. (Read across.)

-*a*ble	-*i*ble	-*a*ble	-*i*ble
laud*a*ble	aud*i*ble	depend*a*ble	extend*i*ble
reconcil*a*ble	indel*i*ble	return*a*ble	discern*i*ble
advis*a*ble	divis*i*ble	condens*a*ble	respons*i*ble
cross*a*ble	poss*i*ble	pass*a*ble	pass*i*ble
adapt*a*ble	corrupt*i*ble	detest*a*ble	digest*i*ble

6. This catch-all group represents hundreds of words which are often misspelled because our memories fail us. (Read down.)

consist*e*nt	defer*me*nt	abund*a*nt	err*a*nd	better*me*nt
inst*a*nt	dorm*a*nt	depend*e*nt	rever*e*nd	inform*a*nt
serp*e*nt	gramm*a*r	calend*a*r	call*e*r	adam*a*nt
verd*a*nt	hamm*e*r	lavend*e*r	doll*a*r	ligam*e*nt

7. Now if you will read along the lines in the following samples, you will hear identical sounds in the last syllables:

a	*e*	*i*	*o*	*u*
dioces*a*n	loos*e*n	peps*i*n	ars*o*n	Whits*u*n
bant*a*m	tot*e*m	vict*i*m	cust*o*m	sept*u*m

8. Finally, the vowels before final -r all spell the same sound in these words:

-ar	-er	-ir	-or
burgl*ar*	pli*er*	kaf*ir*	doct*or*
nucle*ar*	runn*er*	elix*ir*	don*or*

-ur	-yr	-ure	-our
fem*ur*	mart*yr*	pict*ure*	glam*our*
sulph*ur*	zeph*yr*	pleas*ure*	hon*our*

If you have a keen sense of hearing and if you will record the sample words in this chapter and then play the tape a few times, it is probable that you will detect a slight difference between the normal schwa sound and the sound which precedes the /r/ sound in group 8 (above). Some language experts, including some lexicographers, distinguish between the two types of sounds. In any event, I have listed in the above group samples of most of the /ər/ spellings. Otherwise I believe your recording will be a waste of time because the schwa sound is the schwa sound, no matter how we spell it.

Now you can more easily believe me when I say we have huge numbers of words with one schwa, many thousands with two, many hundreds with three, and even a small number with as many as four. Examples:

Two Schwas

*a*ccust*o*m	App*a*lachi*a*	*a*rithm*e*tic	c*o*urag*eo*us
eq*u*ilibri*u*m	gel*a*tine	imped*i*ment	mischi*e*vo*u*s
p*a*ran*o*ia	p*a*ss*e*ng*e*r	reg*i*on*a*l	vill*ai*n*ou*s

Three Schwas

*a*nal*o*go*u*s	*a*n*o*nym*ou*s	*a*sp*a*r*a*gus	c*a*pit*u*l*a*tion
c*o*lloqui*a*lis*m*	c*o*mpat*i*ble	C*o*nn*e*ctic*u*t	l*e*vi*a*th*a*n
m*o*lybd*e*n*u*m	p*a*rishi*o*n*e*r	p*e*nins*u*l*a*	Pr*e*sbyteri*a*nis*m*
s*o*ci*e*t*a*l	s*u*scept*i*bl*e*	t*e*mp*e*r*a*ture	t*o*p*o*graph*e*r

Four Schwas

*a*b*o*m*i*n*a*ble	c*o*nsid*e*r*a*bl*e*	pr*o*f*e*ssi*o*n*a*lis*m*
c*a*p*i*t*a*liz*a*tion		C*o*ngr*e*g*a*ti*o*n*a*lis*m*

FIVE SCHWAS

A*meric*a*n*izatio*n*

When the thirty-four sample words are spoken, the schwa sound is heard ninety-seven times. It is spelled fourteen ways; by the six vowel letters, by six digraphs, by the *-ble* situation (four times), and by the strange combination *-sm* (four times). Even though we do not use a vowel to spell the sound, we do indeed hear it in hundreds of words between *s* and *m*, e.g., cha*sm,* enthusia*sm,* optimi*sm,* pessimi*sm,* reali*sm,* sociali*sm,* etc. We also hear the schwa between *th* and *m* in the words logari*thm* and rhy*thm.* It is understandable that children (and some adults) spell *rhythm* as *rithum.*

Incidentally, in the thirty-four words almost two-thirds of the vowel letters (66 percent) spell the schwa sound.

There is no reason to deplore the presence of the schwa sound, but it is deplorable that we have so many ways to spell it. In Chapter 3 you saw how we use all six vowel letters. Now we see that the "final *e*" rule (making the preceding vowel sound "long") is violated again, as it usually is in unstressed syllables. Here we see five more ways to spell the sound: vowel letter plus final *e* with an intervening consonant or consonants:

a-e:	pir*a*te, reli*a*nce	*e-e*:	lic*e*nse, sci*e*nce
i-e:	eng*i*ne, fac*i*le	*o-e*:	purp*o*se, wholes*o*me
	u-e:	fig*u*re, press*u*re	

This brings us to a total of eleven ways to spell the schwa so far, by the six single vowel letters and by the five combinations illustrated above. In addition, we have these fairly common ways to spell /ə/:

ah:	Jon*ah,* Jud*ah*	*ai*:	Brit*ai*n, mount*ai*n
au:	*au*thority, rest*au*rant	*ea*:	Ele*a*nor, hydrang*ea*
eo:	lunch*eo*n, surg*eo*n	*ia*:	Georg*ia,* plag*ia*rize
io:	cush*io*n, fash*io*n	*ou*:	envi*ou*s, previ*ou*s
ue:	etiq*ue*tte, masq*ue*rade	*uo*:	lang*uo*r, liq*uo*r

Still other ways are found in a few words, but good readers must learn most of these words: *ae*: Mich*ae*l; *ia-e*: colleg*ia*te; *eau*: bur*eau*crat; *ei*: rev*ei*lle; *eu*: chauff*eu*r; *ie*: sold*ie*r; *iu*: Belg*iu*m; *oa*: cupb*oa*rd; *oi*: conn*oi*sseur; *oi-e*: tort*oi*se; *ua*: piq*ua*nt.

We find that the names of forty of our states and seven of the Canadian provinces have at least one schwa sound, e.g., Ariz*o*na, Flor*i*da, Minn*e*sota; Man*i*toba, etc. Of course many English names contain the schwa sound, especially given names, and in some, as we might expect, the letter *e* spells /ĭ/. You will recognize these names from an earlier chapter. I promised to return to them:

Helen	/hĕl′ ən/	Dor*o*thy	/dôr′ ə thē/	Margaret	/mär′ gə rĭt/
Laur*a*	/lô′ rə/	Sus*a*n	/soo͞′ zən/	Karen	/kăr′ən/
Thom*a*s	/tŏm′ əs/	Tim*o*thy	/tĭm′ ə thē/	Richard	/rĭch′ərd/
William	/wĭl′ yəm/	Kenn*e*th	/kĕn′ ĭth/	Micha*e*l	/mīk′ əl/
Rhod*a*	/rō′ də/	Sar*ah*	/să′ (sâ) rə/		

What is the extent of the role played by the schwa in English? I made a count of a hundred pages, twenty pages in each of five college dictionaries and found the ratio of words with the sound compared with words which do not have the sound to be 1.5 to 1. This means there are more words with schwas than words without them, and I included in my count words of one syllable, where there can be no schwas. We must conclude that the schwa plays a major role in both the spoken and the written language.

It is ironic that the spellings of our weakest vowel sound serve as one of the major roadblocks in the rocky path of children learning to read. Now you can better understand why Professor A. G. Kennedy used strong adjectives in describing English spelling. We find them in *Current English* (p. 121). He said it is

(a) unsystematic: If it were systematic, one symbol would represent the schwa;

(b) inadequate: If it were adequate, we'd have a special symbol to spell our most frequently heard vowel sound;

(c) illogical: If the spelling of the sound were logical, it would not be spelled in thirty ways, at least fifteen of them common ways;

(d) misleading: When children see a letter, for instance *a,* they should be able to expect it to stand for /ā/ or /ă/, and certainly not /ə/, as it does in literally thousands of words. And when it does, it is misleading.

(e) absurd: It is absurd to have four or five ways to spell a sound. Since we have six times that many, then the situation is worse than absurd; it is preposterous, nonsensical, and irrational.

I have said before that if Ichabod and Johnny spoke a language whose words were spelled phonetically, they might well become good readers. If we now apply the Mencius plan, we can readily see why such a statement is logical. We'll restrict our comparison to common spellings of just two sounds in Table 10, even though good readers in English must learn to read twice as many spellings.

Table 10

Common Spellings of /ə/ and /ɪ/ in Four Languages

LANGUAGE	WAYS TO SPELL /ə/	WAYS TO SPELL /ɪ/	TOTALS
Dutch	2 (Since 1947)	1	3
German	1	1	2
Swedish	1	1	2
English	15	9	24

Do you wonder that Johnny can't read?

CHAPTER 14

A Good Word for the Bad Speller

A whole lot of good spellers think the ability to spell well is a sign of high intelligence and that poor spellers are less intelligent. If the ability to spell correctly is a sign of intelligence, why are spelling words never found on intelligence tests? Technical details could easily be worked out; for instance, examiners might offer words in phonetic spelling and require test takers to write the conventional spellings:

/ĕk′ stə sē/   /ē′ kwə tôr′ ē əl/   /ə kwīr′/

/fə zĭsh′ ən/   /ĭg zôs′ chən/   /bĭ gīl′/

(Words: ecstacy, equatorial, acquire, physician, exhaustion, beguile)
Spelling could be graded quickly and objectively. Furthermore, there would be a limitless supply of words; if twenty words were used each year, the supply would last for many a millennium. But the results would be reliable only for SPELLING!

We don't find words on IQ tests because the ability to spell is not a valid measure of one's intelligence.

Humans are often strange and illogical. Who hasn't heard an adult say rather boastfully, "I'm no good in math. I never was any good in it." Being poor in math is a kind of honor, a badge worn with pride. Why do we pleasantly and somewhat admiringly accept a person's failure in math, which is, after all, based on logic and is regular and consistent, and then be contemptuous of a person's poor performance in spelling, an area where there is so little logic?

When I was chairman of a large college English department for many years, at least a dozen colleagues at one time or another came to me in distress because one or more of their superior students couldn't spell well. The colleagues were concerned because they assumed excellent students in composition or literature courses should be able to spell

A Good Word for the Bad Speller

impeccably. The unfortunate students, along with roughly fifty million other Americans, were not endowed with a particular kind of visual perception and a good visual memory. It goes without saying that top-flight students with keen minds can be poor spellers because such a high proportion of our words cannot be spelled logically.

The supercilious attitude of good spellers toward poor spellers developed in the eighteenth century. Even in the seventeenth century a great many words were spelled two, three, and more ways. But finally convention took over and deep-froze spellings. So "height" became the only correct spelling, even though earlier spellings, "heighthe" and "highth" had been widely used. By analogy, many people thinking of "bread*th*," "wid*th*," "dep*th*," and "leng*th*," say /hītth/ today, as earlier generations did. "Colledge" and "knowlege" were fairly common spellings and, certainly, phonetically, were no worse than current spellings, "college" and "knowledge." Compare /kŏl′ ĭj/, /nŏl′ ĭj/.

The spellings of the schwa sound, as I have noted before, result in many of the greatest problems as I now wish to demonstrate, both dramatically and convincingly.

Realizing I'd get out beyond my depth if I attempted to work independently with mathematical probabilities, I went to my grandson Tim, who knows a great deal more about them than I do and put to him this question: What chances would a person have to spell the schwa sound correctly in six entirely unknown English words if each one has a single schwa sound? I simplified the problem by choosing words in which the sound is not spelled by the letter *y* or a digraph (*ai, ou,* etc.). Thus, in each of the six words there were only five possibilities, one of the simple vowel letters *a, e, i, o,* or *u*. My grandson said the chances are

one in 15,625.

The premise has to be that a person has never once seen the words. With known words there would be no great challenge. Obviously, in these samples

/ō′ mə hô (hä)/ is Om*a*ha /ŏm′ ə lĭt/ is om*e*let
/ŏm′ nə bŭs/ is omn*i*bus /ō′ nəs/ is on*u*s
/ō′ pəl/ is op*a*l /ŏp′ə zĭt/ is opp*o*site

Here are six unknown words with one vowel letter missing:

1. /ŏn′ ə jər/   on_ger   2. /ŏl′ ə vēn/   ol_vine
3. /ŏn ə măs′ tĭks/ on_mastics 4. /ō′ lə fĭn/   ol_fin
5. /ŏp′ sə nĭn/   ops_nin   6. /ŏm′ fə ləs/ omph_los

If the words are new to you, would you care to try your luck and fill in the spaces? Pure chance will determine your results! Presently I'll give the missing letters.

Grandson Tim said the outcome would be more dramatic if I were to double the number and use twelve unknown words. A person's chances of guessing the spelling of all twelve schwas correctly would be minute, for the chances are only
one in 244,140,625.
Would you care to try to beat the odds (there is absolutely no skill involved) with these six additional words?

7.	/ō′ ə līt/	o_lite	8.	/ō ŏg′ ə məs/	oog_mos
9.	/ŏf′ ə klīd′/	oph_cleide	10.	/ŏn tŏj′ ə nē/	ontog_ny
11.	/ō′ ə sīt′/	o_cyte	12.	/ŏp′ ə lāt/	opp_late

In order to spare you the trouble of looking up the spellings, here you have the missing letters:

1. *a;* 2. *i;* 3. *o;* 4. *e;* 5. *o;* 6. *a;*
7. *o;* 8. *a;* 9. *i;* 10. *e;* 11. *o;* 12. *i*

Lest you think my (my grandson's) figures—one chance in more than 240 million of getting all twelve spellings correct—are theoretical but wrong, I made a sampling to see if I dared print the astronomical figures. I gave the twelve words to 218 college students in nine English classes. To make sure that everybody knew what was wanted, I gave the six sample words you have seen, *Omaha, omelet,* etc. I used the pattern shown above, but in addition I dictated each of the unknown words three times. All the students had to do was to try to fill in the blanks with the proper letters. All the students knew what a schwa is and what was wanted. Every one cooperated. If you are mathematically inclined, you will not be surprised to learn that more than two-thirds of the 218 students misspelled the schwa sound in eight or more of the twelve words. The one who missed the fewest, four, said she knew three of the twelve words.

The point of the experiment was to show that *nobody* can spell all of our words! Skeptics may wonder how many years I spent looking for such difficult words. That was no great accomplishment; I merely looked in the area from *ol-* to *op-,* and on just seven successive pages (927–933) of the College Edition of the *Random House Dictionary of the English Language,* took the eighteen words, the six known ones and the twelve less well known ones. I looked primarily for words of three syllables,

A Good Word for the Bad Speller

in which the middle syllable has the schwa sound. Three of the words have four syllables, and one of the three I selected for a special reason, which will soon become apparent.

I have told how some parents think we spell most of our words as they are sounded. But parents aren't the only ones. Syndicated columnists and editorial writers keep the fiction alive. One such example may be found in an editorial in the *Phoenix Gazette* of June 30, 1973. The writer congratulated a girl who had participated in a spelling bee for having spelled the prize-winning word correctly. Asked how she had been able to spell it, she replied, "You spell it like it sounds." This was the editor's reaction: "That remark made the Gazette's editorial heart leap up."

The sound which the winner's predecessor had spelled incorrectly and which the girl winner spelled correctly was a schwa. Good grief! How can we hear how a schwa is spelled if we haven't previously seen the word? Well, we can't, and the editorial writer obviously doesn't know what the schwa sound is, let alone that it is spelled in two dozen ways. When I think of the young contestant's spelling of the schwa sound, I am reminded of a phrase in *My Fair Lady,* "With a little bit of luck." As you have seen, this is an understatement; with the spelling of the schwa sound we need more than just a little bit of luck.

We live in a blissful unawareness of language reality. The writer of the editorial was convinced that "The teaching of phonics in the grammar schools . . . is the child's key to unlock a treasure trove of knowledge." The editorial ends with the glad words that it was wonderful "To be able to congratulate the young spelling champ, who's living proof of what a wondrous system phonics is." That editorial deserves more than just a passing word. The writer used many words which will baffle learners. In the following twelve words we find twenty-nine obvious unphonetic spellings:

Words:	Unphonetic Spellings:
Phoenix	*ph* spells /f/; *oe* spells /ē/
Gazette	*a* spells a schwa; the second *e* is a wasted letter
editorial	The first *i* spells a schwa; the second spells /ē/; *a* spells a schwa
heart	*ea* spells /ä/
congratulate	*o* spells a schwa; *t* spells /ch/; *u* spells a schwa
treasure	*ea* spells /ĕ/; *s* spells /zh/; *u* spells a schwa; the final *e* is wasted.
of	*o* in *of* usually spells a schwa; *f* spells /v/
knowledge	*k, w,* and *d* serve no phonetic function and are wasted letters; the first *e* spells /ĭ/

young	*ou* spells /ŭ/ but should spell /ou/ in phonetic spelling
who	*w* is wasted; *o* should be "long," as in *go*
wondrous	*o* spells /ŭ/, should spell /ŏ/; *ou* represents a schwa
system	*y* spells /ĭ/ but should spell /y/ (*yes*). Do we also accept /ī/, as in *my,* /ē/, as in *Amy;* /ə/, as in *Sibyl;* and /ĭ/, as in *system.* Phonetic spelling does not allow such choices; *e* spells a schwa

The word which the winner of the spelling contest spelled correctly was number three in the experiment above, *onomastics*. With one schwa sound a person has one chance in five of getting its spelling right (if only five vowel letters are used); but the girl had one chance in four because the boy before her had used up one of the five letters when he misspelled the word.

In her mind the young lady might well have associated the first four sounds in "*onom*astics" with the spelling of words she had heard and learned to spell, as in "astr*onom*y," "aut*onom*y," or "ec*onom*y." For that reason she spelled the four sounds as she had learned them and she "spelled it like it sounds."

If she had been spelling the word "hum*a*n," she'd have spelled the schwa "like it sounds," but she would have used *a* and not *o*. The last three sounds in "omen" are the same as the last three in "human," but she now would spell the schwa with an *e*. And if we take a word which is derived from "om*e*n," namely, "om*i*nous," the second vowel sound remains the same, a schwa; however, the letter is no longer *e* but *i!* (/ō' mən/, /ŏm' ə nəs/). Our eyes and our memories (and our dictionaries) have locked in the spellings, as irrational as they are.

Since the emphasis here is on spelling, it might be well to remind you that from earlier chapters we have seen how we have to memorize Franc*e*s and Franc*i*s, Mari*a*n and Mari*o*n, and capit*a*l and capit*o*l. But they are merely samples; we have to memorize the spelling of *every* schwa sound we write. Here is additional evidence:

  a in div*a*gate   *e* in congr*e*gate   *i* in nav*i*gate
        o in der*o*gate   *u* in corr*u*gate

These six words are excellent evidence:

  neg*a*tive   compar*a*tive   sep*a*rate
  pos*i*tive   compar*i*son   desp*e*rate

In practice, children hear shortened forms of the last two words more often than the three syllable words: /sĕp' rĭt/, /dĕs' prĭt/. Who needs

A Good Word for the Bad Speller

additional proof that too often children can't simply spell sounds; they have to learn, memorize, and remember spelling.

In Chapter 9 I told of a continuing tendency, which started a thousand years ago, to shorten spoken words by dropping unstressed syllables. Previously, I offered two dozen samples. Here are twelve more:

bound*a*ry	corp*o*ral	fed*e*ral	hist*o*ry
lib*e*ral	mem*o*ry	quand*a*ry	temp*e*rature
the*o*ry	usu*a*l	vet*e*rinary	We*d*n*e*sday

Words ending in *-ically* (and some in *-ally*) appear to be losing the schwa sound; here are six additional samples:

| drastic*a*lly | fantastic*a*lly | gener*a*lly |
| optimistic*a*lly | realistic*a*lly | sarcastic*a*lly |

You will seldom hear the schwa uttered in such words, and there are some 300–500 of them. I'm sure you'll hear /bās′ ĭk lē/ for basic*a*lly; you'll even find it in some dictionaries. But the classic example of our dropping sounds is found in the word "goodbye" ("goodby," "good-bye"), which is a contraction of "God be with you (ye)." In Britain, children have to learn more dropped syllables than our children do, as in diction*a*ry, laborat*o*ry, and medicine /mĕd′ sĭn/. They also have to spell more words in which the letters *h* and *r* spell no sound. As I have said, even in standard American we could easily drop the final /r/ sound. If two or three Presidents were to fail to pronounce a clear /r/ sound at the end of words and syllables where the spelling calls for it, many people might try to emulate their speech, and that would be still another of the many burdens on our children learning to read and spell.

We have now seen how we have to learn to spell (a) a sound, the schwa, which can give us no guidance whatever, and (b) lost sounds (or silence). In the past, there have been efforts to eliminate useless letters. Noah Webster for a while wanted to establish a "federal" language in the United States, and he hoped to achieve "perfect regularity." In so doing, he planned to rid the written language of all wasted (that is, "silent") letters. He advocated such changes as these: h*ea*d to hed; h*ea*lth to helth; giv*e* to giv; beli*e*ve to beleev; activ*e* to activ; fri*e*nd to frend; tong*ue* to tung; *w*rong to rong; *w*ritten to ritten; *k*nee to nee; la*ugh* to laf; da*ugh*ter to dawter, and so forth.

Unfortunately for our learners, he turned conservative and abandoned all of his proposed sweeping changes. He settled for a few minor ones. But you can see how English might have had many fewer nonfunctional letters if Webster had carried through and made a success of his original intent.

There are many letters which, from the standpoint of phonetics, are also wasted, and some of them you may have given little thought to. Here is an indication of that problem: In column A is the letter in question, and in columns B and D you see it in words. The words in columns C and E show how we spell the identical sounds without the letters in column A. Again you will see how we spell words, not sounds (as we should):

A	B	C	D	E
c	ascetic	antiseptic	scepter	beset
c	excellent	execute	excerpt	exercise
c	account	academy	occasion	acacia
c	crack	squeak	lock	look
d	ledge	allege	judge	refuge
e	foe	hobo	hoe	alto
e	turkey	lucky	galley	jelly
g	gnome	Nome	gnarled	snarled
k	tack	lilac	tick	synthetic
s	grass	gas	canvass	canvas
s	bliss	crisis	kiss	tennis
s	discuss	focus	fuss	virus
s	across	epos	moss	cosmos
t	batch	attach	witch	sandwich
w	shadow	torpedo	swallow	solo

Apparently future generations will continue to write the *e* following the letter *v* because they think it must be there for a good reason, and will be too conservative to change; and they (and we) will continue to waste time, paper, ink, and energy (that is the word of the hour) writing it. If it had been dropped a hundred or more years ago, huge forests as well as lakes of ink would have been saved, and these words would look perfectly natural to us: groov, hav, liv, nerv, twelv. Convention calls for the *e* and habits will keep it. IF language experts were to agree

A Good Word for the Bad Speller

that the preceding vowel is "long" when followed by *e* in the same stressed syllable, it would survive, as in pav*e*, Stev*e*, fiv*e*, and stov*e*. But where it is downright misleading, it certainly does not help in the slightest, and this is true in many hundreds of words. Surely it would help readers as well as spellers if it were dropped. What phonetic function does it serve in such words as these:

| detectiv*e* | expensiv*e* | expressiv*e* | nativ*e* | oppressiv*e* |

Is the letter *e* not equally misleading in these words:

agat*e*	anis*e*	climat*e*	considerat*e*	disciplin*e*
exquisit*e*	fortun*e*	genuin*e*	hypocrit*e*	imagin*e*
immediat*e*	local*e*	perjur*e*	preterit*e*	requisit*e*

There are still more problems with which poor spellers (and poor readers) have to contend. Perhaps an outstanding example is the large number of homophones. Everybody will agree that those words must be memorized, certainly if they have to be written, and there are at least twenty-five hundred of them. Examples: /o͞o/ *wood* and *would*; /ŭ/ *none* and *nun*; /û/ *serf* and *surf*; /ə/ *mustard* and *mustered*; /k/ *chord* and *cord*; /t/ *missed* and *mist*, etc. In Chapter 7 there were twenty sets of "triplets," and here are a half dozen more:

/ā/	raise	rays	raze	/ā/	main	Maine	mane
/ā/	nay	nee	neigh	/ī/	aye	eye	I
/o͞o/	slew	slough	slue	/ō/	doe	dough	do (music)

"Quads":

| /ī/ | right | rite | write | wright |
| /s/ | cense | cents | scents | sence |

There are good reasons for our having far more homophones than Dutch and German combined. The Great Vowel Shift, the acceptance of various spellings and dialect forms from different parts of Britain, and the borrowing of so many words are the chief causes. An example of our borrowing is found in /sīt/: *sight* came from Old English, and we borrowed *cite* and *site* from French and Latin.

You will find staunch supporters of homophones on every hand. They say the spellings enable readers to know instantly which word the writer had in mind. That is true. But what about our oral language? Are we super intelligent when we listen and know which word the speaker had in mind, but stupid when we read? In all events, our many homophones reveal that we have an oversupply of ways to spell our sounds.

Another bothersome spelling problem is to know when consonants are written singly or doubled. Here are a few samples:

eminent	inoculate	emigrate	omit
imminent	innocuous	immigrate	commit
chagrined	eradicate	inordinate	disaster
grinned	desiccate	innovate	dissolve

Who hasn't had problems with a*ccomm*odate, emba*rr*ass and para*ll*el?

The spellings in the following words simply have to be memorized. If men*t*ion is correct, why is it not ten*t*ion instead of ten*s*ion? And why must it be pen*s*ion and not pen*t*ion? It is ambi*t*ious, but we must not follow the pattern and write con*t*ious because it is con*s*cious. Do we *chute* the *chutes* or *shoot* the *chutes* or *chute* the *shoots?* Why don't we write *lizzard* and *gizard* instead of *lizard* and *gizzard?* But I must not give more examples; there are limits to space and to your patien*ts*. Sorry, patien*ce*.

The spelling of vowel sounds is just as confusing. If poor spellers write *speach* for *speech,* some good spellers cluck as if the bad spellers had committed a grave crime. If only the clucking would stop! We write *each* and add a *p* and have *peach.* Why can't we add an *s* and have *speach?* After all, it is *speak,* and it doesn't make sense to say we can't write *speach.* Only convention dictates that it must be *speech.* If it must be *speech,* then we ought to write *eech, peech,* and *speek.*

When I have said on several occasions that lots of people don't even try to look up words in a dictionary because too often they can't find the words, my listeners have looked at me as if I were benighted. That is a word that might be hard to find, partly because the letter *e* spells /ĭ/ and because one might assume the spelling is "beknighted" /bĭ nī' tĭd/. But suppose a poor speller wanted to find these six words: *mosquito, ghost, adjourn, renege, audience,* and *amiable.* Poor spellers might well try to look for these spellings first: *musketo, goast (boast, coast), ajurn, rinig, oddeeance,* and *ameeable.* If there is an Amy in the class, chances are children will try *amyable.* Why not?

At least two publishers recognize how difficult it is for bad spellers to find words in dictionaries. Believe it or not, they have published dictionaries in which thousands of words are purposely misspelled! The words are spelled in the ways poor spellers might be expected to look them up. In an adjoining column the correct spelling is given. The appearance of the two books on the market was both humorous and sad, humorous to think any such book would be needed for the language of an enlightened people, and sad to think they are truly needed. They do a pretty good job, helping with thousands of words.

Suppose somebody doesn't know how to spell "marine." A poor speller is likely to think of *mureen* or *mareen* or *marean.* Each one of those spellings is listed in *The Perfect Speller* by Harriet Wittels and Joan Greisman (Grosset and Dunlap, 1973). Each misspelled entry is printed in black, and alongside it is the correct spelling, printed in red. "Muscle" might be hard for Ichabod. The compilers know he is not likely to be looking for the fish "mussel," and they properly, in red, give him what he is looking for. "Mutual" may also be hard for Ichabod. By analogy, *mew* and *pew* give him the clue, and he looks for *mewchual*. There it is in black, and beside it is *mutual* in red. He wants to spell "lymph glands." He can spell *glands,* but he assumes "lymph" is spelled *limf,* as it is in phonetic spelling. Without the "crutch" dictionary he would be lost and frustrated; with it, he can spell the word as custom requires. (Yes, "require" is in red and *rekwire* and other misspellings are there in black. Finally, "measles" is given in twenty-four incorrect spellings, e.g., *measals, meazols, meesuls,* etc.

However, nothing is really perfect, not even *The Perfect Speller.* And so at least a dozen possibilities for the misspelling of "measles" are not there, e.g., *mesles, mezuls,* etc. Nor is *inger* there. Ichabod can't find "injure"; and as he knows the word "ginger," he takes for granted that he will find it minus the *g*. But the book with 330 large pages and six columns on the page, three in black and three in red, cannot help, cannot possibly help, with all of our mixed-up spellings of words. (Incidentally, the other of the two books is *The Misspeller's Dictionary* by Peter and Craig Norback, published by Quadrangle.)

The presence of the two unusual books is a true indication of the erratic state of our spelling. In Italy and Spain as well as in countries speaking Germanic languages other than English, they aren't necessary, not even conceivable. In these countries little time is spent teaching spelling, and spelling bees are completely unknown. As Professors Robert M. Gorrell and Charlton Laird write in their *Modern English Handbook,* "Learning to spell in Spanish or German is relatively easy." (p. 507)

The following four quotations were made by seven professors of English:

1. Two British scholars, H. A. Treble and G. H. Vallins, in their highly successful book, *An ABC of English Usage,* give two reasons for the difficulties of English spelling: "(i) The alphabet is defective . . . and (ii) English spelling is etymological rather than phonetic." (p. 167)

2. Three professors whom I have previously quoted, Norman Foerster, J. M. Steadman, Jr., and James B. McMillan, said, "It is impossible to determine how an English word is spelled by hearing or pronouncing it."

They went on to say, "Every word must be remembered visually." *Handbook of Writing and Thinking.* (p. 272)

3. Under the caption, "Spelling a Problem," Professor Margaret M. Bryant wrote as follows in her book, *Modern English and Its Heritage:* "The worst feature of our present alphabet is the burden it places upon generation after generation of school children learning to spell." (p. 181)

4. The Columbia University professor of Romance Languages, Mario Pei, did not pull any punches: "The fact remains that our spelling is more than irrational—it is inhuman, and forms the bane not merely of foreigners, but of our younger generations, compelled to devote interminable hours to learning a system which is the soul and essence of anarchy." *The Story of the English Language,* p. 338

An analysis of each of the following words will show why the experts came to their conclusions:

seize, siege, fierce, weird, niece, foreign, forfeit, sieve, believe, receive, consensus, acquiesce, conquer, vermilion, numskull, crummy, picnicking, ecstacy, tendinitis, chilblain, bellwether, quandary, twelfth, threshold, chipmunk, exhilarating, scissors, stomach.

Is it *preceed* and *proceed* or *precede* and *procede?* Why is it *precede* and *proceed?*

You will note the list contains no really unusual words, such as *gouache* /gwäsh/, *orgeat* /ôr′ zhăt/, *ouachita* /wŏsh′ ĭ tə/, *oubliette* /o͞o′ blē ĕt′/.

In this chapter on the difficulties of English spelling it would be a major blunder if I failed to remind you of the computer study of 17,310 words (Chapter 4). You will recall how the programmers established 308 spelling rules, and with all those rules the machine was able to spell correctly only 49 percent of the words. It is small wonder that there are at least fifty million adults in the United States who do not spell well.

In conclusion, I have this question: Has it ever occurred to you that our spelling is a curse on everybody who writes (and learns to read) English? In our dictionaries one of the definitions of the noun "curse" is this: "Any cause of trouble, evil, injury, or misfortune." Based on that definition, we must agree that the mixed-up ways we write our words are the cause of trouble for all of us, and, therefore, at least a mild curse. And at the other end of the scale our spelling is a cause of misfortune for many millions of people wherever English is written, and to many it is an intolerable, a terrible curse.

If you are a poor speller and are or have been a bit embarrassed or ashamed, you have no reason to suffer such feelings any longer. Who is ashamed of an inability to carry a tune? Of being tone deaf? Of being color blind? Of being unable to play the piano? Of not being able to paint a landscape or a portrait? If the answer is nobody, or at least nobody should be ashamed, then I ask you if you should be ashamed or embarrassed because God or nature did not endow you with a particular type of perception and the necessary visual memory? This is especially true with a language whose spelling is "the soul and essence of anarchy."

CHAPTER 15

The Second Great Big IF
(The Price We Pay—I)

Now it is necessary for us to turn to another highly important subject. In addition to having by far the most difficult spelling system, English has a second cruel handicap: It has by far the most difficult vocabulary to master.

How many times have you read or heard of the glories of the tremendous English vocabulary, the largest one of all the world's languages? Who doesn't know about our marvelous stock of words?

Have you ever considered the other side of the coin?

The overwhelming size and especially the nature of our vocabulary have contributed, are now contributing, and will continue to contribute to the failure of millions in their efforts to learn to read well. The nature of a majority of the words in the English language is unquestionably the second cause of so much functional illiteracy and is the reason it is hard for nearly everybody to acquire an adequate and satisfactory vocabulary.

IF most of our words had come down to us from Old English or were composed of native English elements, there would be far fewer functional illiterates in the English-speaking world because it would be incomparably easier to acquire satisfactory vocabularies.

In the many books I have studied on the English language I have repeatedly read of the inestimable advantages our language affords writers and speakers, enabling them to express themselves with remarkable exactness and accuracy, to achieve the subtlest shades of meaning, and to enjoy a wealth of words unmatched in any other language.

On the other hand, few writers recognize or give much space to the profound disadvantages which came about from our extensive borrowing of so many scores of thousands of words and resulted in such a vast vocabulary. With few exceptions writers do not discuss this aspect of the subject, even though it is of tremendous significance. It deserves your thoughtful consideration.

The Second Great Big IF

The small amount of space which I am giving the matter could give you a false impression. As a practiced reader you now feel comfortable with the way our words are written, and it took many chapters to demonstrate to you that our writing symbols are inadequate and much too often are used irrationally. But if you are thoroughly satisfied with the extent of your present vocabulary and know the meanings of all the words you read, you are a most unusual individual and are indeed fortunate. Most people, however, feel less than completely satisfied with the size of their vocabularies; and for such readers only three chapters will be needed to make the point. I will do my best to demonstrate to you that we pay a high price, a heavy penalty, for having borrowed so many foreign words.

In short, we'll consider the negative aspects of our having such a gigantic inventory of words, which consists of many more foreign than native words.

There is a danger that you will think I am exaggerating because we are inclined to relate what we read to ourselves, and you do not come close to having the problems which poorer readers and nonreaders of the English-speaking community have. We are thinking primarily of the plight of the millions of frustrated individuals who are functionally illiterate or come close to being in that deplorable state.

First, let us take a brief look at the type of word we are NOT talking about. A high percentage of the words our children hear and use in the home, on the street, on the playground, and in the first two or three years of school came down to us from Old English. They are easy words, of which these are samples:

mother	father	sister	brother	water	milk
bread	day	night	eat	drink	sleep
love	hate	hot	cold	young	old

It is also necessary for us to remember that we have a considerable number of borrowed words which have become completely naturalized from the standpoint of use in daily conversation. These words are usually, although not invariably, short and, to lay persons, look for all the world like words which came down from the dialects of the Anglo-Saxons. These are samples of words which have become completely naturalized:

| chair | city | close | face | fine |
| gentle | nice | past | place | sure |

Naturally we hear and use the words in both preceding groups hundreds of times a year. But we see such words as are in the following group much less often:

adroit	audacious	avid	dispense
euphonious	garrulous	interminable	limpid
lucid	opaque	poignant	predecease
prodigious	profound	profuse	propagate

On a relative basis, we may call the words in the first two groups "easy" words to learn, and the words in the third group "hard" for our children to learn, especially the slower ones. Thus, we must conclude that some words are harder to learn and some are easier.

*We must never assume a word is a word and
one word is as easy to learn as another.*

There are two reasons why words in the third group are harder: (1) Most of us don't often see, hear, or use them; and (2) The words themselves offer us no associations to help us understand them; most people can't relate one part to another because they don't know either one. The words and their component parts are foreign to our past and to our thinking.

Well over 400 years ago, Roger Ascham, a writer who would have liked to weed out foreign words from English, had this to say on the subject:

> He that wyll wryte well in any tongue, muste folowe thys councel of Aristotle: to speake as the common people do, to thinke as wise men do; and so shoulde every man understande hym . . . Many English writers have not done so, by usinge straunge words as latin french and italian do make all thinges darke and harde.
> (*Toxophilus*, p. 18, Arber Edition. Written in 1545)

In 1901, two Harvard professors expressed the thought I want to develop. I have previously quoted them, J. B. Greenough, professor of Latin, and G. L. Kittredge, professor of English. They collaborated on a book, *Words and Their Ways in English Speech*. In one chapter in particular, "Learned Words and Popular Words," they made the point I wish to put across. By "learned" (pronounced /lûr′ nĭd/) they meant scholarly words which are hard to learn because they are seldom heard in conversation. They are either not known or not well known to those who have a limited education; they are words we learn in reading. "Popular" words, the authors said, "Belong to the people as a whole" and are used in ordinary conversation. They conclude, "In English it will usually be found that the so-called learned words are of foreign origin. Most of them are derived from French or Latin, and a considerable number from Greek." (p. 21) The two professors offered these samples:

The Second Great Big IF

Popular	Learned	Popular	Learned
brave	valorous	learned	erudite
building	edifice	secret	cryptic
queer	eccentric	behead	decapitate

The following fifteen words also typify the kind of words the authors had in mind. All of them came into English from Latin and were taken from the first part of Roger Angell's superb and trenchant book (1977) on baseball, *The Five Seasons:*

resolutely	lateral	lepidopteran	fatuity	modicum
obdurately	torpid	felicitous	expunging	palpable
crepuscular	desultory	progenitors	resilient	stegosauri

Incidentally, in the book there are some 360 more borrowed "learned" words like these fifteen, nearly one to a page. It is self-evident that many English-speaking people would recognize very few of the words, and that is what Greenough and Kittredge said.

Professor Otto Jespersen (1860–1943), whom I have previously quoted two or three times, writing in 1905 in his *Growth and Structure of the English Language,* expressed plainly what I am saying. He spoke of "easy" and "difficult" words. Discussing words borrowed from Latin, he said a great many of them are difficult because English-speaking people cannot easily associate the ideas with the foreign word symbols.

He explained how tempting it was for Renaissance scholars to introduce great numbers of Latin words into English. At the time of the borrowing, every educated person had to know Latin well; it was a basic requirement. As I have previously said, in all of Europe professors and students in universities spoke Latin, lectures were given exclusively in Latin, and professors and students wrote in Latin.

Nevertheless, Professor Jespersen criticized the scholars for having introduced into English so many Latin words and for being so inconsiderate of the great majority of people, the nonscholars, most of whom couldn't even read English. Jespersen spoke of "unborn generations whom the scholars forced by their disregard for their own language (English) to carry on the burden of committing to memory words and expressions which were really foreign to their idiom (language)." (p. 133)

Jespersen goes further; he tells what is wrong with having such immense numbers of foreign words in English:

> The worst thing, however, that can be said against the words that are occupying us here is their difficulty and their undemocratic character which is a natural outcome of their difficulty. A great many of them will never be used or understood by anybody that has not had a classical education (that is, one which has included the study of Latin and Greek). There are usually no associations of ideas between them

and the ordinary stock of words, and no likenesses in root or in the formative elements to assist the memory. We have here none of those invisible threads that knit words together in the human mind. Their great number in the language is therefore apt to form or rather to accentuate class divisions, so that a man's culture is largely judged of by the extent to which he is able correctly to handle those hard words in speech and in writing—certainly not the highest imaginable standard of a man's worth. (pages 147, 148)

In this quotation, made more than 75 years ago, we see how the great Danish scholar recognized that our vocabulary has an undemocratic quality because so many words are beyond the reach of huge numbers of people in the English-speaking community. Who can argue with him? Who can claim that citizens living in democratic countries should be deprived of the privilege of recognizing a majority of words in their mother tongue? Jespersen tells us plainly why so many adults are functionally illiterate; too many words are too hard for too many people. We surely agree with him when he deplored the tendency to judge the worth of individuals by their inability to cope with difficult words taken from foreign languages. Bless his memory.

I am impelled to repeat this thought: The general education we acquire in school certainly should include more information about our language because it is so important and because our language is such an intimate part of us. We should be taught that where Romance and Germanic languages other than English are spoken people do not have to struggle against such heavy odds. We should be taught how much harder it is for our people to learn 25,000 or 40,000 or more words in English than it is for natives of France or Italy or Holland or Austria to learn the same number of words in their respective languages. All children should be taught that these conditions prevail and why they do.

To be sure, nearly all educated English-speaking people are aware of the fact that our language has a sizable number of borrowed words, but few realize that English has a preponderance of them and, above all, that they are much harder to learn. Usually we are not taught that the French, Italian, Dutch, and German languages, for example, employ far fewer words borrowed from foreign languages.

If we are given and accept the facts, we'll realize how much more time and effort must be spent in building satisfactory vocabularies. Teachers should spend more time teaching the most essential foreign stems, prefixes, and suffixes. Children might also be taught to look for etymologies; as it is, they quickly avoid them. And because we can't know how to pronounce so many of the "foreign" words, all teachers should work with pupils on the symbols used by dictionaries to show pronunciations. If people were more knowledgeable, they might also be inclined to be more tolerant of those who misuse or mispronounce a word.

The Second Great Big IF

It is also possible many people would use the dictionary more often in their daily lives.

This is vital information: *About three-fourths* (75 percent) *of our words were borrowed from other languages.* So if Dutch and German borrowed between 15 and 20 percent of their words, English has approximately four times as many borrowed words! Surely it must be obvious that Dutch and German learners have fewer problems and have to do much less work to acquire satisfactory vocabularies in their respective languages. This subject will be discussed in the following chapter.

A majority of the words in Romance languages stem from Latin, which lives on in her daughters, French, Italian, Portuguese, Romanian, Spanish, etc. As a consequence, a great majority of words in those languages cannot be regarded as borrowed words. Indeed, scholars often cannot tell whether a borrowed word came into English from French or Latin; a large number of words in the two languages are that similar. But it makes no difference to our poorer (or even to most) learners which language a word came from. After all, it is a borrowed foreign word, whether it came from French or Latin.

You may recall the first group of "difficult" words in this chapter. It contained sixteen words, such as *adroit, avid, euphonious,* and *limpid.* All of the sixteen words came into English from French. But this is important: Whereas few of our *twelve*-year-olds would be able to define half of the sixteen words, nearly all of the sixteen words are in the active vocabularies of most *ten*-year-old French-speaking children, meaning they not only can read them, but they can and do use them in their conversation. My neighbor, Marcelle Crook, whose native language is French, assures me this is definitely true. As a matter of fact, she selected the words so that she could be on safe ground in giving me the information.

So we ask ourselves, How many "difficult" words are there in English? Professor Axel Wijk, a Swedish expert on English, wrote as follows: "It has been estimated that out of the 20,000 *commonest* words in the language (English), about one-third are Germanic, while two-thirds are of Romance or Latin origin." (*Regularized English,* p. 37)

When we go beyond the words most frequently used, the number of borrowed words increases because of the type of words we took in from Latin; more of them are abstract and scholarly. In 1915, F. H. Vizetelly, editor of the *Standard Dictionary,* made a study of about 20,000 random (not the commonest) words and found only 19 percent of them came from Old English! (*Essentials of English,* pp. 159–173) The British lexicographer and etymologist W. W. Skeat, using his own dictionary, also made a count, and he found that about 22.6 percent of English words came from Old English. (In the back of Skeat's *An Etymological Dictionary of the English Language,* Fourth Edition, pp. 761–776)

Based on the latter two reports, Professor A. G. Kennedy concluded that "At least three-fourths of all words in the dictionary are borrowed words." (*Current English,* p. 366) Professor Mario Pei concurred, when he wrote that "Our vocabulary is at least seventy-five percent borrowed." (*The Story of the English Language,* p. 310)

If you think the percentages of native words are low, you might make a cursory count in your dictionary on ten or twenty pages. If you use an unabridged dictionary, you will find relatively more borrowed words than you will find in a college dictionary because the percentage of native words decreases in the larger dictionary. The Old English words are the more basic ones, the kind we use every day. I made a count of twenty pages in each of five college dictionaries and became completely convinced of the correctness of the figures of Skeats and Vizetelly. Without doubt, critics will scoff to think I wouldn't take the word of such outstanding authorities. I merely felt I owed the effort to this undertaking. If you make a count, you should do it on ten widely separated pages because if you restrict your checking to words beginning with the letters *sh-* or *wr-,* you'll find a higher percentage of words which came down from Old English. But if you make your count on pages beginning with *comm-* or *cond-,* you'll start to wonder if all our words were borrowed. If you spread your work, it is unlikely to be above 25 percent of words which came down from Old English.

In any event, authorities are in complete agreement that words taken from foreign languages are, in general, more difficult than native words to learn.

Here are statements by two respected linguists, Morton W. Bloomfield and Leonard Newmark, whose thoughts support the theses of this book. They wrote in their *Linguistic Introduction to the History of English* that English is difficult "Because of the large degree of arbitrariness of English spelling, the many specialized meanings of words, the very large vocabulary in English (and) the great number of 'hard' words." (p. 320) A few pages later they say our "Borrowing has created most of the English hard words." (p. 332)

When we study a foreign language, we take for granted that a major part of the work is the learning of foreign words. Has it ever occurred to you that when we study our native language beyond, say, the fifth grade, a good part of the work is also learning largely a foreign vocabulary?

We'll now see specific examples of what Jespersen meant when he said we have a hard time associating elements of the foreign words with known elements because all the elements are foreign and have to be learned. This true story illustrates his point. When one of my daughters was in a first-year Latin class in junior high school, her teacher aroused

The Second Great Big IF

great enthusiasm among the members of the class. Just before a one-week vacation, she announced the children wouldn't have to come back to school for two weeks if they would sign a petition, which she would take to the principal, assuming, of course, they would abide by the terms agreed upon in the petition. It made the rounds, and all children signed it—with one exception (alas, not my daughter). One boy was unwilling to sign anything with a proviso which he didn't understand. In exchange for the additional week of vacation, the children had agreed, upon their return after the lengthened vacation, to "decapitate" themselves. In that word there are no threads that knitted together in the children's minds the word with its meaning. If the teacher had used "behead" instead of "decapitate," I'm quite sure many of the children would have thought twice before signing the petition. It is clear that the children had jumped to the conclusion that they were promising to work hard, to exert themselves, when they returned to school.

Nearly all of us mislearn some of our hard words and have a bad time getting rid of the wrong meaning (just as we have a hard time ridding ourselves of incorrect pronunciations we pick up). For instance, some people think the opposite of "debilitating" is "enervating." I know this from experience. Several patients who have gone to therapeutic swimming, where I have been obliged to go since an accident, have told me when they have come out of the pool how much good the exercise, that is, the swimming, has done them and how wonderful they feel because, as a few have said, the experience had been "enervating." I'm sure they have meant "energizing" or "invigorating."

In truth, the type of reader—poor reader—we are concerned with doesn't even try to use a word like "enervate." We aren't often in a position to know how large or small the vocabularies of other adults are. High school and college teachers, especially English teachers, are in a better situation to evaluate the strength and weaknesses of the vocabularies of young adults. I was in that position for many years. Young people (and older ones as well) don't like to use dictionaries. It was made plain to TV watchers of one program how difficult many of our borrowed words are. The producers used borrowed words to get cheap and unfair laughs by showing up the inadequate vocabularies of their contestants. I became acquainted with the program under less than ideal conditions. Having been struck by a car, I was lying for many weeks in a hospital with my arm in traction hanging in front of my eyes. Naturally I couldn't read. I liked sports and my roommate liked game shows. I agreed to watch his games if he would watch my football. Well, I half watched the programs peering under the inert arm.

Very often in a day game show the producers, as I have said, played a dirty trick on the participants, who were probably between eighteen and twenty-five years of age. The young people were frequently fed words which the producers assumed, at least hoped, the participants would not know. I recall that a majority of the young people on various days (not the same people) did not know these words: *cliché, collaborate, commemorate, cuisine, elite, equestrian, facsimile, lethargic,* and *provocative.* One contestant thought *nostalgia* was *carsickness;* and in reply to the question, "How many *decades* old was your mother when you were born?" one young man replied seven, one said eight, and a third answered ten! Note these are all borrowed words; all can be considered to be in the "hard" classification for those young people. The odds were stacked against the participants; the producers used the English language to embarrass them.

The word "decade," which is easy *to us,* is a good example of what Jespersen meant by a "difficult" word. We can tie the known element of *dec(a)* with *Dec*ember (the tenth month of ancient Rome), the *deca*thlon (ten events), *dec*ennial (ten years) and *deca*gon (ten angles, sides), but there are millions of English-speaking adults who have never read or been told about the Greek form and haven't the vaguest idea that it has something to do with *ten.* Incidentally, the words haven't always been self-evident to us; we had to work to learn the words, many of us the hard way.

The very least we can do is to tell our learners why the acquisition of a good reading vocabulary in English is so difficult. I imagine millions of people who have never been told that three-fourths of our words came from foreign languages feel inferior because of their poor vocabularies and assume they must be stupid.

Great numbers of our foreign words, which we now call "English" words, are long, and they are really hard to learn because we do not know (a) what they mean, (b) how they are spelled, or (c) how they are pronounced. Our authorities had a point when they talked about "learned," "difficult," and "hard" words.

Based upon the conclusions of Professors Greenough, Kittredge, Jespersen, and others, I will, in the next two chapters, call the "easy" or "popular" words "conversation" words because we learn them naturally and effortlessly in conversation in the home or school, or with other children. I will call the professors' "hard," "difficult," or "learned" words "book" (or sometimes "learned") words because in practice we ordinarily encounter them in print, either in books or in periodicals. Naturally many "book" words find their way into erudite conversations, and books could not be written without using "conversation" words. There is no clear line of demarcation between the words in the two groups; a word can be "easy" to one child and "learned" to another. In a home where parents are highly educated and literate, children will no doubt learn in conversa-

The Second Great Big IF

tion a great many words which children of deprived homes won't ever hear. But if you will accept the general principle, you will better understand the problems children have in acquiring words which they ordinarily do not hear in conversation.

In concluding this chapter, I will offer a generous baker's dozen of examples to illustrate this theme. My notebooks contain so many examples of borrowed "book" words that I have had difficult decisions. Possibly you will think of many words which seem to you to be superior to mine; and if you do, you are helping to strengthen my claim. I offer these fifteen samples:

1–3. I am sure the important words *epiglottis* and *trachea* remain mysteries to millions of people, including many educated ones. Even the word *pneumonia*, although freely used, is not well understood because it is not self-explanatory. We'll return to these three words in the next chapter.

4. *Cordial* illustrates what may be considered a "conversational" word, but many speakers who use it and even more listeners who hear it do not connect it in any way with the Latin *cor* (gen. *cordis*), from which it came, meaning "heart." Thus, *cordial* and *hearty* greetings are synonymous and mean the same thing.

5, 6. Sufferers who have a form of arthritis often do not know whether they have *osteo-* or *rheumatoid* arthritis. Even when they find out, they know only that one form is worse than the other, but they are still left in the dark, just as thousands of foreign words leave so many of us in the dark.

7, 8. In the same vein, a good many people have a hard time distinguishing between an *acute* and a *chronic* illness. They are more likely to find out when they suffer one or the other type of illness.

9. I'm reasonably sure many people do not connect the word *portable* (French *porter*) with the word "to carry." Many assume a "portable" TV set is a small one, perhaps a table model or one with rabbit ears.

10. An excellent example is the word *hypodermic* (needle). In the minds of many this word simply represents an instrument used to give an injection. Professor Jespersen's point, and mine, is that great numbers of individuals do not, because they cannot, associate the foreign elements, in this instance Greek, with known elements for the reason that they don't know what either element means. If the Greek elements *hypo* meant "under" and *derm* meant "skin" to all speakers of English, then there would be the threads to knit together in our minds the word with its meaning. As it is, if we learn the word, we must memorize it, too often not knowing what the two parts mean, and that takes effort and a certain kind of intellectual ability. In the hospital at different times I asked two aides and a nurse what *hypo* and *dermic* mean. None of them knew,

but I especially liked the answer the nurse gave. She said they were Greek to her. How true!

11–13. The words *fatal*, *lethal*, and *mortal* are confused and hazy in the minds of many adults. We have all heard the "joke" told about the man who asked if the "fatal" accident was a really serious one. (*Critical* also gives some individuals trouble.) In order to supplement the easy word "deadly," which requires little or no effort to learn because it means what it says, we have to learn three more words, all of which by themselves are quite meaningless. Even *mortal* is confusing. If we don't know French or Latin, how can we know by looking at the word "mortal" that it is a synonym for "deadly"?

14. If you want a choice example of our uncertainty about the meaning of many of our words, ask a goodly number of lay persons and then the same number of lawyers to define the word *indictment*. The lawyers will know what the word means; many of the lay persons will give confused, even incorrect answers.

15. Please indulge me for offering as the last example in this chapter the word *mortuary*. In the last few decades here in America it has changed from a coined "learned" word to a "popular" one. But I am including it because it helped me to discover the wide disparities which exist in the vocabularies of college students.

In the thirties we usually used the word "undertaker," although the word *mortician* was beginning to be used more and more often. During the Depression my German class was reading a disquieting essay about machines replacing workers and causing unemployment. A good many members of the class were deeply concerned; where would the male students find employment after graduation? One clever young man offered the suggestion that, since everybody had to die, they might become morticians. His classmates thought it was a terrific joke. Obviously, however, one young man had not understood the word because the next day in class he triumphantly raised his hand and volunteered that the young men could become undertakers. A hush fell over the room, and there were some nervous titters and laughs. As you may have guessed, I was mortified.

The episode shook me up. I had assumed most students had much larger vocabularies than they actually had. Surely it is clear that we should attempt to get all of our young people to establish the dictionary habit early.

It seems to me that the habit is a good one when we consider that the English vocabulary is comprised of a great majority of words which do not tell us naturally what they mean.

CHAPTER 16

On a Silver Platter
(The Price We Pay—II)

The Anglo-Normans and the Renaissance scholars placed a heavy intellectual burden on every English-speaking individual. This truth has been more evident since everybody has been expected to learn to read. What they did was to make every single one of us work much harder to acquire a satisfactory vocabulary than would have been necessary if they had used native English elements and had formed new words from them instead of bringing in the floods of foreign words. In this chapter, and the next, I wish to demonstrate how much harder our task is and why we have so many functional illiterates.

If you have not studied Latin (or French), you probably do not know what *potare* means. Because our word "to drink" is not *potare*, there are millions who haven't the slightest idea what *potable* means. If we had not imported the foreign word into our language, we wouldn't use *potable*, but "drinkable" exclusively. Now we have two words, one hard, one easy. Similarly, *edible*, based on Latin *edere*, became an English word (I'd like to say a Latin-English word); and so all who master English must learn, in addition to the respectable word "eatable," the foreign one, *edible*. "Drinkable" and "eatable" come to us naturally; in order to learn *potable* and *edible*, we have to expend added time and effort and then memorize the "book" words. These two samples are representative of a majority of our words. In fact, we have left in our language only borrowed words with which to express many thoughts.

Scholars have known for a long time what I am saying, but they have written to a limited circle of readers. Many teachers have told their students the facts; but it is time for everybody to know how hard it is to acquire a rich vocabulary. For millions it is difficult to gain just an adequate vocabulary in English. We can more easily accept this truth if we do what good old Mencius told us to do, to make a comparison. Well, a great many German words are considerably easier to learn, and satisfactory vocabularies in German are easier, much easier, to acquire by natives where German is spoken than English vocabularies are where English is spoken.

For instance, German uses German words for "potable" *(trinkbar)* and "edible" *(essbar).* Here are possibly more convincing examples. We'll return to "epiglottis," "trachea," and "pneumonia." In the original Greek, and then in Latin, they were self-explanatory, as the corresponding words in German are because they were translated into meaningful, self-explanatory German words. We learn—or attempt to learn—Greek words.

Greek:	German equivalents translated into English:
epiglottis	throat lid (or cover), i.e., the cover which keeps food from going down into the lungs *(Kehldeckel)*
trachea	air tube (or pipe) *(Luftröhre)*
pneumonia	inflammation of the lung(s) *(Lungenentzündung)*

Three examples, a bit more earthy, might not have been appropriate in such a book as this one fifty years ago. They speak for themselves:

constipation	obstruction, stoppage (Ver*stop*fung)
diarrhea	through fall *(Durchfall);* original Greek "through flow"
laxative	remedy (for) leading away *(Abführmittel)*

We'll see many more examples showing how fortunate German-speaking people are because scholars and writers developed great numbers of new German words, using their native ingredients, that is, their own stems (roots), prefixes, and suffixes.

Several authorities have expressed the thought impersonally and objectively without indicating how lucky German children are when they learn their words. We find it stated, for instance, in Henry Bradley's *The Making of English,* where we read how German scholars "Supplied the need for new words by forming compounds and derivatives from the words belonging to the native German stock." (p. 74) Bradley was repeating what he had said earlier, namely, that German (and Dutch) found "expression for new ideas by development of their native resources, instead of drawing on the stems of the Latin vocabulary." (p. 66)

This fact must be stated clearly: German did borrow thousands of words from other languages, especially in technical and scientific fields. It borrowed them chiefly from Latin and Greek. In addition, in a majority of secondary schools leading to university eligibility, an elitist educational system has emphasized the study of either the classical or modern languages and has produced graduates who often (sometimes too often) employ foreign words which the average German doesn't understand.

But German equivalents for overwhelming numbers of borrowed words exist and are quite generally used, certainly in elementary schools. At all events, the extent of the borrowing was minor compared with that of English, which took vastly more foreign words. Professor Mario Pei told of the range of borrowing: "The English language acquired such an extensive body of French and Latin words . . . that present-day English is best described as a fundamentally Germanic tongue with an imposing Romance superstructure." (*The Story of Language*, p. 18) Such a statement could in no way be made of any other Germanic language.

In the words "imposing Romance superstructure" Pei illustrated, perhaps subconsciously, what he was explaining. Here are four words borrowed from French and Latin. They represent the differences in our words. Undoubtedly the most common one today is *super*, now that we have elevated hundreds—or is it thousands—of athletes to the rank of "super stars." We also go to the supermarket, or we even feel "super"! So it has become an easy, a "conversation" word. The other three words, "imposing," "structure," and "Romance" (in the sense used by Pei) are surely not used in daily conversation by a majority of our adults.

In order to illustrate the additional amount of time and effort we must expend when we learn many of our borrowed words, I have put together twenty-five sentences, using native words (in italics) in the sentences, and then, following the sentences, using borrowed synonyms. To make the samples more interesting to you, I have speculated on the degree to which the borrowed words have become easy, conversation words, not in *your* vocabulary, but in that of people who read little. For instance, the word "unspoken" is manifestly understood more readily than the borrowed word "tacit," which must be considered a "book," a "learned," word. I have used a scale from 1 to 10, 1 being easiest and 10 being hardest, i.e., recognized and used by fewest people.

1. It is an *empty* house.   a *vacant* (1)
2. The whole act was *laughable*.   *ridiculous* (1, 2)
3. They were *all naked*.   *completely* (2), *nude* (2, 3)
4. It was a *holy* spot.   *sacred* (2, 3)
5. They *climbed down* the stairs.   *descended* (3, 4)
6. The instructions were *unclear*.   *indefinite* (3, 4)
7. Bears *spend the winter* in caves.   *hibernate* (5)
8. He was *thrown out of* the house.   *ejected from* (8 in 1920, 5 today)
9. The work was done *by hand*.   *manually* (5)
10. That is *unbelievable*.   *incredible* (10 in 1920, 5 today)
11. The *outside* walls were painted green.   *exterior* (6)
12. She *put* her hand into the hot water.   *plunged* (5) *submerged* (7)

13. Their treatment of the prisoner was *unbearable.*   *intolerable* (7)
14. The first two days were cold; the *following* ones, warm.   *subsequent* (7)
15. He has a *liking* for classical music.   an *affinity* (8)
16. She showed *endless* patience.   *infinite* (8)
17. It's a *new* way to learn words.   *novel* (9)
18. It was a *true* field day for them.   *veritable* (9)
19. She has an *inborn* genius for music.   *innate* (9)
20. He is just a *beginner.*   *novice* (10)
21. It was a *harmless* prank.   *innocuous* (10)
22. There was an *unspoken* understanding.   a *tacit* (10)
23. They believed him to be *almighty.*   *omnipotent* (10)
24. The din was so *harsh* that my ears ached.   *cacophonous* (10)
25. English has far fewer *of our own* words than borrowed ones.   *indigenous* (10)

We all know that words in a language tend to take on special meanings, even special meanings to every individual. You will, therefore, not agree with me about all the synonyms I chose. My sole goal was to reveal how much harder many of the borrowed words are to learn. The operation would be much more convincing to you if you were to compose twenty-five sentences and were to try to match native words with foreign borrowings. It is a good deal easier to find synonyms where both words are borrowed!

The examples in the sentences are merely the tip of the iceberg. Here are two dozen more examples, but this time with English translations of words used in German for the foreign words of English.

Borrowed Words	Translations from German	Borrowed Words	Translations from German
ambidextrous	both-handed	armistice	standing still (stopping) of weapons
carniverous	meat eating (devouring)	century	hundred year(s)
counterfeit (money)	false (money)	deter	hold back
gregarious	sociable	hearse	dead car
index finger	pointing finger	ineffable	inexpressible
irretrievable	"unbringbackable"	nodule	little lump, small knot

On a Silver Platter

Borrowed Words	Translations from German	Borrowed Words	Translations from German
orchard	fruit garden	pedestrian	foot walker
pediatrician	children doctor	pedometer	step counter
peninsula	half island	porcupine	prickle pig
precocious	early ripe (mature)	prescience	knowing, seeing beforehand
pyromania	(sick) urge to set fires	suicide	self-murder
to suture	to sew	ubiquitous	all (everywhere) present

If you will go back and spend two or three minutes studying the list, you will more easily accept the thesis of Professors Greenough, Kittredge, Jespersen, Pei, Bradley and others: a whole lot of our words found more often in reading are truly much more difficult to master than their German counterparts are. Obviously some of the borrowed words are used in conversation, e.g., *century, counterfeit, orchard, pedestrian, peninsula,* and *suicide.* But note this fact: Not one of the twenty-four words is self-explanatory in English. On the other hand, few, if any, of the German words need to be explained to German-speaking children. So while our children are learning scores of "book" words, German-speaking children are learning a dozen "book" words and hundreds of "conversation" words, and the latter are easy to learn simply because they have instant meaning to them.

Incidentally, in the English translations from the German we find a demonstration of what I was just saying: It was necessary in the translation columns to use a dozen borrowed words! Native English words simply can't do the job; too many of our own words and ingredients to form new words were pushed aside centuries ago. Of course some of the borrowed words, as I have previously noted, are now completely naturalized and are conversation words, e.g., *count, doctor, fruit,* and *point.*

In listing the examples I was also attempting to show that if our forebears had used English resources, we'd have much larger vocabularies than we have now. The British scholar, Barbara Strang, has expressed this view. She wrote, "To a considerable extent . . . the speaker of modern English needs more education to (have) a fair range of English vocabulary than the German speaker to reach a similar level in his own language. The gap has certainly widened in the last six centuries." (*A History of English*, p. 251)

As you no doubt know, we didn't take all of our words ready-made from Latin and Greek. In the present century there have been vast numbers of words formed from Latin and Greek elements when new words were needed to express new ideas. This has been especially true in the world of science and technology, and to a considerable extent these words have found their way into other Germanic languages. Some of the compounds they have formed with the foreign elements have come into English. Thus, these compounds, which were formed in relatively recent times, are found in both English and German:

eugenics   genetics   hypodermic   periscope   telescope

It goes without saying that the average German doesn't know the basic meanings of the foreign elements any more than the average English-speaking person does. I do not say this contemptuously of either group, and for good reason. When a "pneumothorax" instrument helped to save my life a long time ago, I didn't know or think to find out the meanings of the two elements of the compound which, by the way, was then a word which only a short time before had been developed.

There is still a strong tendency in German to form new compounds from German elements. This is true, for instance, even of "hypodermic" and "periscope." The better-known word in German for "periscope" is *Sehrohr,* or "see tube" or "pipe." The latter word clearly has more significance to most learners, and certainly it is easier for them to learn. No doubt the originator who compounded the two elements in "periscope" was proud of himself (herself?), and the word would be a good one if it were self-explaining, but most adults don't know what "peri-" means, and not many more know the meaning of "scope."

In a number of earlier examples you have seen technical and scientific terms which are commonly used in English, but whose German counterparts are composed of German elements. Examples: "pediatrician," "to suture," "pedestrian," and "pedometer." Here are four more examples to show how much easier the German words based on German elements are than our words because they tell more about themselves to learners: In German the word for "vacuum cleaner" is "dust sucker" *(Staubsauger).* In due time we find out what a "child prodigy" is, but surely the German equivalent tells German children more quickly what a *"Wunderkind"* is, for both elements are used in conversations of children. We even coined difficult words when the words "to escalate" and "escalator" came into being. (The latter word was a trademark.) Our children learn what an escalator is by seeing one, by having one described to them, or by riding on one. But what is an escalator if not a "rolling staircase"? And that is what the word is in German, a *Rolltreppe.*

Perhaps the best example is the German word for "submarine." We practiced readers think children OUGHT to know the meanings of "sub" and "marine," but on reflection we realize many sixth-graders don't really know the meaning of either word. Note how easy the corresponding German word is: *Unterseeboot.* The three-word compound, very clearly, is "under sea boat."

Since a great majority of our "book" or "learned" words are used most often in books and periodicals, it follows that those adults who rarely read books or even periodicals have little chance of developing large vocabularies. Even those of us who read widely develop our vocabularies gradually, and most of us learn many words, both meanings and pronunciation, tentatively and uncertainly. It has been demonstrated that many readers simply skip over unknown words, often the same words, and then suddenly "discover" them. When I was an academic counsellor for a few years at a major university, I offered a no-credit course which I called "Effective Study Methods." In some sections I found that half of the members of the class would not know where the Iberian Peninsula is, even though the term had been used seven times in the chapter they had only recently read, and it had been used repeatedly in the Western Civilization lecture they had attended the day before.

It is easy to understand, therefore, why a good many readers are unable to learn correctly the words "extenuating" and "mitigating." A student once told me he had looked up both words in his dictionary and had found that the words have opposite meanings and are antonyms. That being true (which is not so), the one would mean "favorable" and the other "damaging" or "harmful." An English-German dictionary gives the same German word for both English words, *mildern,* "to make mild," "to ease," "to soften," "to temper." It is possible to have the wrong conception for years because the words themselves do not tell us what they mean, or we are too lazy to consult a dictionary, and we are too embarrassed to ask. And that is one of the penalties we pay for enjoying the mixed blessings of having so many foreign words in our language.

If we return to the thirty-one words found in the first two groups of "book" words in the previous chapter, we find good examples of the point I am trying to make. (I am referring to the sixteen words my neighbor furnished me and the fifteen words from Angell's book.) I looked up the thirty-one words in the *Schöffler-Weis* English-German dictionary, which has 134,000 entries, to see how many of the thirty-one words are listed there in the original French or Latin—or related forms. There were only two.

We can see what German scholars did by examining eight of the words, four from each group.

English	German	Meanings of German Words
expunge	ausstreichen	to cross out, erase
fatuity	Albernheit	stillness, foolishness
felicitous	gut gewählt	well chosen
garrulous	schwatzhaft	chatty, talkative
interminable	endlos, unendlich	endless, unending
limpid	klar, durchsichtig	clear, "seethroughable"
lucid	klar, hell, deutlich	clear, bright, distinct
modicum	Kleinigkeit, bisschen	trifle, little bit

If we examine the eight borrowed words closely, we may remember the quotation by Otto Jespersen; he said, "A great many of them (borrowed words) will never be . . . understood by anybody (who has not studied Greek and Latin)." In effect, we who do learn the words have been studying Latin and Greek! He said further, "There are usually no associations of ideas between them and the ordinary stock of words, and no likenesses in root or in the formative elements to assist the memory."

Now we'll look into Jespersen's "formative elements." When we think of compounds, we think first of two words joined together, as in these examples:

bloodthirsty	cloudburst	doghouse	downfall	foresee
homework	moonlight	newcomer	offset	outlook
overtake	sunshine	uphill	waterfall	windshield

These are all "conversation" words, and no wonder; all elements have been in the language since before the Norman invasion. But now we'll take a brief look at German compounds. Nearly everybody has heard of German's long compounds, words consisting of two and three words written together. Mark Twain, among others, poked fun at that phenomenon in German. And it is no great feat to find words twenty to twenty-five letters in length, as in

Lebensversicherungsgesellschaft (thirty letters)
life   insurance   company

But German children don't get unduly upset when they see long words, mainly, I'm sure, because in so many of those long words—as in short words as well—every letter spells its assigned sound. We adults can work out "lifeinsurancecompany," but our children would not find it so simple.

This is a little known fact:

English has scores of thousands of compounds.

They are, in the main, the type of compounds Jespersen was writing about, and only relatively few adults recognize the words as com-

On a Silver Platter

pounds. They go unrecognized because a majority of our adults do not know the individual parts. So if we were to ask a hundred persons who haven't studied Latin or Greek or a modern Romance language if the following words are compounds, their answers would likely be in the negative:

    apparatus   debate   despise   distress   evoke

Their answer would reveal either they don't know what a compound is or they don't recognize many of the integral parts of borrowed words (or both). A compound word is one that has two or more parts or elements. All five sample words have more than one part. Our readers are more likely to recognize the prefixes in the following groups of words:

English Words Learned the Hard Way	Equivalents Learned by German-Speaking Children the Easy Way
pre- (before)	
precede	to go before, ahead
precursor	a person or thing that goes before
preface	a word before, in front of
premeditate	to think about before(hand)
re- (back)	
rebound	to bounce back
reclaim	to gain, win back
recoil	to pull back
reimburse	to pay back
sub- (under)	
subscribe	to write under (sign)
submerge	to dive, plunge down, under
subsonic	under (the speed of) sound
subterranean	underground
ex- (out)	
exclaim	to cry out
exhibit	to place, put out
expose	to set, put out
extend	to stretch out

In an abridged English-German dictionary I found more than a hundred entries in which English words beginning with the prefix *ex-* are represented by the German prefix *aus* ("out") and eighty-two entries in a smaller English-Dutch dictionary in which *ex-* represents Dutch *uit* ("out"). *Ex-* is a meaningless syllable to most young readers of English, even to many older ones, while *aus* and *uit* are basic, common "conversation" words in German and Dutch respectively; and when they are used as prefixes, they have immediate meaning to young and old readers alike in their languages.

Perhaps the point will now be better understood if we focus our attention on another prefix, the letter *e-,* which is a less well known prefix. If we restrict our samples to carefully chosen words, we adults come quickly to the conclusion that it also means "out." In the translations you will see how easy the German words are to understand and learn.

eject	to throw, drive, let out
emerge	to rise up (out of water), surface, turn up
emit	to throw, let out (a shout), send out
erase	to wipe out
erupt	to break out

We move to a second group and find the meanings somewhat more difficult to figure out:

egress	exit, way out
elect	to choose, select (out)
elude	to avoid skillfully, get around
eradicate	to root out, destroy completely, get rid of, wipe out
evade	to get out of the way of, avoid

Finally, even the knowledge of the meaning of *e-* helps very little (in English) to understand these whole words:

ebullient	edict	editor	educate	effect
effeminate	effervesce	efficient	effigy	effluence
effort	effusive	elicit	eliminate	elision

Unfortunately, as you see, even if learners know the meanings of the prefix *e- (ef-),* they still won't know the meanings of words if they don't know the meanings of the stems (roots).

The foreign stems create far more problems because there are so many of them.

The Stem (Root) -pend-

The word "bridge" and its counterparts in other languages are conversation words. In Dutch it is *brug,* and in German it is *Brücke.* With no other knowledge of Dutch or German you may well be able to figure out what a *hangbrug* is in Dutch and a *Hängebrücke* in German. In French a bridge is a *pont.* The verb "to hang" in French is *pendre (suspendre),* and French children can easily imagine what a *pont suspendu* is, even if they have never seen one because they learn both words in conversation, and they expect the adjective to follow the noun. So Dutch, German, and French children don't have to learn what a "hanging bridge" is. Our children wouldn't either if we actually used the term "hanging bridge" instead of "suspension bridge."

Our children do not automatically associate the foreign stem *-pend- (suspend-)* with our root "hang." Nor do they automatically make the connection in other words containing the root, as in *append, appendage, appendix* (in a book or person), *depend, pend, pendant, pendent, pendentive, pending, pendulous, pendulum, propend,* etc. Using an English-German dictionary, I looked up all these words and didn't find the French root in any of them; I found only the root *häng;* and in an English-Dutch dictionary I could find only the root *hang.*

The Stem -viv-

The French and Latin stem *-viv-* has given us at least a dozen words. French-speaking children know right away that words using this stem have something to do with "life" or "live," because that is what *-viv-* means to them. If you will look up our words such as *revive, survive, survivor, vivacious, vivacity,* and *vivid* in an English-German dictionary, you will find the stem *-leb-* ("life," "live"), and in an English-Dutch dictionary, you will find the stem *-lef-* ("life," "live") in every word. Again, it is clear where French, German, or Dutch are spoken the words are learned in the home or early in school; and, again, our poorer learners may never make the connections and the words they learn are the result of work, effort, and memorization.

The Stem -ced- (and the Forms -ceed and -cess-)

We find the stem *-ced-* or the two other forms, *-ceed* and *-cess-,* in some eighty English words, and yet (a) millions of English-speaking people who could read acceptably well have gone to their graves not knowing the basic meaning of the stem of the words; (b) millions of readers (and nonreaders, naturally) are alive today who don't know it either; and (c) in the year 2020 millions more will be in the same unknowing state. We have so many compounds that don't tell us what they mean that we don't even expect them to do that. Blessed are children whose words reveal their meanings. Roman children knew what the verb forms meant; they couldn't have communicated very well if they hadn't known *cedere,* which meant "to go." See how easy these words would be for all to learn if everybody knew natively that *cedere* means "to go":

ante*ced*ent	ex*ceed*	ex*cess*	inter*cede*	pre*cede*
pre*ced*ent	pro*ceed*	pro*cess*ion	re*cede*	re*cess*ion

Surely it is clear that that vocabulary acquisition in English for all whose linguistic abilities are limited is exceedingly slow and painfully difficult.

The Prefix *dis-* and Several Stems

So far you have seen five prefixes and three stems. Now let's look at combinations of prefixes and stems. We'll start with words in which the prefix and the stems are easy. In the samples to follow the prefix "dis-" is easy because it simply reverses the meaning of the stem. The stems all came into English from Old French, and, therefore, they have been in English for many centuries and may be considered to be naturalized and conversation words:

disagree	disappear	disapprove	discharge
discontinue	discourage	dishonest	dissatisfy

Now we'll take a dozen words that are less well known; they are "book" words; and although the force of the prefix is the same on most stems, we recognize at once how difficult words are when we don't know all the "formative elements."

disabuse	disaffected	discomfit	discommode
discrete	disencumber	disingenuous	disparage
disparate	dissemble	dissimulate	dissuade

Once again we'll see how much easier it is for German-speaking learners to gain a large vocabulary with much less effort; and because of the comparison, which is far more important, how much time and effort we must expend. Here are the same words, together with the words Germans learn, translated, of course:

disabuse	to free from error
disaffected	unfriendly, not satisfied
discomfit	to frustrate, thwart somebody's plans
discommode	to trouble, bother, inconvenience
discrete (not discreet)	separate, distinct, not attached to others
disencumber	to release, set free
disingenuous	not frank, insincere, not straightforward
disparage	to put down, discredit
disparate	unlike, unequal
dissemble	to conceal under a false appearance
dissimulate	to hide one's feelings, intentions, by pretense
dissuade	to advise against, talk someone out of something

The Prefix *"co-,"* *"com-"* and Several Stems

It would be illogical to pass over what must be the most frequently used borrowed prefix in English, *co-* and its variants. Including only main entries, I counted in a college dictionary 939 compounds whose first element is a form of the prefix *co-*.

Most of our poorer learners, I am sure, do not know or even sense that the following words have something in common:

cohere	collaborate	collect	collide	compose
condole	consume	contain	convene	convoke

Some of us who are more fortunate realize that in the ten words the prefix *co-* (usually plus consonant) means "together." So the ten words are all compounds. The word "compound" itself is a compound, meaning "put, placed together." In the Roman Empire people knew these easy, conversation words: *cohere:* to stick together; *collaborate:* to work together; *collect:* to gather together; *collide:* to strike together; *compose:* to place together; *condole:* to grieve together; *consume:* to take together; *contain:* to hold together; *convene:* to come together; *convoke:* to call together.

As reinforcement for the ideas expressed in this chapter, I now offer another group of words which demonstrates anew how much more ability our children must have to learn words that German children with much less ability can learn in their language:

Our children learn these words with no help from the words themselves:	German-speaking children readily understand and learn these compounds:
adult	*Erwachsener:* a grown up one
adultery	*Ehebruch:* marriage break, breach
burglar	*Einbrecher:* ("inbreaker") one who breaks in
calm	*Windstille:* wind stillness
collapse	*zusammenbrechen:* to break together; Latin: to fall together
dentist	*Zahnarzt:* tooth doctor
dictionary	*Wörterbuch:* words book
dirge	*Grabgesang:* grave song
divorce	*Ehescheidung:* marriage separation, parting
emigrate	*auswandern:* to travel, go, wander out
fail (an examination)	*durchfallen:* to "fall through"
generosity	*Freigebigkeit:* "freegivingness"
hypocritical	*scheinheilig:* appearing holy, sacred
(sanctimonious	*scheinheilig:* appearing holy, sacred)
native	*Eingeborener:* "inborn one"; person born in
obituary	*Todesanzeige:* death notice
surname	*Familienname:* family name
surrender	*übergeben:* to give over, up
survivor	*Überlebender:* one living on, over
(survivor	*Hinterbliebener:* one left behind)
umbrella	*Regenschirm:* rain protection
(parasol	*Sonnenschirm:* sun protection)
(parachute	*Fallschirm:* falling protection)

Several times after I have spoken on the subject of how hard it is to acquire a respectable vocabulary in English, even though I have made many comparisons with German, people have wanted more examples. They have a hard time accepting the fact that words aren't simply words and one is not as easy to learn as another. In short, German bases thousands of compounds on German conversation words and elements. For instance, with the German words for "to come" and "to go" German uses prepositions, adverbs, and other prefixes to form more than 200 verbs and nouns. Whereas an English college dictionary will cover the uses of the two words in a total of three columns, a similar German dictionary *(Wahrig)* devotes dozens of columns to the German words. Or while we have the foreign prefix *co- (com-)* in hundreds of words, German uses the equivalent prefix, *ko-* in fewer than a third as many words. Instead, German uses native German prefixes that are prefixed to incredible numbers of words. Words beginning with *aus* ("out") cover forty-five

On a Silver Platter

columns, and the prefix *ver-* which alters the meaning of stems in a half dozen ways, is prefixed to words covering ninety-four columns.

The message of this chapter is this: When it comes to learning words in countries where Germanic languages other than English are spoken, children have (a) considerably less to learn, and (b) far more self-explaining words. In order to be able to read well, German-speaking children (and children in Iceland, Holland, Sweden, etc.) need to learn only a fraction of the foreign stems and affixes our children must learn. In those countries, relatively speaking, children have many thousands of their words handed to them, as it were, on a silver platter.

CHAPTER 17

Their Name Is Sisyphus
(The Price We Pay—III)

Most English-speaking adults have heard of the Norman Conquest, which took place in 1066. I think we might call that military victory the "First Invasion." There was another invasion, and we would do well to call it the "Second Invasion." It dealt with the vocabulary of the English language; its effects, which have been favorable to some and seriously detrimental to others, have been felt by every English-speaking person ever since. It was the beginning of the movement which resulted in our having so many more foreign than native words.

In practice, this is how it worked. Until the thirteenth century—the Second Invasion did not really start until then—the English people ate *swine* (or *hog*) meat, *sheep* meat, and *calf* meat. This was beneath the dignity of the Norman lords and ladies. In the kitchens the English-speaking staffs cooked or baked *swine, sheep,* and *calves;* but when the food was served to the fine people upstairs, it was elevated into the French words, *pork, mutton,* and *veal,* since the masters and mistresses wouldn't have been caught dead eating that other stuff. Eventually, the members of the staffs, imitating the lords and ladies, also ate *pork, mutton,* and *veal.* And so three unnecessary words to represent the same things were added to the words which must be learned in English.

Now we have developed negative feelings toward those good native words, and we more or less shudder at the thought of eating "swine meat." If you go to Germany, however, you'll find that the good burghers there don't look down their noses at the word *Schweinefleisch,* which is "swine meat," because that is the German word for "pork." (And, yes, the cognate for *Fleisch* is "flesh." "Meat" was once used to designate food in general (cf. Gen. 1:29), and then changed and took over the limited function of representing our concept of "flesh.") Anglo-Normans preferred their own words because they had more feeling for them, and, moreover, their own words had greater significance to them.

Several writers have commented on the subject of the proliferation of "English" words. Barbara Strang, a British scholar, wrote as follows:

Their Name Is Sisyphus 163

"It is often, quite wrongly, supposed that English borrowed items it lacked. . . . In fact, hordes of the French words which swept into the language . . . were synonymous with perfectly good words already established in English. . . . This redundant borrowing was on a very substantial scale." (*History of English,* p. 251) Dr. Strang named an author whom I have previously cited: "The change of emphasis from word-formation to borrowing as a source of new words established what Jespersen has called the 'undemocratic' quality of cultivated English vocabulary." Although the Second Invasion did bring in a number of words which were needed, it forced onto English a great number of words which were not needed at all. This fact is important: Instead of developing new words from native sources, the shapers of the language let the new words inundate the language. This basic pattern changed the course of English. Thus, the Anglo-Normans elbowed aside valuable and important resources which otherwise could have been used to develop new words. By introducing so many new words with entirely disparate elements—stems, prefixes, and suffixes—they reduced the number of English stems and affixes considerably. Because the many native elements were brushed aside, large numbers of them fell into disuse.

Sometimes one or two native words survived, but they were supplemented again and again. For instance, the words "to end" and "to stop" stayed alive. But English took over six new words from French: "to cease," "to close," "to complete," "to discontinue," "to finish," and "to quit." Now shouldn't eight words be enough to express a thought? One would think so, but the pattern had been established, and three new synonyms were brought in from Latin, "to conclude," "to intermit," and "to terminate." So now we have eleven words, and surely four or five should have sufficed. In the *Schöffler-Weis* English-German dictionary not one of the French or Latin borrowings is given as the equivalent German word. German's words to express the thought are native German words.

When I have discussed our borrowings, friends have been curious about good Old English words that were displaced. Here are examples of new words, all borrowed from the French: "aunt," "cousin," "nephew," "niece," and "uncle." Words which maintained themselves are these: "brother," "daughter," "father," "mother," "sister," and "son."

Often when I have spoken on the *subject,* "Our Over*power*ing *Vocabulary,*" somebody has *disagreed* with me. Therefore, in my *memory* I can *conjure* up your *protests.* You want me to *point* out the *plus aspects* of the *picture.* You are *quite correct.* But I have *previously discussed* the *marvelous merits* of our *vast store*house of words. English is blessed with *probably* the richest and *largest treasure* of words of all *languages.* This *exceptional advantage* gives writers and speakers the tools to *create fine* *precision* and *discrimination, superior flexibility,* and *remarkable variety* of *expression.* It is *easy* to *extol* the *tremendous benefits* of our *unparalleled reservoir* of words. Even when we already had a number of words to *express ideas,* we have often taken in two or more *synonyms* for the same word from *Latin* and French or from French alone, a great many of which, of *course,* came *originally* from *Latin.* Your *"profound gratitude"* may have more *significance* than "deep *appreciation"* to both you and the *recipient* (or *receiver*) of your *message,* just as *"significance"* may have more meaning than *"importance."* There is nothing wrong with "thankfulness," which is a *native* word, or even with the less *formal* "thanks."

This doesn't mean there is a *paucity* or *scarcity* of *synonyms* in the *Romance* or other *Germanic languages. Obviously it* is a *fact* that English *possesses* a *plethora* of them. When a *language* does not have a *synonym* for a learned word, it may *express* the same *idea* clearly and well *simply* by *using* a *definition.* Paucity, as given in *German,* means a small number or *amount,* a short*age,* or a lack; and *plethora* means an overfullness, a *superabundance.* Such writing does not always *result* in an *economy* of words, but it nearly always makes the understanding *easi*er for the *average* reader, as the *samples demonstrate.*

No doubt you were struck by the large number of words printed in italics in the two preceding paragraphs. English borrowed all of them, and I believed by your seeing them in italics you could more easily appreciate the extent of our borrowing. In the lists below you will see the same basic words, together with the language from which we assume they came. F, L, and G stand for French, Latin, and Greek, respectively.

subject (F)	power (F)	vocabulary (L)
disagree (F)	memory (F)	conjure (F)
protest (F)	point (F)	plus (L)
aspect (L)	picture (L)	quite (F)
correct (L)	previous (L)	discuss (L)
marvelous (F)	merit (F)	vast (L)
store(house) (F)	probably (F)	large (F)
treasure (F)	language (F)	exceptional (F)
advantage (F)	create (L)	fine (F)
precision (F)	discrimination (L)	superior (F)
flexibility (F)	remarkable (F)	variety (F)
expression (F)	easy (F)	extol (L)
tremendous (L)	benefit (F)	parallel (L)
reservoir (F)	express (L)	idea (G)
synonym (G)	course (F)	original (F)
profound (F)	gratitude (F)	significance (L)

appreciation (L)	recipient (L)	receive (F)
message (F)	importance (F)	native (F)
formal (F)	paucity (F or L)	scarcity (F)
Romance (F)	obvious (L)	fact (L)
possess (F)	plethora (G)	express (L)
simpl(y) (F)	use (F)	definition (F)
amount (F)	short*age* (F)	super (L)
abundance (F)	result (L)	economy (L)
easi(er) (F)	average (F)	sample (F)
Latin (L)	demonstrate (L)	create (L)

Our preponderance of words of foreign origin is so little noticed and rarely considered for two reasons. First, the use of our spoken language surpasses by a wide margin that of written language. There are few individuals who write more words than they speak during the day. And there are billions of adults in the world who never or rarely write more than a few lines. Even highly educated adults use the spoken word much more than the written one. And when we talk, we ordinarily use "conversation" words.

Studies have shown that the *speaking* vocabulary of most individuals is restricted to a few thousand words. To be sure, there are some who have 40,000 or 50,000 and more words at their command while they are speaking. But there are hundreds of thousands, probably a few million English-speaking adults whose speaking vocabularies are limited to fewer than a thousand words. However, the majority of us fall somewhere between the extremes, and we get along with a rather modest number of words.

Even the *writing* vocabularies of most of us are not large and do not go far beyond the range of our speaking vocabularies. We write mostly about commonplace things and events, and we rarely extend ourselves. The meagerness of vocabularies is nowhere better in evidence than in composition classes when college freshmen are required to write weekly themes. (This is no longer a common practice in many colleges!)

So in most of our speaking and even most of our writing we get by with a few thousand words, with "conversation" words; and, in the main, they are words which have been in the language hundreds of years, either as native or as thoroughly naturalized words.

Our *listening* vocabularies are undoubtedly considerably larger than our speaking and writing vocabularies. We are helped, as we all know, by the context in which the words are spoken. But when we are watching television or listening to the radio, our vocabularies are not greatly taxed because those who are in control of the two media make sure that the appeal is to the lowest common denominator in order to include the widest possible audiences.

Reading vocabularies are something else. They vary exceedingly widely, even within families and communities and among college graduates. In order to be able to read on a highly literate level, most individuals have reading vocabularies ranging from two to thirty times the size of their speaking vocabularies. It is clear that hosts of adults who have speaking vocabularies of two or three thousand words do not have the requisite training or ability to understand many of the words in a complete newspaper or in a weekly newsmagazine.

When we talk we simply call on the words we know to express our thoughts as best we can. On the other hand, when we read, there are many factors beyond our control. The type of material may range from (a) the comics or sports pages to (b) a novel by a popular author to (c) a novel by Henry James or editorials on serious subjects to (d) highly technical matter or the philosophy of Kant or Santayana or Heidegger. The style may be simple, direct, flowing, and lucid; or it may be involved, ponderous, cryptic, and opaque. Then there are writers who want to be read and understood and choose simple, effective words to express their thoughts; and there are other writers who choose to show off their erudition by using as many difficult words and expressions as they can find in an unabridged dictionary, books of synonyms, and a thesaurus.

Above all, our "book," our "learned" words represent a gigantic barrier to our children in school and to most of our adult population; and they will continue to be a barrier to English-speaking people in the future, in the year 2000 and in the year 3000.

It is a pity that so few are fully aware of our basic problem.

Nearly everybody who is conscious of weight or certain health problems reads labels on packages in supermarkets to learn the ingredients, which are listed in descending order. Now if we were to find the sources of English words listed on such a package, we would not, as you know, find English (Old English) at the top in first place—or even in second place!

What can we expect of our slower learners when we borrowed three-fourths of our words, scores of thousands of which are not naturalized?

As we have seen, and as you can easily verify, if you haven't already done so by consulting a dictionary like *Webster's New World Dictionary,* Latin would stand at the top of our hypothetical list. Next would come French, for, as you may recall, Professor Charlton Laird has written, "More than a quarter of our vocabulary comes to us from French." (*The Miracle of Language,* p. 131) (Old) English would stand third with 22.6 percent, as researched by Professor W. W. Skeat, the foremost English etymologist.

And which language would stand fourth? No, not any of the related

Germanic languages, and not even a combination of them. One of them probably would stand first if the other more dissimilar foreign languages had not intruded—if there hadn't been the First and Second Invasions. As it is, all evidence shows that Greek would stand fourth.

Why doesn't every educated person know this information and, from the standpoint of language, know what the penalties are for English to have such illogical, irrational, and disparate sources?

Yes, I must frankly admit that I had to work my way through to knowing the things I am writing about. Nearly thirty years ago I still didn't recognize how much easier most German words are for Germans to understand than our words are for us. About a dozen years ago I found confirmation for what I had by then come to believe. The linguists Morton Bloomfield and Leonard Newmark say in the book from which I have previously quoted, "Educated speakers of other important languages rarely consult a dictionary of their own language." (p. 320) They could easily have said, ". . . rarely *need* to consult . . ."

I know from a first-hand and painful experience that their observation is correct. About twenty-five years ago, in Germany, on the occasion of the birthday of a German friend, I thought I'd please him by filling what I considered to be a gap in his library. There was no all-German dictionary in it, and I gave him one as a present. His sickly smile when he thanked me revealed his true feelings; he was downright offended. To think that he, an educated man, needed a German dictionary!

The second reason we don't notice so many "learned" foreign words in our reading is that "conversation" words are mixed with them and play an important part. If you were to make a frequency word count in a newspaper, magazine, or novel, you'd find the easy, conversation words are the ones used most frequently—and by far. However, if all words were to be listed in alphabetical order, you would find that the conversation words would represent only a fraction of the total. What is so confusing is that the easy words occur so frequently among the running words that they give a deceptive impression.

In a year's time most of us skip over quite a few "book" words, knowing only vaguely the meanings of some and not knowing the meanings of others. Although relatively very few readers know all the words in an average weekly newsmagazine, the context fortunately comes to the aid of the rest of us in many, many instances. I'll show what I mean; I'll take the simple words out of context and reveal to you what the problem is for a fair percentage of all our adults. These are samples of "learned" borrowed words which I found in four issues of periodicals. The second and fourth columns contain corresponding native or naturalized words:

Borrowed	Native	Borrowed	Native
badinage	banter	intrepid	fearless
ancillary	helping	trenchant	keen
clement	mild	arrant	out-and-out
dextral	right-handed	arcane	hidden
acute	sharp	asperity	harshness
ephemeral	short-lived	adept	skilled
dormant	sleeping	pertinacious	stubborn
redolent	sweet-smelling	artifice	craftiness

Borrowed	Naturalized	Borrowed	Naturalized
abrogate	cancel	convoluted	coiled
bestial	savage	distrait	absent-(minded)
ebullient	high-spirited	dissidence	disagreement
ineluctable	certain	contumacious	disobedient
convivial	sociable	intransigent	refusing to agree

Actually, the above twenty-six sample words are only representative of many more words which I found in four issues. You'll find half that number on just two pages of *Time,* December 26, 1977, pages 70 and 71. Here they are: *helots, nascent, heinous, inept, innovative, indubitably, ebulliently, insurrectionary, subverts, luminous, flaccid, saturnine,* and *convoluted.*

In the preceding chapter I said it is usually easier to find synonyms where both words were borrowed. Now I'll demonstrate the fact. In order to give a visual illustration of the vast numbers of borrowings which good readers must master (and which many learners with limited capacities cannot master), I'll show the borrowed words in lower case (small letters), and I'll give words which came from Old English in capital letters. These synonyms and analogous words are taken from college dictionaries:

PEAK	acme	apex	apogee
climax	crest	culmination	pinnacle
summit	TIP	TOP	zenith
HIGHEST point			

flexible	BENDable	ductile	elastic
LIMBER	LITHE	malleable	pliable
pliant	resilient	supple	tractable
YIELDING			

change	alter	convert	metamorphose
modify	transform	transmogrify	transmute
vary			
beg	adjure	BESEECH	conjure
entreat	implore	importune	petition
plead	pray	request	solicit
supplicate			
calm	collected	composed	COOL
halcyon	impassive	noiseLESS	pacific
peaceFUL	placid	quiet	serene
STILL	tranquil	UNdisturbed	
UNtroubled	SELF-possessed		
disproportionate	excessive	exorbitant	extravagant
extreme	immoderate	incommensurable	
incommensurate	inordinate	UNdue	UNreasonable

Since the definitions of "conversation" and "book" words depend on each individual, it would be impossible to agree on the number of "book" words in the above groups. Better readers who were excellent students in Latin and one or two Romance languages in high school and/or college will not see the words in the same light as poor readers in the fifth or sixth—or even in the twelfth—grade. In any case, there must be no misunderstanding; *point, elastic, change, beg, peaceful,* and *quiet,* for example, are naturalized words and must be considered "easy" words. Nevertheless, in two groups I searched in vain for a single native synonym.

The ratio of eleven words to sixty-four borrowed ones in the six groups is about what we might expect if we are to believe an authority, Professor Albert C. Baugh, who wrote in his *History of the English Language* as follows: "An examination of the words in an Old English dictionary shows that about 85 percent of them are no longer in use." (p. 63)

For me the most dramatic examples of difficult borrowed words follow; they are found where we have good native nouns and have borrowed foreign "book" adjectives. Fortunately there are not many of them. Here are twenty samples:

NATIVE	BORROWED	NATIVE	BORROWED
book	literary	daughter, son	filial
ear	aural	eye	ocular
father	paternal	house	domestic

Native	Borrowed	Native	Borrowed
island	insular	land	agrarian
mind	mental	Middle (Ages)	medieval
money	monetary	moon	lunar
mother	maternal	mouth	oral
nose	nasal	ox	bovine
sea	marine	sound	sonic
star	stellar	sun	solar

Also these: sense of hearing: auditory; sense of smell: olfactory; sense of taste: gustatory; sense of touch: tactile.

The second major barrier to our learning the foreign words is that when we see them for the first time, we not only don't know what they mean (and can't work out the meanings), but we don't know how to pronounce them either. In earlier chapters I quoted a half dozen authorities who said we must first hear a word before we can know how to pronounce it. Here is further evidence.

If our spelling system were regular and reliable and if we had altered the spelling of foreign words to fit into the system, children would be able to use phonics and at least arrive at correct pronunciations of words. But the spelling changes were not made, and we know how utterly impossible it is for beginning learners to "sound out" most borrowings. When you see the word "bouquet," you now automatically think /bōō kā′/ or /bō kā′/, but that is only because you learned one pronunciation or the other. You may recall my friend asked me which pronunciation was correct. How can there be a correct pronunciation when none of the four vowels spells a nonexistent spelling rule? Even "-quet" does not always spell /kā/. Compare "quet" in ban*quet* /băng′kwĭt/ and cou*quet* /kō kĕt′/.

The word "opaque" didn't have the *-que* ending when it came into English from Latin. Surely the change to the Frenchified spelling didn't help our children. Compare "cla*que*" /klăk/ and "pla*que*" /plăk/. The two sample words were also borrowed by German, and necessary spelling changes were made. The stress on loan words in German is on the last syllable. Thus, *Bukett* has to be, and is, /bōō kĕt′/; and *opak* has to be, and is, /ō päk′/.

The location of the stress on our borrowed words is the source of a great deal of trouble. If we knew in advance, as the Finns do, where the stress falls and if we didn't have such an intolerable number of schwas, it might be possible for us to work out pronunciations. Even closely related words cannot be worked out. Here are ten in alphabetical order: *benediction, benefaction, benefactor, benefic, benefice, beneficent, beneficial, beneficiary, benefit, benevolent.* You did not come by the pronunciations naturally; you had to learn all ten of them, and the situation is not like that in other Western languages. Perhaps if I group the ten words according to the location of the stress, the problem will become more apparent:

> First or third syllable: benefaction
> First syllable: benefice, benefit, benefactor
> Second syllable: benefic, beneficent, benevolent
> Third syllable: benediction, beneficial, beneficiary

Did I say we have an intolerable number of schwas? In the ten words there are eighteen of them; and schwas, as you know, cannot be sounded out.

In another group of words we again see that even though the language environment is the same, we cannot know where the stress falls. We simply have to learn each individual word:

First Syllable	Second Syllable	Third Syllable
intellect	intelligent	intellectual
intercom	interrogate	interrupt
interest	interior	intermediary
interpol	interpret	interpose

To be sure, three or four of the twelve words may, in general, be considered "conversational," and many learners can, therefore, more easily learn to read them, but if you will experiment and purposely put the stress on the wrong syllables in other words, you may get an idea of what learners are up against. Incidentally, in the twelve words the first letter *e* in each word spells sounds as follows: /ĕ/ twice, /û/ once, /ĭ/ once, and /ə/ eight times.

We are all aware that the location of the stress is not always the same in British English as it is in American English. It would serve no purpose to discuss the differences here, but the mere fact that there are differences brings out clearly how unfortunate it is for our learners to have no rule to follow, only usage and local usage at that; they must learn where the stress is located in borrowed words of two or more syllables.

Here are fifteen words for which many people assume there is only one acceptable pronunciation—theirs. They are wrong. Please note that here, as before, I am offering the consensus of five recent, dependable, college-edition dictionaries, according to which the words do indeed have at least two accepted pronunciations:

abdomen	acclimate	adult	angina	cerebral
decadence	defense	detail	eczema	exquisite
hegemony	incognito	precedence	recluse	respiratory

Even the word "vagary" has two (or three!) accepted pronunciations!

In addition to the location of the stress, which plays a major role in our learning the pronunciation of our borrowings, there are many other problems. As you know, we have quite a few words in which the vowel or even the consonant quality has not yet stabilized. Here are fifteen samples, some of which you may question:

*A*llah /ă/, /ä/; anti- /ĭ/, /ē/, /ī/, /ə/; c*ou*pon /o͞o/, /yo͞o/; cynosure /ĭ/, /ī/; d*a*ta /ā/, /ă/, /ä/; d*i*gress /ĭ/, /ī/; d*i*lute /ĭ/, /ī/; *e*conomics /ē/, /ĕ/; e*x*it /gz/, /ks/; f*e*cund /ē/, /ĕ/; f*e*tish /ĕ/, /ē/; grim*a*ce /ə/, /ā/; l*e*ver /ĕ/, /ē/; ob*ei*sance /ā/, /ē/; qu*a*si- /ā/, /ä/; qua*s*i- /zē/, /zī/, /sē/, /sī/.

Even a native word such as "dour" gives us trouble: /o͞o/, /o͝o/, /ou/. Take your choice; your listeners will marvel to think you dared use the word.

There is a tendency to assume words which came from French may have strange spellings and Latin words are more likely to resemble ours. Well, let's take six words whose spellings came into English from Latin virtually unchanged: *animal, inertia, material, mysterious, recipe, superior.* On the surface, these words look innocuous. But if we analyze the sounds the twenty-three vowel letters spell, we become distressed. It can be argued that in four instances vowel letters spell their assigned sounds, although two are dubious. We become so well acquainted with the spellings of thousands of words, e.g., "recipe," that we think they simply have to be phonetic spellings as well. If you still believe that the final *"e"* indicates the preceding vowel is "long," then what about the sound spelled by *"i"*? Here are phonetic respellings:

animal /ăn' ə məl/   inertia /ĭn ûr' shə/
material /mə tĭr' ē əl/   mysterious /mĭs tĭr' ē əs/
recipe /rĕs' ə pē/   superior /sə (/o͞o/) pĭr ē ər/

Please note (a) the nine schwa sounds; (b) the spelling of /ĭ/ by *e* in three words; (c) the spelling of /ē/ by *i* in the same three words; and (d) the fact that not one of the eight vowel letters in two of the words (m*a*teri*a*l and s*u*peri*o*r) spells the properly designated sound.

Now we understand why the British scholar Logan Piersall Smith made the following statement (in 1910): "This fancy for preserving the alien forms of borrowed words . . . is tending to make our language more difficult and undemocratic than is at all necessary." (*The English Language,* p. 18)

Most of our learning of our vocabulary after the third or fourth grade is much like putting a jigsaw puzzle together; it is largely a haphazard procedure, a gradual matching process. This is slow, laborious,

Their Name Is Sisyphus

tedious, unpleasant, and thoroughly inefficient learning. We must continue to teach reading as a formal subject much longer than we do in many, probably most, of our schools.

A language, both oral and written, deals with symbols; a group of printed letters represents a group of sounds, which represents a thing or an idea. When printed symbols cannot be sounded out correctly with any degree of certainty, children are not learning anything if they try and fail; and even when a group of sounds results in a correct but meaningless word, there still has been no meaningful learning. Neither the erratic printed symbols nor the uncertain sound symbols have value to a good many learners, especially the poorer ones, and the whole operation becomes too abstract and confusing. The end result is that slower learners are left behind as illiterates or functional illiterates.

In the final chapters I will ask you to consider a complementary way of teaching reading.

We might compare the work required to learn to read Finnish and English with the rolling of a rock up an incline. The Finnish incline is merely a hillock, and ours is a massive, steep mountain. The rock the Finnish children roll is small and smooth and round and requires little effort to roll. Our rock is angular and jagged and so large that some of our children can push it no more than a few feet.

In Greek mythology Sisyphus was compelled to push a rock up the side of a mountain. However, each time he reached the summit, the rock would roll back down to the bottom. He had to return to the bottom and start over again. He was condemned to repeat the futile task forever.

When I have seen some of our illiterates, I have been reminded of Sisyphus and his dread fate. Our unfortunate failures are condemned to live incomplete, frustrated, and unfulfilled lives.

Their name is Sisyphus.

CHAPTER 18

Low Test Scores

Our concern in this book is with all young people, but particularly with those at the lower end of the reading scale. However, since the low test scores made by college-bound high school students you have been reading about in recent years tie in with the subject of the three preceding chapters, I believe a short digression is called for.

In the verbal portion of the tests, which represents at least half of each test, a high proportion of the words used are "book" or "learned" words; and, as we have just seen, we cannot deduce the meanings of such words without a great deal of work, help, and practice. And most of that practice comes from reading adult material. In the "good old days" reading did not have to compete with television. Therefore, there was immeasurably more time to read then, and children had far better chances of learning such words as *neophyte, tyro,* and *novice.* That kind of word is rarely heard on TV, and the following words aren't TV fare either: *vacuous, specious, scrofulous, furtive, impecunious, mesmerized, surfeit, cartographer, entourage, unregenerate, vicarious,* and *ineffable.* These twelve words and at least a dozen others not used in daily conversation by high school students are found on the first five pages of reading matter in the July 19, 1976 issue of *Time.* It is words like these that young people encounter on the tests.

In my opinion low test scores were and are inevitable results of our young people devoting an inordinate amount of time to watching television, with a corresponding loss of time spent reading.

Our young people are not alone. The British have been expressing dismay in recent years over the deficiencies in language skills among young Britons, even among Oxford students. I have read a number of disturbing reports on the situation in the Education Supplement of the *Times of London.* And an article, easily accessible in the United States, appeared in the *Wall Street Journal* on March 5, 1975. Vermont Royster, former editor of the *Journal* and later a weekly columnist, discussed the state of English proficiency or, rather, deficiency of many students in Britain. The title of the article is, "Why Can't the English?" (taken from

My Fair Lady). He told of a two-year study of the language levels of British students which was launched by Mrs. Margaret Thatcher, Prime Minister now, but then Education Minister. The project was directed by Sir Alan Bullock, vice-chancellor of Oxford. Royster says, "The report was unanimous on one point. Present reading and writing skills . . . are bad. 'Worse than bad' said several committee members."

Looking for reasons, some blamed television, some blamed the use of the look-say (word) method in teaching reading, some blamed the keeping of instruction at the same level for all children in a class (not dividing classes on the basis of ability), and some blamed teachers, who "no longer use enough drill." While not disagreeing, Mr. Royster said, "The root of the difficulty is that the English language, for all its variety and richness, is illogical. There is no way to learn its orthography (spelling)." Good for Mr. Royster! He wrote the very things I said in more than a dozen chapters of this book. He believes excellent teaching, disciplined drills, and constant use are necessary to raise the level of performance.

In addition to too much watching of television and too little reading, there are several other reasons for the decline in test scores. They are of lesser importance, but I think these six should be considered.

1. More young people are now taking the tests who have come from less affluent homes, and those youngsters have not had the advantages of the other high school students—fewer were read to in their early years, they have had more to learn, and in their homes there are usually fewer books and periodicals. There are just too many words on these tests which they have never learned.

2. When mothers watch much television—before World War II there was none to watch—they have less time to read to their children. I know all reading authorities consider it to be an extremely valuable experience for young children to be read to. Among other values, it instills in most youngsters the desire to learn to read, and they recognize early some of the rewards gained from reading. It is also true now that when mothers are free to read, children feel they must watch their favorite programs.

3. As numbers of mothers finding employment outside the home have increased, this development has also deprived large numbers of children of the opportunity of hearing their mothers read to them. In many day-care centers children are read to, but there is not normally the one-to-one relationship nor the personal attention to the reading interests of each child.

4. The decline in test scores was matched by a decline in the foreign language requirement for admission to hundreds of colleges, and a resulting decline in enrollment in foreign languages in our high schools. While studying French, Spanish, or Latin, large numbers of high school students were exposed to many words in those languages which English

has borrowed but which the young people had not yet learned in their own language. Moreover, more time is spent—or was spent—in teaching prefixes and stems which helped in teaching the words of the foreign language and in learning our borrowed "book" words. Yes, I am saying a corollary of their studying a Romance language was that the children enlarged their English vocabularies. They met hundreds or even thousands of our "learned" words while studying a foreign language (or two). Teachers, especially older teachers of Romance languages, will verify this bizarre truth.

The cold truth is that today relatively few students in American high schools and colleges study foreign languages. According to Sally Cates, "Ninety percent of U.S. colleges have no foreign-language requirement for admission; and fewer than 25 percent of high school students now learn a foreign language." ("The Language Gap" in "Sunday Punch" of the *San Francisco Chronicle,* December 14, 1980) That information has been published in a number of newspapers and periodicals; it is undoubtedly true.

5. However, even those children who do take a modern language today in high school no longer learn in the foreign language anywhere near the number of words earlier students did in that language and, therefore, not as many of our borrowed words. Twenty and more years ago the primary goal was quite generally the ability to *read* the foreign language, and learners were exposed to many thousands of words, a good proportion of which English borrowed. Now learners are exposed to a much smaller number because far more emphasis is placed on the ability to speak and understand the spoken word. These goals require more emphasis on pronunciation and a greater control over relatively few words and over grammar (now usually called "structure"). In the time spent in language laboratories, speaking and listening are the goals, and a considerable portion of class time is devoted to the same activities. Meanwhile, the young people have lost one of the great advantages of studying a Romance language, the acquisition of a larger English vocabulary.

6. In years gone by English teachers were severely overworked. Usually they had to teach just about as many hours and almost as many students as, for example, social studies teachers taught. Often the numbers have been the same. But English teachers could not and would not simply give multiple-choice tests. On the contrary, they assigned great quantities of writing. This did not simply mean the giving of a grade; each paper had to be corrected as well; at least the mistakes were indicated. This work meant incredibly long hours of hard work for English teachers. Along with teachers' changing attitude toward the teaching profession, most English teachers no doubt have made fewer writing assignments, and, in addition, students no longer have needed to spend as much time on reading assignments as before, because now in class they "discuss"

what they have read; and with twenty-five to thirty-five in a class, it is easier to get by without careful reading (and, often, without any reading at all). Administrators were more at fault than English teachers; they should never have overburdened English teachers in the first place; and most certainly when administrators saw the signs of changing attitudes, they should have decreased the number of teaching hours and the number of students in each class. With manageable loads, teachers would then, I am sure, have continued to read papers, because English teachers correctly realize their subject is the basic and most important one to most students.

In general, in the past few years there has been a tendency to think children will develop and learn if they are given the opportunity to talk and express themselves orally. The resulting "rap" sessions, with an unmerciful number of meaningless "you know's" thrown in, have, presumably, enriched the lives of the individuals.

But reading and writing are skills. We take practice for granted if we wish to become proficient at cooking, typing, shorthand, swimming, diving, painting, playing the piano, or doing any number of activities where skill is required. We have to work and apply ourselves. So it is with reading and writing—and increasing our vocabularies.

We must realize there will be no turnaround until we make it happen, in the home and in the schools. We cannot control what goes on in other homes, but in our own homes we can at least try to improve conditions. We must not assume teachers alone should be the ones to motivate young people. By setting an example and spending less time watching television and by reading more books, we will discover or rediscover the rewards and pleasures of reading. We may learn again that "A thing of beauty is a joy forever." And we may contemplate the beauty of "The quality of mercy is not strained." We will rediscover that the use of our own imagination is a richly rewarding experience. It goes without saying that we will ourselves set another example and use a dictionary very often and have it where it is easily accessible to all, but especially to learners. We will also take time to read to young children, thereby pointing the way to an acquisition of a satisfactory vocabulary in a language composed of many more foreign than indigenous words.

CHAPTER 19

English Has Many Fifth Wheels

Isn't it ironic that the very language which has the most confusing letter-sound relationships, making it the hardest language to learn to read, also has the most difficult reading vocabulary to master? No other major language comes close in either category!

It is time to return to Ichabod and Johnny, whom we more or less abandoned in our discussion of "book" words, because in the past they haven't been able to advance that far with our conventional teaching methods. In Chapter 3 there were so many ideas which had to be developed briefly in telling the five major reasons why Johnny can't read that it is necessary to return to the third basic reason, the use of vowel combinations to spell a single sound. (They are called digraphs.) They are exceedingly important because we find them in roughly one-fourth of our words and they impose an immense burden on our learners.

If you will look at the examples in Chapter 7, not the running text, you will find there are 183 words containing digraphs—34 different ones—and they spell sounds in 68 ways. The amazing fact is that the word "digraph" isn't even mentioned; digraphs weren't under discussion.

I remind you that vowel digraphs merely duplicate and unnecessarily spell the same sounds single letters do. In other words, they are fifth wheels.

Here is a manufactured sentence: Although they had little money to spend when they got there, the youthful couples would make the journey each year, driving four hours to get to the glamorous city.

In that sentence the combination *ou* occurs eight times; in the word "hours" *ou* is a phonetic spelling; it spells the diphthong /ou/, but in the other seven instances it is a digraph, and each time it spells a different sound! That is a crazy situation, and each word is spelled unphonetically. And in Table 11 you will see how digraphs merely duplicate the work of single vowel letters. Just one letter, *o,* spells every sound the digraph *ou* spells; and that, too, is indefensible. To add insult to injury, I'll also show how the letter *u* spells six of the same sounds!

Table 11
Sounds Spelled in Common by *ou*, *o*, and *u*

	/ō/	/o͞o/	/ŭ/	/o͝o/
ou:	although	youthful	couples	would
o:	go	who	comfort	woman
u:	———	truthful	cup	bush

	/û/	/ô/	/ər/	/ə/
ou:	journey	four	glamour	glamorous
o:	worry	or	tremor	thermos
u:	hurry	———	murmur	virus

As you can plainly see, the *ou* digraph spells words we cannot do without, words that children need to learn early in their reading instruction. They must learn such words as the preceding ones and the following ones as well: y*ou* and thr*ou*gh; th*ou*gh and sh*ou*lder; y*ou*r and t*ou*r; y*ou*ng and en*ou*gh; c*ou*rage and c*ou*rteous; c*ou*ld and sh*ou*ld; *ou*ght and b*ou*ght; and words with the suffix *-ous*, of which we have a tremend*ous* number, e.g., nerv*ous* and humor*ous*. In addition, the diphthong spells invaluable conversation words, as in c*ou*nt, h*ou*se, m*ou*th, *ou*r, *ou*t, s*ou*r, and s*ou*th.

The *ou* digraph is just one of the nineteen digraphs used extensively in English, and only one of our more than fifty digraphs. German has fewer than half of our total number of vowel digraphs, and only eight of them are widely used. What is more important is that each of the eight German digraphs spells only one sound. A few of ours spell only one sound, but since some spell between five and eight sounds, the average number of sounds spelled by our fifty-three digraphs is 3.4!

Do you see why writers of our children's elementary readers have to choose their words so prudently? The facts are these:

   A. WE HAVE FAR TOO MANY DIGRAPHS
   B. TOO MANY OF OUR DIGRAPHS SPELL
      MORE THAN ONE SOUND

You may well imagine how teachers have searched for ways to teach digraphs effectively. They have used many schemes. The one digraph which appears most frequently is *ea*, spelling /ē/. It is found in many words of high frequency, as in *each, east, easy, eat, heat, meat, reach, sea, speak,* and *weak*. Another digraph, *ee,* is also found in many words, as in *beet, feet, meet, see, three,* and *week*. The first letter in both of these digraphs spells the sound /ē/, which is the same sound spelled by the digraph. Educators noted also that there are many words ending in -*ay*, as in d*ay*, m*ay*, pl*ay*, and s*ay*, and again the first letter spells its name, which is the sound /ā/. Likewise the digraph *oa* spells the sound of the first letter, /ō/, as in b*oa*t, c*oa*t, c*oa*st, r*oa*st, l*oa*d, and r*oa*d. It was only natural then that someone composed a catchy couplet which would apparently be the best of all possible ways to teach digraphs. It runs as follows:

> When two vowels go walking,
> The first one does the talking.

Alas! The British educator Vera Southgate, whom I quoted in the seventh chapter, is correct. We can't make valid generalizations, i.e., workable rules. You have just seen how confused and misled children would be if they tried to apply the couplet to the *ou* combination. They would be correct in relatively few words: th*ou*gh, d*ou*gh, d*ou*ghnut, s*ou*l, b*ou*lder, p*ou*ltry, thor*ou*gh, and a half dozen other words, where it spells /ō/. But in incomparably more words, including those where *ou* spells the diphthong /ou/, of course, it spells other sounds.

Professor Theodore Clymer at the University of Minnesota tested the "rule" that the sound of the first letter would be the sound spelled by the digraph in general. He examined 2,600 words in four primary reading series and found the statement to be true in 309 words. But it was NOT true in 377. Thus, in 55 percent of the words in which there are digraphs the "rule" does not hold up. ("The Utility of Phonic Generalizations in the Primary Grades," *The Reading Teacher,* January, 1963, pages 252-258) Dr. Clymer concluded, "An inspection of the data leaves me somewhat confused as to the value of generalizations. . . . It seems quite clear that many generalizations which are commonly taught are of limited value."

We would do well to check on the *ea* digraph because it does spell /ē/ in a good many words. First, we'll have another silly sentence in which the digraph *ea* also spells eight(!) sounds: I h*ea*rd J*ea*nette's throat is completely h*ea*led and she is h*ea*lthy; it will be gr*ea*t to h*ea*r her singing Isolde again with all her h*ea*rt and to see her w*ea*ring the golden crown.

Table 12 will give another good picture of the overlapping and the absurdity of our spelling. For good measure I'll include, in addition to *ea*, two letters, *e* and *a*, and even another digraph *ei*. You will note how the letter *e* spells all the sounds *ea* does, the letter *a* spells seven of them, and the digraph *ei*, which is supposed to occur very rarely and then only after *c*, spells six of the eight sounds.

Table 12
Sounds Spelled in Common by *ea, e, a,* and *ei*

	/û/	/ə/	/ē/	/ĕ/
ea:	heard	Jeannette	healed	healthy
e:	herd	navel	me	tell
a:	———	naval	picayune	any
ei:	———	mullein	protein	heifer

	/ā/	/ĭ/	/ä/	/â/
ea:	great	hear	heart	wearing
e:	carburetor	series	entree	there
a:	flavor	village	art	hare
ei:	vein	counterfeit	———	their

Now you see what a difficult and challenging task reading teachers have.

We adults have a hard time visualizing the problems confronting our learners because, as I have emphasized, we thoroughly memorize so many words. I have observed children agonizing, and I again want to help you feel for a brief moment how children must feel. I have selected eight words whose vowel sounds are spelled by the digraph *ei.* I hope you have not heard all of them. If we are that fortunate, you may gain for a brief moment the feeling of frustration some children feel when they come to new words. Here are the eight words, all containing the *ei* digraph, and in them it spells eight sounds:

serein	enceinte	Eire	nonpareil
leister	surfeit	peripeteia	villein

I hope I am not insulting you by offering the sounds spelled by the digraph; they are in the same order as the words, reading along, /ă/, /ā/, /â/, /ĕ/, /ē/, /ĭ/, /ī/ (or /ē/), and /ə/.

Here are five more digraphs that spell a number of sounds and, in accordance with my previous statement, they are also spelled by single vowel letters:

Sounds	Digraphs	Single Letters	Sounds	Digraphs	Single Letters
	ai			*ie*	
/ā/	pain	stable	/ī/	pie	mind, fly
/ĕ/	said	red	/ĭ/	frontier	hit, symptom
/â/	stair	stare	/ē/	relief	she

Sounds	Digraphs	Single Letters	Sounds	Digraphs	Single Letters
	ai			*ie*	
/ī/	k*ai*ser	r*i*ser	/ĕ/	fr*ie*ndly	r*e*nd
/ə/	capt*ai*n	s*u*ltan	/ər/	sold*ie*r	wag*e*r
/ă/	d*ai*quiri	d*a*gger			
/ĭ/	porcel*ai*n	or*i*gin		*ue*	
			/ōō/	s*ue*	d*o*, d*u*ty
	au		/yōō/	arg*ue*	*u*nited
/ô/	*au*to	*O*tto	/ĕ/	coq*ue*tte	y*e*t
/ă/	l*au*gh	st*a*ff	/ə/	g*ue*rilla	g*e*ranium
/ō/	ch*au*ffeur	s*o*			
/ā/	g*au*ge	h*a*lo		*ui*	
/ə/	*au*thori-tative	*a*stonish	/ī/	g*ui*de	tr*i*angle, dr*y*
			/ĭ/	b*ui*ld	b*i*lled
/ou/	s*au*erkr*au*t	(diphthong)	/ōō/	fr*ui*t	wh*o*, d*u*ly
			/ē/	mosq*ui*to	h*e*

Observe how frustrating it can be to try to "sound out" words with digraphs. The first vowel "does the talking" in just four of the above words, p*ai*n, g*au*ge, p*ie*, and arg*ue*, but in the other twenty-two words the jingle would mislead learners who trusted it.

You may recall the quotation in Chapter 6 by Professors Foerster, Steadman, and McMillan: "English words are spelled inconsistently and unphonetically . . . Every word must be remembered visually." If you have ever had trouble spelling words with *ei* or *ie*, there is the best of reasons. Here is proof that the professors knew what they were talking about: Both digraphs in the first two columns spell /ē/, and in the third and fourth columns both spell /ī/:

/ē/		/ī/	
ei	*ie*	*ei*	*ie*
caff*ei*ne	gr*ie*f	*Ei*nstein	fl*ie*s
cod*ei*ne	pr*ie*st	fahrenh*ei*t	fr*ie*d
conc*ei*t	rel*ie*f	h*ei*st	t*ie*
K*ei*th	sh*ie*ld	Rh*ei*n	suppl*ie*s
Sh*ei*la	th*ie*f	s*ei*smograph	tr*ie*s

One might jump to the conclusion that *ie* in d*ie*s, dr*ie*s, l*ie*d, and t*ie*d always represents /ī/, but that is not true when those letters become parts of other words; then they stand for /ē/:

English Has Many Fifth Wheels 183

/ī/ /ē/
The obituary read, "Bud d*ies* with his budd*ies*."
If the sun dr*ies* your skin, buy lotion in the sundr*ies* department.

Dal l*ied*.   Dal dall*ied*.
He t*ied* one on.   He empt*ied* all the bottles.

We have seen how confusing the *ea* digraph can be, and here are more samples of reasons for children's confusion:

/ē/	I cl*ea*n	I d*ea*l	I m*ea*n	I r*ea*d
/ĕ/	I cl*ea*nse	I d*ea*lt	I m*ea*nt	He r*ea*d
/ē/	Will you l*ea*d the way?		It won't h*ea*l.	
/ĕ/	Will you weigh the l*ea*d?		How is your h*ea*lth?	

Nearly everybody gets the erroneous impression that the digraph *ea* spells /ē/ in almost all words in which it occurs. I made a list of 494 words in which the combination spells a single sound; it does spell /ē/ in 252 of them. However, it spells /ĕ/ in 140. But for learners the hardest spellings to learn are not for /ē/ or even /ĕ/; they are for those other five spellings which they don't see so often, as in st*ea*k, /ā/ (cf. t*ea*k), n*ea*rly /ī/, b*ea*r /â/, h*ea*rd /û/, h*ea*rt /ä/, etc.

Even in the statement of the rule, "When two vowels go walking, the first one does the talking" we find a violation. In "d*oe*s" the sound is not /ō/.

In Chapter 3 I promised to tell more about the frequency of digraphs in words we read. I told about the count of page 1 of the *New York Times*. I have since made a count of another page 1 of the same newspaper, April 20, 1979. That count and the others made on pages I wanted to read anyway were taken as follows: *Time,* September 12, 1977, p. 35; *Sports Illustrated,* September 12, 1977, p. 63; and because pictures partially fill the pages, I counted two pages each in *Newsweek,* September 19, 1977, pages 29 and 30, and *U.S. News and World Report,* pages 58 and 67. Here is what I found:

Table 13

Frequency of Digraphs

	N.Y. Times		Time	News-week	U.S. News	Sports Ill.
Digraphs	1.	2.				
Number of occurrences	442	452	235	265	283	215
Different Digraphs	29	38	25	32	28	27
Ways Sounds Are Spelled by Digraphs	57	66	44	44	54	42

On the eight pages I found a total of 1,892 combinations of vowel letters spelling single vowel sounds, and a total of 44 different digraphs spelling sounds in 89 ways.

Almost a fourth of the running words in our reading matter have digraphs if we do not count the ubiquitous, hard-working little words *a, an, the; and, as, but, for, if, or; at, by, from, in, of, on, to, with; I, me, it, that; is; no,* and *not.* (They are articles, certain conjunctions, certain prepositions, four pronouns, and three other words.) In *Time*, 25.7 percent of the words on the page had digraphs. The conclusion is indisputable: In order to be able to read, it is necessary for English-speaking learners to master a considerable number of spellings of digraphs.

We might be inclined to assume digraphs are to be found more often in "hard" or "learned" words, but that isn't true. I counted two columns each of "Dear Abby" and "Ann Landers" with these results: 27, 22, 26, and 29 percent of the words contained digraphs.

Actually, we have much more convincing evidence that children must be introduced to digraphs early—unfortunately very early. I counted the digraphs in the 2,000 most frequently used words as listed in Thorndike's *A Teacher's Word Book,* which lists the 10,000 words occurring most frequently in more than 4,500,000 running words. It is an old list, but a new one surely would include almost every one of the first 2,000 words. My careful count shows that 518 words contain digraphs. That is 25.9 percent. After completing a second count to make sure of my figures, I realized that children have to learn diphthong spellings, especially *ou* and *ow* (as in br*ow*n); and in fairness to learners, I counted and found 58 words with diphthongs among the 2,000 words. That makes a total of 576 words, or 28.8 percent, that have digraph or diphthong spellings.

We see just how much digraph spellings are needed when we again examine Professor Clymer's work with four elementary reading series. In them he found, as I said, 2,600 words, and among them there were 686 words with digraphs. That is 26 percent, again our one in four ratio. And that is the situation in elementary readers.

You are probably prepared for exceptions because our language is filled with them. Children must learn many exceptions:

(a) When the letter *i* is preceded by *c, s,* or *t* and followed by another vowel the *i* is not part of a digraph. I have previously pointed out that it helps to spell /sh/, /zh/, or /ch/, as these examples illustrate:

	ci	*si*	*ssi*	*ti*
/sh/	artifi*ci*al	convul*si*on	commi*ssi*on	por*ti*on
	defi*ci*ent	exten*si*on	rece*ssi*on	poten*ti*al

ci		si	ssi	ti
/zh/		conclu*si*on	/ch/	inges*ti*on
		divi*si*on		ques*ti*onable

This exception is found in thousands of words, a majority of which end in *-tion*.

(b) In many other words, side-by-side vowels do not serve together as digraphs to spell single sounds. If we take the word "diarrhea," we see four vowel letters, each of which independently spells a sound, even though the letters *i* and *a* and *e* and *a* are adjacent to each other. Good readers don't stop to think that there aren't two digraph spellings in the word. It wouldn't occur to us, and this is additional evidence—as if more were needed—that we learn and memorize huge numbers of individual words. We know that the final two letters do not spell /ē/ alone.

This tale of three cities will show what learners must find out and memorize. "Sea" spells /sē/, and if we add *-t*, we have *seat,* /sēt/. Now if we add *-tle, Seattle,* we do not wind up with /sē′ təl/, but with /sē ă′ təl/. In other words, *ea i*s not a digraph. If we take the plane to Minn*ea*polis, again *ea* spells /-ē ă-/, and does not spell /ē/ alone. We proceed to Montr*ea*l, and now the *a* does not spell /ă/, but /ä/. So if we tell our children *ea* spells /ē/, we must quickly add, "But don't count on it." We do not say /sē′ təl/, /mĭn′ ē pō lĭs/, /mŏnt′ rēl/.

(c) The letter *u* often spells /w/ and is then not a part of a digraph. We learn this to be true when it follows *q,* as in q*u*alify /wŏ-/, q*u*eer /-wĭ-/, and eq*u*al /-wə-/. But *u* spells /w/ in a number of other words also:

c*u*isine	/-wĭ-/	jag*u*ar	/-wä-/	lang*u*age	/-wĭ-/
peng*u*in	/-wĭ-/	pers*u*ade	/-wā-/	sang*u*ine	/-wĭ-/
s*u*ave	/-wä-/	s*u*ede	/-wā-/	s*u*ite	/-wē-/

(d) The letter *i* spells /y/ in a hundred or more words, and often does not combine with the following letter to serve as a digraph. Examples:

| auxil*i*ary | brill*i*ant | conven*i*ent | ingen*i*ous | Ital*i*an |
| mill*i*on | on*i*on | rebell*i*on | sen*i*or | un*i*on |

(e) The letter *i* spells /ē/ in thousands of words. It is obv*i*ous that each one of the following words must be learned separately. Does the *i* spell /ī/ or /ē/?

| /ī/ | pl*i*ant | b*i*as | den*i*al | d*i*al |
| /ē/ | suppl*i*ant | al*i*as | perenn*i*al | custod*i*al |

| /ĭ/ | D*i*ana | def*i*ant | tr*i*al | v*i*al |
| /ē/ | p*i*ano | rad*i*ant | industr*i*al | triv*i*al |

(f) When following c or t, the i may help to spell /sh/ or it may independently spell a sound and is not part of a digraph:

| appre*ci*ate | /-sh ē-/ | benefi*ci*ary | /-sh ē-/ |
| appre*ci*able | /-sh-/ | benefi*ci*al | /-sh-/ |

| offi*ci*ate | /-sh ē-/ | ini*ti*ate | /-sh ē-/ |
| offi*ci*al | /-sh-/ | ini*ti*al | /-sh-/ |

Additional evidence that we spell words, not sounds, may be found in these words, in which /ē/ is spelled by both e and i in the same language environment, and both side-by-side vowel letters do the talking, i.e., represent sounds, the second spelling a schwa in each instance:

| cer*e*al | erron*e*ous | funer*e*al | spontan*e*ous |
| ser*i*al | harmon*i*ous | arter*i*al | stud*i*ous |

| lin*e*al | met*e*or | simultan*e*ous | vitr*e*ous |
| colon*i*al | meat*i*er | ceremon*i*ous | fur*i*ous |

It was suggested to me that I make a count of a longer article, one to which critics might have access to verify my count. Because many libraries keep in their stacks old copies of *Sports Illustrated* and because my grandson, Tim, had a clerkship in neurosurgery under the author, Sir Roger Bannister, M.D., the first man to break the four-minute mile barrier, I chose an article by him, "Beyond the Barrier." You will find it in the August 13, 1979 issue. There are not quite 3½ pages of text (not counting pictures and ads). I copied each word with side-by-side vowel letters and then made the count and found these results:

Number of digraphs	550
Diphthongs /ou/ *ou* and *ow*, /oi/ *oi* and *oy*	69
Number of side-by-side vowel letters where both letters spell sounds	87
Total number of side-by-side letters	706
Number of different digraphs	40
Number of ways forty digraphs spell sounds	76

What this boils down to is this: *Every word which has side-by-side vowel letters has to be learned individually.* Here are a few possible misreadings of words taken from the article:

1. st*ea*dfast is not /stēd′ făst/
2. r*ea*lity is not /rēl′ tē/ or /rē′ əl tē/
3. *ea*rly is not /ēr′ lē/ or /ĭr′ le/
4. forf*ei*ting is not /fôr′ fē tĭng/ or /fôr′ fī tĭng/
5. Sov*ie*t is not /sō′ vĭt/ or /sō′ vēt/
6. mill*io*n is not /mĭl′ lī ən/ (cf. "lion")
7. bel*ow* is not /bĭ lou′/ (cf. all*ow*)
8. nicet*ie*s is not /nīs tīs/ ("nice ties")

Before we leave the subject of digraphs, it is again necessary to reply to a protest which I have heard repeatedly, often expressed vehemently. A number of people who have heard my message stoutly defend digraphs, saying they are needed because we are conditioned to reading words as they are now written. That is absolutely correct. But we ought to accept digraph spellings of vowel sounds for what they are: necessary evils—traps which play a not insignificant role in conquering many slower learners and increasing our number of illiterates each year. We must find better ways to teach our unphonetically spelled words.

CHAPTER 20

Marvelous Memories

This is the last chapter to reveal eccentricities of the ways we spell our words. I'll keep two promises made in earlier chapters, and I'll add three thoughts which I have been saving until now.

In Chapter 3 I named as the fifth reason why Johnny can't read the incongruous locations of the stress in huge numbers of words and the shifting of the stress in related words. Of course the many schwas which precede and/or follow stressed syllables were listed as Public Reading Enemy Number One. There I showed how German children have no problems in learning to read, understand, pronounce, or spell their words for *monotone* and *monotonous*. The first three vowel letters in our words spell different sounds in each word, and that is most inconsistent and illogical.

By pronouncing *monogamy* (/mə nŏg′ ə mē/ we conceal the meanings of both the prefix and the stem. Logically, *mono-* should be /mō′nō-/ (or at least /mŏ′ nō-/), and then we'd hear that *mono-* means "one." Because the stem vowel in *-gamy* spells a schwa, we don't have a chance to hear what the stem is. No wonder few people readily recognize the fact that *-gamy* means marriage. That is truly irrational.

We learn *prevail* /prĭ vāl′/ and *prevalent* /prĕv′ ə lənt/, but, as with thousands of words, many learners do not learn them by association—the easy way. They can't. When we speak the two words, we don't hear the prefix in one, and in the other the stem remains an unknown quantity. Because there was so much ground to cover in Chapter 3, I did not place enough emphasis on learning meanings. There I gave six samples of pairs of words in which the stress shifts, and here are a half dozen more. Please note how the vowel sounds in the prefixes and stems change, even though the words are related, and this places a great burden on learners.

*a*dapt	/ə/, /ă/	c*o*nsole	/ə/, /ō/
*a*daptation	/ă/, /ə/	c*o*nsolation	/ŏ/, /ə/

Marvelous Memories

declare	/ĭ/, /â/		defer	/ĭ/, /û/
declaration	/ĕ/, /ə/		deference	/ĕ/, /ə/
excell	/ĭ/, /ĕ/		propose	/ə/, /ō/
excellent	/ĕ/, /ə/		proposition	/ŏ/, /ə/

In the first pair, *adapt* and *adaptation,* we cannot know what the prefix is; in the first word it sounds as though it might be *a,* and in the second it seems to be *ad-*. In all words the weakened sound causes problems in understanding and in spelling.

The addition of the prefix *in- (im-)* to a few words reveals the inconsistency of our use of the stress and of our spelling of sounds. Here are the three best examples that I have been able to come up with:

famous	/fā′ məs/		infamous	/ĭn′ fə məs/
pious	/pī′ əs/		impious	/ĭm′ pē əs/
potent	/pō′ tənt/		impotent	/ĭm′ pə tənt/

Why in the world does the *i* in imp*i*ous spell /ē/? Note how the *a* in inf*a*mous and the *o* in imp*o*tent spell schwas.

In the earlier chapter I offered five pairs of words in which three vowel letters represent different sounds in related (derivative) words, and I promised twenty more. So here are twenty-one. We begin with *maniac* and then wonder what *maniacal* will sound like. Compare:

maniac	/mā′ nē ăk′/
maniacal	/mə nī′ə kəl/

You will probably notice that all of the words where the sounds vary with the shifting stress are borrowed words:

anesthetic	/ă/, /ə/, /ĕ/		aroma	/ə/, /ō/, /ə/
anesthetist	/ə/, /ĕ/ /ə/		aromatic	/ă/, /ə/, /ă/
astronomy	/ə/, /ŏ/, /ə/		authorize	/ô/, /ə/, /ī/
astronomical	/ă/, /ə/, /ŏ/		authority	/ə/, /ô/, /ə/
barometer	/ə/, /ŏ/, /ə/		confiscate	/ŏ/, /ə/, /ā/
barometric	/ă/, /ə/, /ĕ/		confiscatory	/ə/, /ĭ/, /ə/
cylinder	/ĭ/, /ə/, /ə/		declaration	/ĕ/, /ə/, /ā/
cylindrical	/ə/, /ĭ/, /ĭ/		declarative	/ĭ/, /ă/, /ə/
democrat	/ĕ/, /ə/, /ă/		derivation	/ĕ/, /ə/, /ā/
democracy	/ĭ/, /ŏ/, /ə/		derivative	/ə/, /ĭ/, /ə/

der*o*gate	/ĕ/, /ə/, /ā/	excl*a*mation	/ĕ/, /ə/, /ā/
der*o*gatory	/ĭ/, /ŏ/, /ə/	excl*a*matory	/ĭ/, /ă/, /ə/
expl*o*ration	/ĕ/, /ə/, /ā/	m*o*lec*u*le	/ŏ/, /ə/, /yo͞o/
expl*o*ratory	/ĭ/, /ô/, /ə/	m*o*lec*u*lar	/ə/, /ĕ/, /yə/
*o*blig*a*tion	/ŏ/, /ə/, /ā/	*o*rig*i*n	/ô/, /ə/, /ĭ/
*o*blig*a*tory	/ə/, /ĭ/, /ə/	*o*rig*i*nal	/ə/, /ĭ/ /ə/
path*o*logy	/ə/, /ŏ/, /ə/	ph*o*t*o*graph	/ō/, /ə/, /ă/
path*o*logical	/ă/, /ə/, /ŏ/	ph*o*t*o*graphy	/ə/, /ŏ/, /ə/
psych*i*atry	/ə/, /ĭ/, /ə/	rep*e*t*i*tion	/ĕ/, /ə/, /ĭ/
psych*i*atric	/ĭ/, /ē/, /ă/	rep*e*t*e*tive	/ĭ/, /ĕ/, /ə/

Please don't get the impression that there are large numbers of related words in English in which three sounds change with a shift in the location of the stress and with no spelling changes. There aren't. There are, however, a good many related words in which the shift in stress brings about the change of two vowel sounds. I gave the above examples because they are dramatic and convincing. The point is that we have much more to learn and remember than would be true if there were no shift in the position of the stress and the spelling were reliable.

Looking at the matter objectively, we reflect on this strange phenomenon and come to the conclusion that the unreliable spellings make a mockery of the use of letters to represent sounds. The identical spellings OUGHT to spell identical sounds.

In those forty words there are fifty-nine unstressed syllables, of which fifty-three have the schwa sound and six the /ĭ/ sound (spelled by *e*). For the record, the schwa is spelled by letters as follows: *a* 18, *au* 1, *e* 7, *i* 8, *o* 16, *u* 1, and *y* 2.

If we connect these undependable spellings with the teaching of reading, we come to a second conclusion: There are great numbers of words which could be learned more efficiently and pleasantly if they could be taught in the written and spoken forms simultaneously. It is obvious that children need all the help they can get because, as you know, a great majority of our words were borrowed and are not self-explanatory, and a great majority of our words are not spelled phonetically.

Another promise which I made earlier was to show the sounds spelled by the letter *u*. It would take most children a very short time to learn the spelling if *u* spelled just two sounds, as it does in many languages, "long," as in *truth* and "short," as in *butter*. But in English the letter *u* spells six times two sounds, a total of twelve! Here are samples:

*u*se	J*u*ne	br*u*sh	p*u*sh	s*u*btract	lem*u*r
/yo͞o/	/o͞o/	/ŭ/	/o͝o/	/ə/	/ər/

Marvelous Memories

occupy	hurt	mature	quilt	busy	burial
/yə/	/û/	/yo͞o/	/w/	/ĭ/	/ĕ/

If you wish to demonstrate how a single vowel letter spells two or three sounds in single words, you might select words from this group of fifteen. In twelve of them one letter spells three different sounds, and in each group of three words each vowel letter spells six sounds:

```
a:   A b r a h a m        m a n a g e a b l e    b a r b a r i a n
     /ā/   /ə/ /ă/         /ă/ /ĭ/    /ə/         /ä/   /â/   /ə/

e:   e m e r g e n c y    u k e l e l e          r e v e r b e r a t e
     /ĭ/ /û/    /ə/        /ə/ /ā/ /ē/           /ĭ/ /û/    /ər/   /–/

i:   c i v i l i a n      i n f i r m i t y      v i c a r i o u s
     /ə/ /ĭ/ /y/           /ĭ/ /û/    /ə/        /ĭ/    /ē/

o:   T o r o n t o        p r o m o n t o r y    o f f-c o l o r
     /ə/ /ŏ/   /ō/         /ŏ/  /ə/   /ô/        /ô/  /ŭ/ /ə/

u:   c u c u m b e r      E q u u l e u s        s u c c u l e n t
     /yo͞o/ /ŭ/              /w/ /o͞o/ /ə/          /ŭ/    /yə/
```

It isn't easy to find the letter y three times in a single word, though syzygy and polygyny both qualify. But they spell the same three sounds, /ĭ/, /ə/, /ē/. Instead of separate words, I'll offer this sentence, in which y spells seven sounds: Y es, Eth y l B y rd owns four cars:
                                        /y/   /ə/   /û/
a Chev y, a Chr y sler, a Pl y mouth, and a Zeph y r.
        /ē/   /ĭ/   /ĭ/   /ər/

One of the basic messages of this book is to say that letters should be reliable guides to pronunciation and that the letters of English are much too often unreliable. Children SHOULD be able to "sound out" words they have never seen or heard before. One of the main thrusts of the book is to prove that it can't be done. Here is almost my last opportunity to show something that ought not be possible in an alphabetic language. How should children read the following words aloud?

Tereus   teredo   neroli   feral   terato   gerent   verism

How is it possible that the letter *e* in the same language environment spells four different sounds and does it an even dozen times? Between a preceding consonant and the letter *r*, the letter *e* accomplishes what should be impossible. The following forty-eight words show that anything is possible in English:

	ber-	cer-	der-	fer-
/ĕ/	beriberi	ceremony	derelict	ferule
/ə/	beret	cerise	dermapteran	ferocious
/ĭ/	bereave	cereal	derive	feral
/û/	berth	certify	dervish	fertile
	ger-	her-	mer-	ner-
/ĕ/	Gerald	herald	merit	neroli
/ə/	germane	heraldic	meridian	neritic
/ĭ/	gerent	heroic	mere	Nero
/û/	German	hermit	mercy	nervous
	per-	ser-	ter-	ver-
/ĕ/	perish	serenade	terato	verify
/ə/	perhaps	serene	teredo	veranda
/ĭ/	periodical	serious	Tereus	verism
/û/	pert	sermon	terminal	verb

To be sure, only half of the forty-eight words will occur early—say by the fourth grade—but I had to replace a dozen easy words because they would have been repeaters, and I have tried to avoid repeating sample words when possible. But we must *not* stop teaching reading at the end of the third grade. Our language does not permit that luxury. Therefore, the inclusion of the less-well known words is justified. (And they actually make the demonstration more convincing.)

Finally, I am going to do what a number of readers probably have been waiting for, namely, what George Bernard Shaw did when he said "fish" could be spelled "ghoti." He defended the spelling by using this key:

/f/ from *gh* in rou*gh*; /ĭ/ from *o* in w*o*men; /sh/ from *ti* in na*ti*on

However, Shaw made two fundamental errors: At the beginning of a word *gh* never spells /f/; and the combination *ti* spells /sh/ only medially, never at the end of a word.

Instead of spelling a single word, I have developed a whole sentence which, incidentally, makes sense and expresses a truth. In it I'll use spellings you are accustomed to seeing in other words and in the same locations, that is, at the beginning, in the middle, and at the end.

Jong Rhoechens pteik leace tuymn tough lourn tue wreid.

Marvelous Memories

We accept without reservations these spellings of sounds in other words; we have memorized them there, but they are incomparably more difficult here because we have not learned these spellings in these words. If you are unable to decode all the words in the sentence, you may for a moment better understand the problems of Ichabod and Johnny.

Here is the sentence in standard spelling:

Young Russians take less time to learn to read.

The statement is factual because a high percentage of Russian words are spelled phonetically. Here is the key:

```
   J o n g      R h o e c h e n s      p t e i k      l e a c e
   1 2          3 4 5 6                7 8            9 10
   t u y m n    t o u g h              l o u r n  t u e    w r e i d
   11  12       13                     14         15       16 17
```

Item	Spells	Sample	Item	Spells	Sample
1. J	/y/	Jugoslavia	2. o	/ŭ/	among
3. rh	/r/	rheumatism	4. oe	/ŭ/	does
5. ch	/sh/	echelon	6. ens	/ənz/	gardens
7. pt	/t/	ptomaine	8. ei	/ā/	vein
9. ea	/ĕ/	bread	10. ce	/s/	slice
11. uy	/ī/	guy	12. mn	/m/	damn
13. ough	/o͞o/	through	14. ou	/û/	flourish
15. ue	/o͞o/	true	16. wr	/r/	write
17. ei	/ē/	leisure			

Before crying "unfair!" let me remind you that you are not used to seeing those ways to spell those sounds *in those particular words*. Specifically, for instance, #14, the spelling of the vowel sound /û/ by *ou* in the fabricated word "lourn" is no more illogical than in the real word "flourish" or in "nourish" or "sojourn" or "discourage" or "scourge" or "journey." Simply stated, in all of the sample words the spelling is equally illogical, and that is the reason language authorities have said our spelling is irrational. You have learned and memorized "flourish" and accept it; you have never learned or memorized "lourn" and for that reason say it is a stupid spelling.

It is clear that all English-speaking adults who read well, have to remember what many thousands of irregularly spelled words look like, know how most of them are pronounced, and understand what they mean. They must have marvelous memories.

CHAPTER 21

Clearing the Way

Before we tackle the problem of how to improve our method of teaching reading, we must discuss briefly problems connected with reading instruction.

First, what justification is there for calling vowel letter sounds by their present names, "long" *a*, "short" *a*, "long" *e*, "short" *e*, etc.? When I strike the note *a* on the piano and hold it four seconds and then hit the *same* key and hold it for one second, I can say that the first *a* relative to the second was long, and the second one short. But if I strike *a* and hold it for four seconds and then strike *c* and hold it for one second, I can't say the second note was a "short" *a*. You would wonder if I had made a mistake and had struck the wrong key—or if I weren't very bright.

Now that is exactly what we do when we speak of our vowel sounds. We say /ā/ and call it "long *a*." Then we talk about "short *a*" and still pronounce it /ā/. Of course we want to distinguish between sounds spelled by the same letter, and in doing so have not seen the paradox. Spoken vocal sounds should be properly differentiated and identified, just as musical sounds are.

The point is that our terminology is incorrect and misleading, doubly so in the beginning, and must confuse learners, especially the slower ones. Why not call the /ă/ sound /ă/? Naturally we'd also speak of the /ĕ/, /ĭ/, /ŏ/, and /ŭ/ sounds.

There is another reason for eliminating the "long" and "short" vowel terminology. We often do not make much of a distinction between "long" and "short" sounds, especially in comparison with German speakers in their language. In general, German "long" vowel sounds are held longer than our "long" vowel sounds are, and German "short" vowel sounds are held much shorter than ours. Therefore, the distinction is considerably greater in German. If we were to make a comparison with music, we might say German "long" vowel sounds are like half notes, and "short" sounds are like eighth notes. Ours are more like dotted quarter and dotted eighth notes.

Clearing the Way

Moreover, the consonants following the vowels influence the length of the vowel sound. Children can't hear—in terms of length—much distinction between *mate* and *man; leaf* and *led;* and *boat* and *log*. There is a greater difference in these pairs: *lame* and *bat; leave* and *let; bone* and *lot*. Frequently our "long" vowels are quite short in duration, and our "short" vowels may be quite long. Once I fell headfirst into a lake after starting the motor in my boat. The area was rectangular, closed off by docks, and the empty boat was circling at full speed, sometimes directly over my head. I was terrified and when I surfaced, I let out one of the longest "short" vowel sounds in history. I shouted "H-e-e-e-e-e-e-elp!"

It would not alter one whit the length we hold our vowels if we were to stop talking about "long" and "short" sounds. It would help our children.

Second, we would do well to develop names for all our sounds. What, for instance, are the names of these sounds:

/ä/ as in t*a*r, *e*nsemble /â/ as in r*a*re, wh*e*re
/o͞o/ as in t*o*, tr*u*ly /o͝o/ as in p*u*t, w*o*lverine
/û/ as in j*e*rk, sh*i*rk, w*o*rm, p*u*rpose, m*y*rmidon

Isn't it curious that we have hundreds, even thousands, of names for plants and insects, but something as close to us as our language languishes without much-needed terminology, especially for use in instructing our children?

Third, we should recognize that the names of the letters of the alphabet do not do as much good when children are trying to work out the sounds of words as we think they do. Horace Mann emphasized this point when he said that the word "leg" spelled /ĕl ē jē/ sounds more like "elegy" than "leg." When do we use the sounds /āch/ for *h*, /kyo͞o/ for *q,* and /wī/ for *y* in our words? I think it was Mann who liked to show how the names of letters do not produce assumed results. I'm not sure of his examples, but they could have been these names: "William Young Wood" is spelled—

W double yo͞o   Y wī
i eye   o ō
l ĕl   u yo͞o
l ĕl   n ĕn
i eye   g jē
a ā   W double yo͞o
m ĕm   o double
                   o ō
                   d dē

Fourth, and this is merely a summary of what has been said in this book, we must develop an understanding of the lamentable and formidable difficulties our writing system places on learners, and we must exercise boundless and abiding patience when dealing with our children learning to read (and to spell), particularly the slow learners. Having memorized thousands of words, you find it almost impossible to see what children must contend with. Note how not one of these words will give you any problems:

(a) You scarcely notice the *u* in guard, guest, guild, guinea, guide.

(b) You don't have to stop to work out the role of *i* in bil*i*ous /y/ env*i*ous /ē/ contag*i*ous(–).

(c) You can read the following words as fast as you see them: pigeon, doe, yeoman, canoe, leotard, people, poem, amoeba, leopard, Phoenician. You were probably not aware that four words have the digraph *oe,* four have the digraph *eo,* and in two words the side-by-side letters *o* and *e* and *e* and *o* spell individual sounds. The eight uses of the two digraphs spell eight sounds. Not one of the words is spelled phonetically.

(d) In "familiar" and "peculiar" you don't even see the word "liar." Don't blame children if they do; our language permits such quirks.

(e) Words which aren't confusing to you may be to other adults and certainly will be to children. Take *desert* and *dessert.* The two words are homophones when *desert* is used as a verb, /dĭ zûrt′/. Children should not be expected to read such words until they have thoroughly learned them in reading context, as here:

The men were without water while in the hot sun out on the *desert.*

He was extremely selfish and cruel when he decided to *desert* his family.

While eating, the children looked forward to the birthday cake, which was to be their *dessert.*

CHAPTER 22

Methods of Teaching Reading

This is an apparent enigma: All normal people with no hearing problems learn to understand our *spoken* language. But millions of otherwise normal individuals in the English-speaking world who have no uncorrectable visual problems are unable to read and, therefore, understand, our *written* language.

Quite logically, one might expect the same conditions to prevail where other languages are spoken and written. As you know, however, in all countries where other Germanic languages are spoken, people learn not only to understand their oral language, but they also learn to understand their written language—because they learn to read it. This is indisputable: Relatively few normal, native-born individuals in Austria, East and West Germany, Holland, Switzerland, and the Scandinavian countries, including Iceland, cannot read.

There can be only one reason for this disparity: The erratic and confusing spelling of our words defeats the efforts of many when they try to learn to read. More than thirty authorities quoted in this book have told of the flaws in the representation of our sounds. Professors Morton W. Bloomfield and Leonard Newmark, whom I have previously quoted twice, make the point for us, offering the two extremes, Finnish and English. They wrote, "Finnish children, whose language is written in a very consistent alphabetic system, need spend only a few months learning to read and write the language they speak." Then the authors continued, "English-speaking children suffer from the fact that their basically alphabetic system is used so inconsistently that they must spend years memorizing what are actually largely logographic conventions." (*A Linguistic Introduction to the History of English*, p. 31) By "logographic conventions" I am sure they meant "whole-word symbols (not phonetically spelled) accepted by usage."

Let no one say that educators haven't tried to be successful in teaching all children to read. Eighty years ago, John Dewey observed that no matter what teaching method was used, many children labored and strove in vain to learn to read. He concluded that we ought not even attempt to teach children to read at the age of six or seven. In the *Forum,* May, 1898, he called the teaching of reading "lifeless." He elaborated: "Methods of teaching reading come and go . . . They all lack the essential of any well-grounded method, namely, relevancy to the child's mental needs." He summed up his thoughts in these words: "No scheme for learning can supply this want."

Now it is necessary to consider some of the methods which our teachers have employed and see how educators have struggled mightily in their efforts to help every child learn to read. I'll outline briefly a number of the many reading programs which have been used here and in other English-speaking countries.

1. The alphabet method, which was used before phonics and word methods were developed. It is no longer found in our schools or in Europe.

2. Various phonics methods, in which children are taught not to think of the names of the letters of the alphabet, but are to think of the sound which each letter or combination of letters is supposed to represent and then to convert each printed symbol into its proper sound, moving from left to right. This is a letter-sound progression.

3. Whole word (or configuration) methods, in which children are taught to recognize whole words, with initially, at least, minor emphasis on letter-sound relationships. (There have even been sporadic attempts to teach reading by using short sentences rather than just words.)

4. The i.t.a. (Initial Teaching Alphabet) method, in which a revised, more nearly phonetic, spelling of a very considerable number of words is employed. The present revised alphabet was based on one which A. J. Ellis and Sir Isaac Pitman prepared and which Ellis used in the book, *The Alphabet of Nature,* which was published in 1845. In the book Ellis tells us that he knew of twenty-seven earlier revised alphabets, and that his and Sir Isaac's was the twenty-eighth one. Sir James Pitman, who devised or revised the i.t.a., was the grandson of Sir Isaac. Of course you have heard of George Bernard Shaw's desire to have a completely phonetic alphabet prepared so that by using it, we could spell all English words phonetically. Not much came from that attempt. Many well-known personages have supported spelling reforms; they include Dryden, Wordsworth, Prime Minister Gladstone, Benjamin Franklin, and President Theodore Roosevelt. The Initial Teaching Alphabet is a compromise; devised simply to introduce children to reading English, it is a more nearly phonetic spelling than our conventional spelling is. It has been used in the teaching of reading in hundreds of classrooms on four continents. At the end of one year or sometimes two years, children are transferred to conventional spelling.

Methods of Teaching Reading 199

5. Linguistic methods, in which words introduced in early lessons are all spelled regularly and are usually short. Unfortunately, authors soon run out of phonetically spelled words, and then children still must learn our hundreds of spelling exceptions in thousands of words, large numbers of which are high frequency words.

6. Life or language experience methods, in which children in a class are called upon to tell of their activities, and the words they use are introduced into the reading program. The new words are generally written on the board and are often duplicated and handed out to classes, as a rule in sentences. The obvious problems are these: (a) too many of the newly introduced words are spelled irregularly; (b) the words come in larger numbers than a good many children are able to handle; (c) frequently the new words are not repeated often enough for the children to learn them; and (d) there is a dearth of reading material and repetition in this plan. Moreover, it creates a heavy burden on the teacher. Days are too short to take care of all the added work. Only experienced, outstanding teachers can employ this method with any degree of success.

7. Words in Color is a method in which each of our sounds is represented in printed letters by one color, no matter what the spelling. This method, like the i. t. a., word, and some other methods, was based on the premise that a great majority of our words are not spelled phonetically and for that reason, it is assumed, are too difficult for slower children to learn in conventional spelling with no aids. This is how Words in Color operates. When letters spell the /ā/ sound, they are always printed in a certain shade of green (pea green). Children are supposed to memorize which colors represent which sounds. Thus, if they know that pea green spells /ā/, they are supposed to recognize these written representations, of that sound, all printed in pea green: *a*ble, m*ay,* f*ai*l, h*a*te, th*ey,* str*aigh*t, *eigh*t, and gr*ea*t (and caf*e,* r*ei*n, buff*et,* crep*e,* entr*ee,* risq*ue,* f*eig*n, etc.) A shade of red is used for the letters which spell the /ē/ sound, ocher for /ō/, and pale green for /yo͞o/.

In his book, *Reading with Words in Colour,* Caleb Gattegno gives his readers samples to show how colors chosen to represent sounds are consistent, but the spellings by various letters are not. Writing for the benefit of adult readers, he offers words to show how the /ĕ/ sound is spelled ten ways: "He s*a*ys m*e*n s*ai*d m*a*ny fri*e*ndly l*eo*pards b*u*ry h*ei*fers d*ea*d from h*ae*morrhage." (p. 81) Being British, he used British spellings, as we would expect. But I g*ue*ss he overlooked the *ue* spelling and must have considered seven or eight other spellings to be too unusual to include. Later, he shows how one spelling, the letter *o,* represents several sounds, as in "This is *o*ne *o*f the w*o*men wh*o* w*o*rked f*o*r *o*nly a m*o*nth." (p. 166) My goodness! Where is the schwa sound, as in *o*ppose or opp*o*site?

There are nineteen wall charts, and they are supplied to all schools which order the textbook series. The charts are hung in each classroom to help children learn to match the colors with the sounds they represent.

8. Fry's "Diacritical Marking System" also uses conventional spelling, but learners are guided to the proper pronunciation of words by diacritical marks. For example, the virgule or slash, (/), is found across all "silent" letters; a macron, or bar, above a vowel indicates that the vowel letter represents a "long" sound (as used in dictionaries); and a dot above a vowel letter indicates that it spells a schwa.

9. There are, of course, combination methods, and one of them is "Learn English the New Way" by Frank C. Laubach. He respelled many words to make the letters conform more closely to phonetic spellings, and he also used diacritical marks. For example, he used the virgule (slash) following vowel letters that spell "long" sounds.

10. The most recently developed method and not well known is based on an alphabet devised by Dr. Bamesh Hoffman, a mathematician. Using it, Dr. Elaine Newman wrote the *Self-Pronouncing English Reader*. The alphabet makes use of different typefaces to indicate the sounds the letters represent. For instance, regular, boldface, and dotted typefaces are employed. This method is currently being used to teach English to foreign students at Queens College in New York.

11. The Basal Reader Approach in various forms has been in recent times and presently is the most widely used method. Here, vocabulary is strictly limited in the beginning, very often almost exclusively to words that are spelled phonetically, and words are repeated over and over again. Ordinarily, all of the words introduced in the first small book are repeated in the second book; and the authors generally employ in the third reader all of the words found in the first two books. The major emphasis is not placed upon letter-sound relationships in the early book or books, but sooner or later a definite attempt is made to teach the phonetic values of the letters, and therefore phonics is combined with a whole word method. The extremely limited vocabulary results in what my neighbor said is inane, insipid, and uninspired reading matter. In almost every book there are appealing pictures, usually of children in action, often with a pet.

There are still other methods, but the ones I have listed give a fair idea of the efforts educators have made to teach all children to read. They know how faulty our writing system is and have made great efforts to compensate for those weaknesses. Some of the methods would be quite inappropriate in teaching reading in Hungarian or even German. For instance, Words in Color would in all probability hold back the relatively easy progress made by the learners who speak those languages.

Even after reading this far, I'm quite sure a good many parents will still ask themselves this question: Why don't teachers simply use phonics

Methods of Teaching Reading

and be done with it? My experiences over the years, especially with concerned parents, confirm what Professor Frank Smith stated in his book, *Understanding Reading—A Psycholinguistic Analysis of Reading and Learning to Read:* "Many people believe the phonics approach is so efficacious, and are so persuaded that words constructed alphabetically ought to be read alphabetically, that they insist that other approaches to reading instruction are unnecessary. Some consider other teaching methods positively immoral." (First edition, pp. 161-162) Nearly all lay people with whom I have discussed the teaching of reading have been of the opinion that phonics has to be by far the best, really the only intelligent, method.

In due time we'll take up other reasons why phonics is not as successful as we wish it were—and some people are sure it would be if it were used exclusively.

In order to determine the best method to teach reading, we might do well to consider how our children learn to understand our oral language.

During most of their waking hours for six years—before they go to school—most learners of spoken English hear normal language, and gradually they pick up and assimilate hundreds and then thousands of words, learning words here and expressions there and, as a guess, between the ages of two and six learning between one and eight (or more) words a day. By and large we do not give our children our spoken language broken down into individual sounds. Granted, they may sometimes hear syllables, as in /bā bē/, /mŏ mē/, and /dă dē/. But certainly 90 to 95 percent of what most children hear is the natural, normal language of their parents, siblings, other relatives, and playmates. They do not all hear the same words, nor do they all learn the same words at the same time. They are not expected to learn "x" number of words in a given time period and "y" number of words in another. They may, and do, take their time. To be sure, children are complimented when they *say* words, phrases, and, finally, sentences, but in general, they do not feel great outside pressure to increase the number of words they *understand*.

If the method of learning to understand oral language is so effective, why do we not follow as similar a pattern as we can when teaching our children to read? It is generally believed we should start with parts, with letters and then individual words. As I have said, we do not attempt to teach children to understand spoken language that way. We do not repeatedly break down scores and hundreds of words for tiny tots and say, /m/ /ĭ/ /l/ /k/ or /w/ /ä/ /t/ /ə/ /r/ or /s/ /ĭ/ /r/ /ē/ /ə/ /l/ *(cereal).*

The hardest part of language learning *should* be behind children when they are able to match groups of sounds with concepts. Learning great numbers of groups of sounds which stand for thousands of things and ideas is a real, an amazing, accomplishment. Now the operation ought to be easier; children need only learn to match unknown groups of letters with known groups of sounds, that is, groups of letter symbols (printed words) with groups of sound symbols (spoken words).

And the operation is indeed fairly easy in numerous languages. Here in the following quotation is verification of an earlier quotation in this chapter. Professor John Lotz wrote as follows in an essay, "How Language is Conveyed by Script": "Finnish represents a very simple alphabetic orthography (spelling)." As a result, "A Finnish child of seven can read without any difficulty." (*Language by Ear and by Eye,* p. 122)

In other words, Finnish children can learn in one year the printed symbols of the words they have taken six or seven years to learn in their oral form. I have previously said it takes German-speaking children a little longer to learn to read than it does Finnish, Hungarian, and Turkish children. Lotz agrees: "The correlation between sound and script is fairly good in German, but with significant differences." Then he concludes, "English probably represents the most irregular system of all." (p. 122) Therefore, as he points out, it costs "The Anglo-Saxon world billions of dollars a year (to teach the difficult English spelling system)."

You probably recall how I propose a method of giving learners an easier and pleasanter way to learn to match the sight and sound symbols: Let them hear what they are learning to read. But before I discuss the merits of that method, I think we should consider the all-important matter of motivation.

As many writers have noted, there is no doubt about the desire of children to learn their *spoken* language, especially when what is said concerns them. They also want to communicate. They want to defend their rights, to have their fair share (and often more), to say they don't want any spinach, but they do want more ice cream. Very often what they hear has relevance in their lives. They speak because they want attention and recognition; through language they gain a feeling of importance. When they can understand language and can express their feelings, their ideas, wants, and needs, their egos are fed; they become full-fledged individuals.

Children are not motivated to the same degree to learn *written* communication. I have never read or heard that most humans have an equal drive, the same powerful urge, to master our written form of communication. We can see this in history. For hundreds of thousands of years writing didn't exist; if the need had been felt to the same degree that we feel the need to communicate orally, writing surely would have been developed much earlier than just some ten thousand years ago. Here is another thought to support that assertion: A few hundred years ago relatively few individuals were able to read or write. If the desire were an overpowering one, undoubtedly many more would have learned to read, even though materials on which scribes wrote were expensive. Today, we who are able to read and write can hardly imagine how we could get along without the two skills. But children of five can be happy and well-adjusted and not be able to read or write. Why, then, should the same children at the age of six suddenly develop a strong urge to learn? Without incentive or desire, many of them feel no need to exert themselves in order to acquire the skills.

As I see it, a great many children will be motivated only if they recognize immediate benefits to them. It is a mistake to assume that all children will want to learn to read merely because they see adults reading. Besides, many youngsters of Ichabod and Johnny's low ability rarely see older people reading, people to whom television and radio bring the news, and in millions of homes there is no newspaper. Furthermore, children usually aren't interested in what adults are reading anyway.

Probably the best motivation for children to learn to read is given when they are read to in the home. It is self-evident that children who are read to nearly every day are much more likely to develop a desire to learn than those who are never read to. I think if parents were conscious of the immense learning difficulties caused by our erratic spelling and were aware of the value of their reading daily to their children, they would make a greater effort to find time and to read to them. It is not easy to find a mutually agreeable time; children have their high priority activities, and one of them is that they simply have to watch their favorite programs on TV; and parents, too, have little free time, and they, too, can't miss their favorite shows. So one day after another slips by without the reading experience.

Not that there were unlimited free times and reading opportunities fifty and sixty years ago. Mothers with their large(r) families always had work to do; fathers worked six-day weeks and longer days; and children had household chores, including doing the dishes, helping with the cooking and clothes washing, ironing, sweeping and dusting, going to the store for groceries, cutting kindling, carrying coal, cleaning walks, doing garden work, feeding farm animals, milking, etc. Finally, there was always practicing on the (often hated) piano.

In any event, great numbers of children have always arrived at school who have not been well motivated. We have expected teachers to do what the home and society have failed to do. And that is a huge order.

Since the main task of primary grades is to teach reading, it is inevitable that children expect to (or think they have to) "learn to read." So now they are going to school, and they assume they will be able to read in a short time. Some of them want instant success. Well, who can blame them? Who doesn't want instant success in any undertaking?

But progress, no matter what method has been employed by teachers, has always been painfully and distressingly slow for many of our children.

With phonics, what motivation and what rewards do they find if they are taught for many long weeks and even months the letters and sounds they ordinarily stand for, perhaps in twenty to forty or possibly sixty words, none of which alone have much significance. They ask themselves, 'Is this reading?'

With electronics, a new day has dawned. In the following chapter you will see how electronics can be put to greater use in the teaching of reading.

CHAPTER 23

The Simultaneous Reading and Listening Method

In order to help greater numbers of young people to become literate (and at the same time to make learning for the other children more efficient), we must compensate for our deficient spelling. Methods of teaching reading that are successful in countries where other languages are spoken are not effective enough where English is spoken. Because some 80 percent of all our words, even an overwhelming percentage of our easy or "conversation" words, are not spelled phonetically, we must develop a more efficacious method, one which will make it possible for our beginners to hear simultaneously what they see in print on the page before them.

We must prerecord our reading material on tapes or cassette tapes; and then while the children listen through earphones to the recorded material, they will follow with their eyes the printed matter in their books.

This proposed method has more than a dozen advantages in its favor. Here are the most important ones.

1. *Interest*—With fewer vocabulary restrictions, the reading matter can, and undoubtedly will, be of interest to a much higher percentage of children. Interest, as we all know, is without question one of the most important factors of learning. I have sampled dozens of children's primary grade readers and have seen how the authors have strained in an unfair contest to write engagingly and entertainingly, but our irregular spellings of words impose vocabulary limits which are unfair not only to the writers, but also to our learners. Take away the lively pictures from primary readers and you will see more clearly what I mean.

2. *Relevancy*—Children will not be required to think mainly of the relationships between letters and sounds as with a phonics method; they will be reading and listening to subjects which will bear a close relationship with their lives.

3. *Attention*—This method is in direct contrast to phonics methods or to the method of the linguists Bloomfield and Barnhart, which I

described in Chapter 5. Whereas they make the letter-sound relationship paramount and ignore interest, certainly the involuntary interest of children, particularly those with few linguistic talents, this method will offer reading material which will catch the attention and maintain the interest of learners.

4. *Involvement*—In a relatively short time learners will identify with the persons and actions they are reading about. They will soon become absorbed and will relate to what is developing. This is basic. Learning, as it should be, will be a pleasure for youngsters, and not something to be disliked and avoided.

5. *First Learning Should Be Correct Learning*—A cardinal principle of good teaching is that teachers should help children avoid as much mislearning as possible, and, conversely, make every effort to direct children's learning to be correct right from the start. Early in the nineteenth century Horace Mann in his *Report of an Educational Tour* wrote, "The child should never have any excuse or occasion for making a mistake." (p. 171) He then added that the child should be "guarded" from making errors.

You have seen in earlier chapters how the use of phonics, of "sounding out" letters, in great numbers of words inevitably leads to incorrect guessing, and certainly that cannot be called learning. For the benefit of those who are still not completely convinced, suppose children see a word beginning with the letters *sho-*. They cannot possibly know what sound the letter *o* represents until they see what letter or letters follow it. This is what they could run into. To *sho-* add:
-al: shoal /ō/; *-e: shoe* /o͞o/; *-ne: shone* /ō/; *-ot: shoot* /o͞o/; *-p: shop* /ŏ/; *-rt: short* /ô/. But the word we have in mind has a *u* following *sho-*. As you have seen, the combination *ou* spells the diphthong /ou/, and what is discouraging, as you know, is the fact that it also spells eight separate sounds. Now what are children's mathematical chances of guessing correctly? Are the children supposed to run through all nine possibilities (including the diphthong)? When you know the next letter is *l*, then you can make a deduction, which children cannot easily make in the sounding-out process. You know that the letter *l* will be followed by the letter *d*. And then we have *should* /sho͝od/. But we're still not home. The word is *shoulder*, and now the combination *ou* does not spell /o͝o/, but another of the eight sounds, /ō/, and the letter *l*, which might be called pollution in "shou*l*d," now spells a sound, as it always should.

The "sounding-out" method or process is a guessing game, and all too frequently the odds favor unphonetic spelling and not our children. Note other possibilities following *sho-*: Add *-ut: shout* /ou/; *-ve: shove* /ŭ/; *-w: show* /ō/; *-wer: shower* /ou/.

With our reading experiences we adults can and do take hundreds of shortcuts in our daily reading. The configuration (and context) tell the experienced reader that *sho-* followed by *-ulder* can be only "shoulder." I submit that neither you nor anybody else learned the words "should" and "shoulder" (and thousands of other words like "other" and "words") by sounding them out. Why should we not make our teaching more logical and efficient? The Simultaneous Reading and Listening Method (SR & LM) forestalls errors and wasteful guessing.

Having taught skill subjects for many years, I consider the advantages of #5 (First Learning Should Be Correct Learning) to be invaluable. We should not make children agonize and try to learn the illogical in an illogical way. As Friedrich Bodmer wrote, "It is easier to form habits than to break them." (*The Loom of Language,* p. 215)

Educators have used many terms to describe the ways children are supposed to sound out or work out words. These are samples: "attack," "decode," "break" or "crack" the "code." This is one of the definitions of the word "code" in our dictionaries: "A system of symbols used in secret writing." How apt the definition is for many of our would-be learners. This, again, is what I mean. We can take any word beginning with the letters *com-*. What are teachers to tell children the letter *o* represents? I counted the words beginning with those three letters in one dictionary, and this is what I found: The letter *o* spells the schwa sound in 55 percent(!) of the words, as in "c*o*mpose"; /ŏ/ in 34 percent, as in "c*o*mposition"; and /ŭ/, as in "c*o*mpany" or /ō/, as in "c*o*ma" in 11 percent. Using phonics and getting too many incorrect guesses and failing to hold the interest of pupils, teachers must have said to themselves, "We must call a halt to the guessing game, to the slow, confusing, unproductive, and much too often fruitless sounding-out process." How must children feel when, as in thousands of words, the chances are not in their favor? Think of the ghastly waste of time which the children suffer when making their guesses; think of the wasted effort; and think of the loss of interest and of the disappointment, discouragement, and frustration resulting from repeated incorrect guesses.

In short, the sounding-out process will work with words that are phonetically spelled; it is a dismal failure with words that aren't. Furthermore, the staunchest supporter of phonics must agree that the sounding-out process presupposes with English words that learners know each word orally in advance or they will have little chance of properly working out unphonetically spelled words.

6. *Use of Two Avenues of Learning*—The two most important avenues of learning, eyes and ears, will be working together. Friedrich Bodmer, whom I just quoted, says, "It is more difficult to learn by eye alone than by eye and ear together." (p. 215) Educational psychologists recommend harnessing as many of the avenues of learning as possible, and here the two will be combined to make the learning process that much surer and faster.

7. *Repetition*—Too often we assume that something which has been taught well will always be remembered. That is a grave error. Children have so much to learn and have so much thrown at them that they need all the repetition they can get. With this method it will be offered in hitherto undreamed of amounts. By this I do not mean the "and he huffed and he puffed and he huffed and he puffed" type. Where that kind is fitting and appealing to young children, it will, of course, appear. But the kind I mean will be judicious repetition in ingeniously worded reading material which will appeal to all children, to boys just as much as to girls, something that cannot be said of a good many current basal readers. The amount of repetition will be many times that which is offered in present series. Now quite a bit of it is forced and synthetic. By the very nature of the new program the increased amount of reading will provide infinitely more natural and profitable repetition. Besides, the material recorded on tapes or cassettes will be read and listened to a minimum of two or three times by the fastest learners and four or more times by the slowest ones.

8. *Reinforcement of Learning*—Reinforcement is more than mere repetition. After it may be safely assumed that words have been taught and taught well, it is necessary to use them again and again, as every good teacher knows. This method is a natural one to make reinforcement of learning extremely easy.

9. *Reduction of Fatigue*—Unless you have recently been around children from six to nine years of age, you may not remember how quickly they tire at tasks. Fatigue is reduced when children are engrossed and doing something they like.

10. *Concentration*—Again, you should observe a class of youngsters and see how quickly many of them lose interest in the work at hand. With this method, concentration can be more complete and held longer. Earphones, which will be necessary in order for children to gain the greatest benefit by listening to work on their own level, will have the added benefit that they will exclude nearly all extraneous sounds, and the most natural thing in the world will be for learners to look at the words while they are hearing them, especially if the material is interesting and not the Dick and Jane kind of pablum.

11. *Immediacy*—Children care little about what they may achieve in six months or in two or three years. Working on relationships between letters and sounds with a promise that their efforts will be rewarded in some vague future, children are less than enthusiastic. They want to see results right away. If they are going to learn to read, they want to be reading now; and they will be doing just that, for learners will be introduced to the genuine reading experience within weeks. They will discover and know from first-hand participation the values, benefits,

rewards, and pleasures of reading. They will not have to wait for that distant future; the future will be now.

12. *Better Use of Time*—With the new method the time of the teachers and of the pupils will be put to better use. Now there are ordinarily three groups of children, divided according to ability; and while the teachers are working with one group, the hope is that the children in the other two groups are using their time well. But frequently they are not. Here they can work with no interruptions and no loss of valuable time. Of course an aide should operate the cassettes or playbacks. Teachers will be able to work with small groups during the reading-listening time and not be concerned about the other children in their classes.

13. *Confidence and Security*—These qualities are essential ingredients in learning, and now they can be developed more easily and more surely because children can be certain they are hearing correctly and making proper associations. Pupils will know they may listen to the same tape again (and again), and this fact will dispel many fears. They can also know that the words will all be repeated many times on future tapes.

14. *Taking an Important Shortcut*—In a phonics method children work with letters and they are, therefore, working with difficult abstractions. That type of operation is hard, especially for youngsters. The children may know the letters and the alphabet song, but still a letter is an abstraction and has no value in itself; it stands for a sound, often the wrong one. Then a group of letters represents a group of sounds which, in turn, stands for a word. Even words are abstractions. Naturally the early words which the children learn to read are known words. Thus, with the Simultaneous Reading and Listening Method, the harder step, from letters to sounds, is not of major importance *in the learners' minds* and is, in effect, eliminated. Therefore, children take a shortcut and proceed directly from the unknown, the printed words, to the known, the spoken words; they do not move from one abstraction to another abstraction and then to the known. The most difficult step is avoided.

15. *Approximating Individualized Instruction*—This method permits more carefully tailored help to each member of a class than any other method does. If there are enough cassettes, cassette tapes, and earphones, there can be more than the three conventional groups. There can, in fact, just as easily be five or six groups of varying sizes, and the fastest readers will not be held back, nor will the members of the slowest group be pushed faster than they can assimilate what is offered them. This program comes as close to offering individualized instruction as we can hope for in a realistic world where we cannot have one teacher for each student.

CHAPTER 24

Support for the Method

Before television, when the radio was a more important means of entertainment, there was a character on one of the weekly programs who was famous for saying, "Ya but," and he became known as Mr. Yabut. Are you saying to yourself as a reaction to the SR&LM "Yes, but . . . ?"

Well, a related program worked beautifully, and a number of authorities have made statements which may surprise you.

First, because it has direct bearing on our subject, I wish to tell you how I taught another skill subject, German. Part of the method I used there is what I now propose for children learning to read. Every bit of the German text was prerecorded by a person with an excellent German pronunciation, and obviously the reader was enjoying the reading material; and all the German was translated into English and was also prerecorded on the same tape. Thus, students could hear the original German while they were reading it; and while they were re-reading the German, they heard an excellent translation. Students were not obliged to go to the listening library to listen, but they found it richly rewarding to do so. They were exceedingly enthusiastic about the method, which was used as long as the primary goal of language instruction was reading. It was also used at other collegiate institutions.

There was a second reason. The recordings and the listening took care of the reading. That left a great deal more class time for the hardest part of learning German, the grammar. Because German grammar is difficult, and because grammar is abstract, I made every effort to explain, clarify, and exemplify. The reason was simple: First learning should be correct learning.

The point here is that the method of reading and listening simultaneously is not an unproven theory. Of course it will work in English. Besides, there is one major advantage. While my students were all listening to the same tape, children in the SR&LM will be listening to tapes on their own level of performance. This flexibility is an absolute necessity and a blessing.

Here are thoughts of four educators who have written on the subject

Support for the Method 211

of reading instruction. I am sure you will find that their thinking prepares us for my proposal.

1. In an essay, "Do you have to be smart to read? Do you have to read to be smart?" Kenneth S. Goodman in *The Reading Teacher* (1975) wrote as follows:

(a) "Language is learned from the whole to the part, from the general to the specific." (p. 628) Phonics proceeds from the part to the whole, from the specific to the general. The whole word, the Basal Reader, and the Simultaneous Reading and Listening methods proceed from the whole to the part.

(b) "From the very beginning, the child needs to be reading whole, relevant, and interesting language that makes sense." (p. 632) The proposed reading and listening method, with its considerable flexibility, is the only way this can be done except on a one-to-one basis, which is not possible in public schools or even in private schools.

(c) "If we keep the focus not on some future need but on immediate pay-off in reading now, then we have self-motivation." (p. 632) Could we ask for stronger reinforcement?

2. Following are some thoughts of Professor Arthur W. Heilman in his book, *Principles and Practices in Teaching Reading* (Third Edition, 1972):

(a) "Emphasis should be on prevention rather than on cure. . . . The emphasis in our schools is still on cure, not prevention." (p. 13)

(b) "One of the most important aims of the beginning reading period is to help the child develop a positive attitude toward reading." (p. 25)

(c) "The main objective in reading instruction is to arouse and sustain the child's interest in reading. When this is achieved, he becomes ego-involved in reading." (p. 164)

(d) "Because of the rigid control of vocabulary in the beginning reading materials, teachers frequently have the problem of arousing and maintaining interest in these materials." (p. 433)

Pardon an interruption here. A common complaint above the third grade, which extends through high school, to college, and, sometimes even to graduate school, is that students can't read and understand enough hard words. The tape program should not end at the conclusion of the first or second year. You have read about our difficult "book" words and know what our children are up against. I consider this additional advantage of the method to be of major importance; it is advantage

16. *The Expansion of Vocabularies of All Children*—The method will not only spare learners the unpleasantness and distress of so many false guesses, it will save tremendous amounts of time; this valuable time

will be devoted to learning far more words than has heretofore been possible. A publishing company that will offer reading assistance by preparing tapes for its books in the fourth grade will not only be rendering a needed service, but will find great numbers of adoptions. Tapes will not slow a program down; they will speed up learning.

Naturally the better readers will not continue in the regular listening program any longer than necessary. Tapes made especially for them will aid them in the acquisition of new vocabulary items, the words being introduced in context to enable learners to learn them more quickly. The poorer learners will, however, need a more complete program through, say, the fourth grade.

(e) "When faced by a complex problem, most people prefer simple explanations and simple remedies. This is true of the complex problem of explaining how and why such a large number of school children with adequate intellectual endowment become seriously impaired readers." (p. 560)

(f) "Practically all teachers have impaired readers in their classrooms." (p. 580)

Few adults who read well can accept the possibility that there are many individuals in every English-speaking country who can't read well. I included the two foregoing quotations for two reasons: (1) to show that there are, and (2) to indicate that we must do something about the unfortunate situation.

3. Here are four quotations from Professor Emerald Dechant's *Language, Phonics, and the Teaching of Reading:*

(a) "Starting with the words and meaning makes learning to read an interesting and rewarding process from the beginning." (p. 4)

(b) "Any method of reading must keep meaning in the limelight. Reading is never complete without the apprehension of meaning. . . . From the beginning the child should be dealing with meaningful language units." (p. 4)

(c) "The pupil needs to learn the phoneme-grapheme (sound-letter) system by induction rather than by deduction." (p. 18) Here he agrees with Professor Goodman. (See the latter's first quotation.)

(d) "The pupil learns by doing; learning under conditions of practice, and overlearning is of crucial importance to poor readers. Children generally become better in word recognition the more frequently they see the word." (p. 131) Who could ask for stronger support of the SR&LM?

Frank Smith, a professor at the Ontario Institute for Studies in Education, has expressed views on reading and learning to read in a number of books that deserve serious consideration. I'll refer to them by using Roman numerals: *Understanding Reading—A Psycholinguistic Analysis of Reading and Learning to Read* (First edition, 1971: I; Second

Support for the Method 213

edition, 1978: II); *Psycholinguistics and Reading,* 1973: III; *Reading without Nonsense,* 1979: IV.

Unlike Professor Leonard Bloomfield, who concentrated on language and didn't take the learners into consideration, Smith begins with the learners and their abilities and limitations. He is strongly opposed to phonics, and in all his books he gives reasons. We practiced readers have trouble seeing what learners have to contend with because, as he says, "Phonic rules look deceptively simple when you know what a word is in the first place." (II: p. 139)

Smith tells about studies with tachistoscopes which were made about a hundred years ago in Paris and Leipzig (and since then in many places). These studies have shown that the eyes do not glide smoothly along a line of print, but make jumping movements, picking up information only when they stop, i.e., make a fixation. It has been demonstrated that readers in one fixation can see some four to six unrelated letters, but if the letters are in words, they can pick up two words, e.g., F U R Y H O R S E S, which may consist of as many as a dozen letters. If words are in context, readers may gather in as many as five words, for example,

> EARLY FROSTS HARM THE CROPS
> KNIGHTS RODE HORSES INTO WAR

It is necessary to know and understand this information because what we see with each fixation and how much our memories are able to retain are factors which play a very important role in the process of reading. Smith discusses the limitations of the short-term memory. If the material we read is connected, we can carry over information and read smoothly with understanding. But if children are required to decode (sound out) words, they are dealing with letters, not meaningful ideas, and their short-term memories cannot provide necessary continuity. Dr. Smith uses telephone numbers to illustrate this point and shows how hard it is to retain them. I believe the numbers we 'carry over' when we add long columns of figures or when we multiply five or six digit figures are also good examples. Do you jot down the numbers that are carried over so that if you forget them you won't have to do the work all over again? If our short-term memories were more dependable and helpful, that would not be necessary. So it is with children learning to read and having to try to hold over earlier and meaningless letters.

"He (the learner) will not be able to read fast enough if he reads letter by letter—by the time he has reached the end of one word, he will have forgotten what he had read earlier—because he cannot hold more than four or five items in his short-term memory." (I: p. 94)

"Reliance on phonics methods will involve a reader in so much delay that his short-term memory will be overloaded and he will lose the sense of what he is reading." (III: p. 89)

"A reader who had to get enough visual information to identify every letter, or even every word, could not be able to read a passage for sense; the limitations of his own memory system would defeat him." (I: p. 220)

"Phonics is a cumbersome and unreliable system for any child, but especially for children finding it hard to make sense of reading." (IV: p. 158)

Professor Smith uses the following example. When children use phonics, they work out the letters they see in one fixation, perhaps E-L-E-P, and then their eyes jump to another fixation, where they see H-A-N-T. But short-term memories often fail to hold the earlier information, and many children cannot make sense of the whole word, E-L-E-P-H-A-N-T.

Of course Smith is fully cognizant of the unreliability of the spelling of our sounds by our letters; he says repeatedly that there are too many rules and too many exceptions for children to learn and apply. He wrote, for instance, as follows: "Attempting to decode isolated words to sound is unlikely to succeed because of the number, complexity, and unreliability of phonic generalizations." (II: p. 150) Several times he makes a point which I have not stressed sufficiently: How is the child supposed to know which, if any, phonic rule applies? "There is no rule that will tell a child whether a word should be regarded as an exception or not, and what is the point of remembering a lot of rules if you have to recognize a word before you can tell whether it follows the rules or not?" (IV: p. 55)

Smith illustrates this point with words beginning with the letters *ho-*. As he indicates, when using phonics, children can only be tentative when they see the letter *o;* in addition, when they are using phonics, they must read not only from left to right, but from right to left! (I have taken the liberty of adding to Smith's 11 examples.)

When reading aloud, we get the following sounds if we add to *ho-* : *a-* : hoarse /ô/, hoax /ō/; *e* : hoe /ō/; *i-* : hoist /oi/; *m-* : homogeneous /ō/, homogenize /ə/; *n-* : hone /ō/, honest /ŏ/, honey /ŭ/; *o-* : hook /ŏŏ/, hoot /ōō/; *ou-* : Houdini /ōō/; hour /ou/, Houston /yōō/; *p* : hop /ŏ/, hope /ō/; *r-* : horizon /ə/, horn /ô/; *s-* : host /ō/, hostage /ŏ/; *t* : hot /ŏ/, hotel /ō/; *w* : how /ou/.

Obviously, if children "sound out" words, they have to work out the sounds which the letter *o* and its helpers spell: eight sounds and both diphthongs, one of them spelled two ways. And note how the letter *h* spells silence in two words, *h*onest and *h*our. The use of *ho-* is not an isolated example; Smith might just have well used another combination, for instance, *bo-, co-, do-, fo-,* etc. Here are samples with the letters *no-* :

Support for the Method 215

nose /ō/, not /ŏ/; noise /oi/; nook /o͝o/, noon /o͞o/; nor /ô/; nothing /ŭ/; noun /ou/, nourish /û/; now /ou/. Children who are taught to expect a "long" vowel sound when a "silent" *e* follows a vowel and a consonant, as in "node," will be frustrated when they try "none," which is /nŭn/ and not /nōn/. The following words also illustrate Smith's point that sounding out leads to errors, despair, and defeat: "notable" is not *not* and *able;* "nothing" is not *no* and *thing;* "notice" is not *not* and *ice,* and "nowhere" is not *now* and *here.*

It would be quite wrong for me to give the impression that most of the ideas expressed in Smith"s books deal with phonics. On the contrary; he develops what you might consider an intriguing idea. He discusses the methods children use to learn to understand oral language, and he uses as one example how children learn to distinguish between cats and dogs. He asks his readers how they would help children make the distinction. He says that only by seeing a number of cats *and* a number of dogs can children establish criteria which enable them to distinguish between the two types of animals. He says the same procedure is followed when children learn to distinguish visually among other animals, faces, furniture, cars, houses, and so forth.

Indeed, he states unequivocally that children also learn words that way when they are learning to read, not by sounding out words, but by learning to recognize them, ". . . 'on sight.' We can recognize the thousands of words with which we are familiar because we have learned what they look like." (IV: p. 58)

His entire emphasis is on meaning. Initially, he calls for very easy reading matter, and he insists that all reading material be interesting so that it will get children involved. And he argues that "There is no essential difference between learning to read and reading. . . . Everyone must read in order to learn to read." (II: p. 9)

"Reading is easiest when it makes sense, and learning to read is also easiest when it makes sense." (II: p. 149)

Smith's constant theme is that "Children learn to read by reading." (IV: p. 69 and in all his books)

"The only way to learn to read is with confidence and enjoyment. . . . Anything that makes reading difficult or unpleasant or threatening makes learning to read more difficult." (III: p. 192)

"The only way to make learning to read easy is *to make reading easy.*" (III: p. 195)

Now if you are wondering how children are to start to learn without any phonics instruction, Smith has this answer: Somebody will read the earliest books for and with children: "If the question arises how children can be expected to read by reading before they have learned to read, the answer is very simple. At the beginning—and at any other time when it is necessary—the reading has to be done for the children. Before children acquire competence in reading, everything will have to be read to them." (II: p. 180)

Children needing help will have "some or all of the book they are expected to read read for them first of all." (IV: p. 35)

"The only way children can become familiar with written language, before they can extend their knowledge by reading to themselves, is by being read to. . . . It is important to read to children, but even more important to read *with* them." (IV: p. 144)

Finally, I offer this quotation because I believe the Simultaneous Reading and Listening Method will offer far more repetition than any other method possibly can: "Feedback is the most important kind of information that a child can receive in any learning situation. . . . Feedback should be given all the time." (I: p. 229)

There are other writers who have expressed thoughts similar to those you have read in this chapter, but I believe I have made my point: There are educators who seem to agree with my proposal to develop a more efficient way to teach reading—namely, by having learners listen as they read and in that way learn what thousands of words look like.

CHAPTER 25

The Direct Method

There is a very good reason why the general reading public believes (a) there was a time when all children learned to read; (b) teachers are to blame for illiteracy; and (c) phonics is the cure-all, the panacea. The reading public is fed a never-ceasing diet of articles and books in which the writers tell how all children once learned to read easily and quickly. And one of two reasons is advanced: Either the teachers then were more competent or they used the only logical teaching method, phonics. Often both "reasons" are given.

The writers never say the faulty writing system is to blame. They see the symptoms and fail to look for the real cause. The same cause was present in the past, and the same symptoms were present 50, 100, and 150 years ago.

Here are sample titles of articles and books that have appeared in recent years:

1. "23 Million Incompetent Americans"
2. "Everyday Skills Lacking for 20% of U.S. Adults"
3. "Johnny's Parents Can't Read Either"
4. "High Schoolers Read Like Babies"
5. "Shocking Los Angeles Report: Students Can't Read"
6. "Shocking Reading Levels"
7. *Programmed Illiteracy in Our Schools*
8. *The New Illiterates*
9. "Are We Becoming a Nation of Illiterates?"
10. *Our Children's Crippled Future*

Before free-lance journalists 'enlighten' their readers with their authoritative pronouncements on the teaching of reading, don't you think they ought to read a minimum of one or two books on the history of the subject, books written by genuine authorities? Too many of them do not. I'd be happy to provide them with twenty or thirty titles. Here are two books in which the authors discuss at length the various methods used in the past in efforts to improve reading instruction: Mitford M. Matthews, *Teaching to Read (Historically Considered);* and Edmund Burke Huey, *The Psychology and Pedagogy of Reading.* The former book is a fairly recent one; the latter appeared in 1908 and was reprinted in 1968. Huey's book is amazingly up-to-date; he discusses reading problems as though he were writing today.

The need to get proper historical background information before writing articles or books may be exemplified by two gross errors found in an article by Frank E. Armbruster, which appeared in the January, 1978, issue of the *Reader's Digest.* The article bears the title, "Why American Education Is Failing." The *Digest* editors introduced the article as follows: "It's time, says the author, to return to traditional teaching that is tried and true." Armbruster's major point was that over the years the classes have become smaller and smaller and at the same time results have become worse and worse. He tells how in classes of eighty and ninety at the beginning of the century "pupils were taught to read and write."

That sounds good, and we want to believe Armbruster, but with his speculation he is perpetuating a myth. As I have pointed out (Chapter 1), census figures prove him wrong. Moreover, if he'd read any one of a number of books written by educators, he wouldn't make such a false assertion. His assumption is that all eighty or ninety in the classes learned to read. Preposterous. It was precisely because so many children failed to learn that in 1898 John Dewey recommended that all reading instruction be postponed until children were at least eight years old.

Now there may have been as many as eighty or ninety in some classrooms at the beginning of the century, but they were the exception and not the rule. My own elementary school was built then, and when I attended it, no room could hold more than thirty to thirty-five pupils. In 1910, when I was in first grade, children filled the room. But when I reached eighth grade, there were only twenty-one children left in the class; the others had dropped out. At that time there was a demand for unskilled labor; and when someone left school, little notice was taken. After all, families needed money. In general, the better pupils were the ones who continued. Incidentally, at that time, out of a hundred children who entered first grade, only seven went on to high school.

Mr. Armbruster informs us further that in the Great Depression "Pupils who couldn't read by the seventh grade were virtually unknown." I defy him to document such a statement. I unequivocally label such a claim as "wild speculation." It is not based on facts. In World War II the Armed Services discovered hundreds of thousands of men who could not read, and most of them were in school during the Depression.

The Direct Method

It is necessary for me to inject personal experiences again. You may remember how I told about my teaching duties in a community college beginning in 1946. By sheer coincidence young people of the very age Armbruster was writing about came to my classes six years after the Depression ended. He said virtually every one learned to read. Well, they must have forgotten how, because when they became freshmen in college a goodly number—a worrisome number—weren't able to read on ninth-grade level, and many not on sixth-grade level.

But I owe you information that can be documented. Writing in *Harper's* in January, 1946, an educator blamed reading failures on the children and their lack of native ability to learn. What he had to say is in direct conflict with Armbruster's claim that almost all pupils in seventh grade at that time were able to read. The author, George H. Henry, was a high school principal, and his figures were based on the "high school rolls of 1940," the last year of the Great Depression. This is what he had to say:

> By testing any graduating class of any high school in the country, the skeptic can see for himself what is an old story for teachers: that a third of the high school cannot read on fifth-grade level . . . Of the six and two-thirds million on high school rolls . . . easily two and one-half million belong to this group. This nonverbal group comprises rich and poor alike.

Although we can argue with Mr. Henry about his statement concerning *any* high school, there is reason to believe his figures were essentially correct. This would mean that in 1940 some high schools had more than a third of its students reading below fifth grade level!

Isn't it unfortunate that Mr. Henry didn't have anything to say about our difficult writing system? Instead, he stated: "The right to learn does not seem to carry with it the ability to learn." It was his conclusion that "The child cannot do the work . . . He is a member of the slow-reading group." His thesis was that teachers and principals should be honest and tell parents their children were unable to do the work instead of saying they could do it if they would only apply themselves.

It is regrettable, I must repeat, that most English language specialists have been content to restrict their writing largely to their esoteric monographs and scholarly books. They should have given the reading public the facts, repeatedly publishing them in widely read newspapers and magazines. And, as I have said, educators are not blameless. They should have made it generally known that our written language is the basic reason for most failures, and, naturally, it has caused proportionately just as many failures in the past as it does today. They should have dug back into books and articles of fifty, sixty, and more years ago and proclaimed again and again this theme: Our written language is flawed and responsible for most of our reading failures. I say the message must be told repeatedly because most people don't want to believe and will forget as fast as they can. Language experts and educators should accept the challenge now and make believers of readers.

Obviously Mr. Armbruster didn't know that in the past 150 years a great many methods have been used in never completely successful efforts to teach reading. Huey and Wilma Miller (*Elementary English Today*, 1972) tell how the word method (sometimes called the "look-say" method) held sway for some 40 to 45 years in the latter part of the nineteenth century, to be replaced by various phonics approaches. But because they were not as successful as had been hoped, the pendulum swung back to the whole word method. Irving Adler in *What We Want of Our Schools* (1957) wrote, "The present method was adopted because there *was* a reading problem under the old methods. The fact that the present method has created new problems should not lead us to ignore the weaknesses of the old methods." (p. 207)

Mathews devoted many pages to Horace Mann. In the 1840s Mann made a study and analysis of phonic and whole word methods. He called attention to the fact that the vowels represent too many sounds, "So that according to the doctrine of chance, it will happen only once in five or six times that he (the child) will be correct (using phonics and sounding out letters)." He also showed how consonant spellings are faulty and, making sure that everybody got the point, he again told of the poor chances a child would have sounding out letters. (*Teaching to Read,* p. 79)

Praising the whole word method, Mann said the advantages were many: "1. Nothing has to be untaught which has once been well taught. 2. What is to be learned is affiliated to what is already known (the unknown tied to the known). 3. The course of the pupils is constantly progressive. 4. The acquisition of the language becomes an intelligible process." He then offered a reason for not using phonics: "The alphabet . . . is wholly foreign to a child's existing knowledge." Finally, he made a bold statement: "I do not see why a child should not learn to read as easily as he learns to talk, if taught in a similar manner." (pages 79, 80) (Isn't that what our proposed SR&LM hopes to achieve?— Well, to approach.)

Professor Mathews quotes a number of nineteenth century educators; and here are thoughts of two of them. Both were stout defenders of the word method. Thomas H. Palmer described phonics as "tiresome drudgery," and he was sure the children's bodies alone were present in the classroom, while their minds were "far distant." (p. 68) He called the whole word approach "the method of nature," saying, "She (nature) always proceeds from the general to the specific. We know a tree and

The Direct Method

can name it long before we become acquainted with its constituents, the leaves, the limbs, trunk, and root . . . a man before his parts, the head, neck, body, limbs, hands . . . and, finally, we have formed a long vocabulary, before we know anything of syllables or letters." (p. 69) In this statement he anticipated Gestalt psychologists, who say we begin with the whole rather than working up from specific elements.

The second educator was the Reverend Cyrus Pierce: "Children begin to *talk* with words and why should they not begin to *read* with words. It is nature's way." (p. 71)

Before leaving Mathew's book, I wish to offer further proof that not all children learned to read during the Depression. At the same time, we see how literacy has been a problem in all English-speaking countries. Speaking about Great Britain, Mathews wrote, "During the war (II) the military authorities in the selection procedures they used to secure the type of personnel needed for particular assignments discovered a surprisingly large number of men who either could not read at all or who read too poorly for practical purposes; that is, they were 'functional illiterates.' The findings at this time in the British Services closely paralleled what had been found to be the case among American soldiers. Even the percentages—twenty-five or thirty percent—were virtually the same." (p. 176)

Speaking before Parliament a few years after the war ended, Sir James Pitman said, "The present (reading) results are so deplorable that this House and the Minister must take notice of them. Some 400,000 to 500,000 five-year-olds begin their schooling every year and some 120,000 to 150,000 are destined to come out of the school system at the other end unable to read properly.

"The same sort of figures happen in Australia and America. It seems to be connected particularly with the English-speaking world, and it is, therefore, important that, since we know there is something wrong somewhere, in our insistence that we do something." (p. 177)

As you have guessed, I am fortifying my case, showing how urgent it is for us to take courageous steps to eliminate as much illiteracy as possible.

Now we turn to Huey's book. It is no wonder that it was reprinted, for it is a valuable source of information. Huey offers not only an excellent survey of reading methods from the earliest days, but he describes the actual state of reading instruction at his time (1908). We get the feeling that he was describing current conditions. So many methods have been tried and found wanting; it's all been done before, and critics have naturally never been satisfied. For instance, "A survey of the views of some of our foremost and soundest educators reveals the fact that the men of our time (1900) who are most competent to judge are profoundly dissatisfied with the reading as it is now carried on in the elementary school." (p. 301) (Mr. Armbruster, please take note!)

Huey devotes considerable space to Horace Mann and John Dewey. Professor Dewey was distressed with the slow progress of young children learning to read. He said, "One can pick out the children who learned to read at home. They read naturally." (p. 305) Huey agreed: "The secret of it all lies in parents' reading aloud to and with the child." (p. 332)

Huey continues: "The best way to get a reading vocabulary is just the way a child gets his spoken vocabulary, by having new words keep coming in a context environment that is familiar and interesting." (p. 348) It is as if he anticipated the Simultaneous Reading and Listening Method: "It is wise that reading should be rather rapid from the first,— that is, that the particular sentences should be taught at the child's ordinary rate of thinking." (p. 350)

Then he came up with this revolutionary thought: "By silently reading meanings from the first day of reading, and by practice in getting meaning from the page at the naturally rapid rate at which meanings come from situations in actual life, the rate of reading and of thinking will grow with the pupil's growth and with his power to assimilate what is read." (p. 359)

How in the world could learners get that type of reading instruction in the classroom? Huey had something else in mind: "The home is the natural place for learning to read." (p. 379)

As we all know, the idea of reading aloud to children while they are following what is being read to them has been done literally millions of times. It has been done in countless homes and numberless times in classrooms at school. But in school, teachers have worked under a severe handicap; while they were reading at a rate satisfactory and beneficial to the middle third of the children, the rate was much too slow for the fastest, who were bored and became disinterested; and it was much too fast for the slowest third, who were frustrated and left so far behind that the reading was a waste of time. That was, no doubt, the genesis of the three groups which have been used in so many classrooms. But the teacher could be in only one place at a time.

In this age of electronics children can read while they are listening to what they are reading. Divided into small groups, and this is important, into groups of varying sizes, children can listen to material tailored to their ability and learn at a rate consistent with their reading level, which is clearly impossible in the whole class situation.

In varying degrees the proposed method has been used in millions of homes. Many years ago, Mrs. Sharp and I had an eager, alert, attentive, and appreciative daughter who loved to be read to. As you would

The Direct Method

surmise, we read certain stories and books to her many times, and she memorized parts or all of them. Then, on her own, when she was alone, she would "read" them to herself, usually aloud, but sometimes silently. We don't know when she started to associate the spoken symbols with the printed word symbols, although we were aware of her looking more and more frequently to our eyes to see where they were directed when either her mother or I was reading to her. But we knew she had started to watch the print carefully. When in her eagerness to learn what happened next in the story we were reading to her, she started to turn the pages for us, we realized that she was actually learning to read. We never showed her the relationships between letters and sounds. Admittedly, she was a quick and an apt learner; she had read independently more than a hundred children's books before she started to school. Ever since, she has been a superior reader.

No, she was not on the Ichabod-Johnny level, but she was not given the basic help which all children should receive under an eclectic method. And of course such a happening is not an isolated instance or it would not be worth reporting. I have been told any number of times how it has been duplicated here, and I have read how it has succeeded in England. I have also been told how it has often taken place in Dutch and German homes, where it would be easier to accomplish. That is how so many Finnish children learn to read before they go to school. The idea is that children can learn to read by a word (or sentence) method. No doubt many of you readers have enjoyed the experience or know someone who has.

No, I am NOT advocating that parents make a conscious effort to teach their children to read. Undoubtedly there is great value to their reading to their children, but reading authorities caution parents against trying to teach reading because they are emotionally involved, they expect too much of their children, they are untrained, and they can easily confuse children. I am saying, however, that it is possible for children to learn words without breaking them down into their component parts. Think of the following words, some of which many children learn as words, not through a knowledge of sounding them out:

STOP	GO	WAIT	WALK	DON'T	GO
ON	OFF	MEN	WOMEN	IN	OUT
UP	DOWN	HOT	COLD	LOUD	SOFT
PUSH	PULL	TOP	BOTTOM	NO	SMOKING
SPEED	LIMIT	BUS	STOP	SLOW	CURVE

Most children aren't concerned about letters or the relationships between letters and sounds. To them, the word STOP and a red light mean the same thing. It is a longer word than GO, which has the same symbolic significance as a green light. It is far beyond the knowledge of most youngsters to know that the *i* in WAIT is a part of a conventional spelling and not a phonetic spelling, and they couldn't care less that the *l* in WALK stands for nothing.

A good many children have learned other isolated words; some may recognize and even be able to print their given names and sometimes their surnames, or the name of a parent; and some may know the name of the street on which they live and perhaps a cereal or two. On the toaster they may learn the words "light" and "dark," and on the TV set they may pick up different words, such as "volume," "color," "contrast," "bright," and "picture." They may learn the names of programs, such as "Sesame Street," and in the newspapers or weekly TV guides they may learn the names of other programs.

Generally they haven't learned the words on a letter-by-letter basis. Instead, they have learned them by their configuration, that is, shape, size, form, just as we recognize, at least in the beginning, certain types of animals, such as dogs, cats, squirrels, sheep, cows, horses, pigs, etc. Clearly, we can and do learn by wholes, and children can learn words by wholes.

It is not easy to disassociate ourselves from the thought that learners don't have to start with letters. We are inclined to think of the groups of printed letters as being the things they represent. We can see words; they are concrete, tangible, and very real. But if we consider five groups of letters which are, by chance, words in two languages, then we will be on our way to accepting the fact that they are truly only symbols. Identical in writing, they have quite different meanings; they are symbols to English-speaking people and symbols to German-speaking people, but with different meanings. The column at the left contains the common symbols. Naturally the explanations are also nothing but symbols, known to you because you learned them, but meaningless to a German who knows no English:

Rat: to us is a *rodent;* to Germans it is *advice, counsel*
Rot: to us means *to decay;* to Germans it is a color, *red*
Kind: to us, as a noun, means a *sort,* and as an adjective, *gentle;* to Germans it means *child* (Cf. *Kind*ergarten)
Mist: to us is *spray,* often associated with waterfalls and rainbows, and usually a pleasant word; to Germans the association is less pleasant; it means *manure*
Tot: an English-speaking adult might wish it were possible to be a little *tot* /tŏt/; a German would not like to be a little *tot* /tōt/, which is quite impossible, because *tot* means *dead*

The Direct Method

No, this is not intended to be a lesson in German. It is nothing but an effort to make the point: words are symbols; they become meaningful to us only when we learn and understand them.

We see, therefore, that the primary goal is to have our learners be able to read words; and if we can teach children to read most efficiently and pleasantly by combining reading with hearing, we are taking a shortcut and using a direct method.

CHAPTER 26

What Are the Alternatives?

"Prove all things; hold fast that which is good."
(I Thessalonians, v. 21)

When I have outlined my proposed supplementary method to teachers, parents, and others, instead of considering the positive possibilities, they have, almost without exception, looked for every possible reason why it should NOT be tried out. These protests I have heard most often:

A. THE METHOD

    (1) is illogical;
    (2) has never been tried;
    (3) is too unconventional and impractical (too visionary);
    (4) is too complicated;
    (5) hasn't the support of authorities;
    (6) would have been tried a long time ago if it is any good;
    (7) would require too much electronic equipment;
    (8) would be too costly.

B. CHILDREN

    (1) would get confused if they didn't learn each word as they went along;
    (2) would just listen and not even try to follow the text with their eyes;
    (3) would get all mixed up and look at wrong words, even wrong lines;
    (4) would change channels and listen to wrong tapes.

In addition, some skeptics have said that if the method should be successful, the gap between the best and the poorest learners would widen and be even greater than it is now because the best learners would probably benefit more than the poorest ones. Well, I do indeed believe

What Are the Alternatives?

all pupils would profit, but surely we should welcome the improvement in learning by the upper half of the children. Isn't the goal of teaching to bring *all* learners up to the highest level of their potential? Shouldn't we rejoice if all children's reading scores are raised? Wouldn't we have good reason to celebrate? We know for a fact that each year under all methods of instruction hundreds of thousands of children in English-speaking countries have been, and still are, destined to be reading failures or near failures.

We will take for granted that the Simultaneous Reading and Listening Method will help good readers become better readers. And let us suppose that on a scale of 0 to 100 children who, with current instructional methods have scores of, say, 60, would raise their scores to around 80. That would be an improvement of one third, or 33.3 percent. That kind of improvement would surely justify the expense and the planning, preparation, and work entailed in the development and use of the method.

Now if the combined reading and listening program were to help children who currently have reading scores of 5 so that they would also increase their scores by 20 points, then their scores would be 25, and there would be real cause for rejoicing. Scoffers might say they still weren't very good readers. But the improvement from 5 to 25 would be 400 percent! And that progress would have great significance in the lives of all those individuals. The improvement points at the bottom represent the primary reason for the program in the first place.

In reality, I see much more improvement than from five to twenty-five for great numbers. I suggested earlier that I believe learning to read may be compared with learning to ride a bicycle. The major problem is to keep one's balance. This is something quite a few learners cannot do at the outset when there is no or very little forward movement. But once riders are able to move faster than, say, two or three miles per hour, they can much more easily maintain their balance; then, to move up to six and eight miles per hour is not a problem because they have momentum. When our readers can read well enough so that they can read for ideas, they will also be on their way; they will also have the necessary momentum. I'm quite sure Professor Frank Smith, whom I quoted at length in a recent chapter, would agree with me.

If children can learn to read the 2,000 most frequently used words, they can learn the next 2,000 words with much less effort and in less time, and that will be decisive. In my opinion, the crux of the problem is in teaching the slower learners the first 2,000 words. Those first 2,000 words represent more than 90 percent of the words on most pages. You might say educators must be ineffective if they can't teach children to read those words in three years. That would be only four words a day (170 days a year times 3 equals 510 days, and 4 times 510 is 2,040.)

But bear in mind that a high proportion of those words are spelled illogically and are, therefore, difficult to remember. We recall that there are great individual differences, and many pupils have little linguistic ability and very poor memories for such things as words and spelling. If you teach words in isolation, you aren't teaching reading; and when you reach the hundredth word, poorer learners will have forgotten many, perhaps a quarter, perhaps half, of the first fifty.

We must give children interesting reading matter that will capture their attention and hold their interest, and we must teach those most essential words intelligently until Ichabod and Johnny recognize and remember almost every one. In reading materials we must establish likable characters, people the children will identify with, and present them in recognizable situations so children will want to read on. Then we'll find a whole lot of children with scores of 40 and 50 who otherwise would have become marginal readers or remained unable to read.

My skeptics have not had the advantage you readers of this book have. You have seen some 3,000 examples of words that are not spelled phonetically and recognize those aberrations are present in a majority of our words. You also read how our words became such enigmas. Many doubters assume that it is immeasurably easier and more sensible to teach the sounds our 26 letters spell than to teach hundreds and even thousands of words. They take for granted that most letters almost always spell sounds consistently and, therefore, children ought to be able to read just about all words after a few months of instruction. That would indeed be true if each letter spelled a single sound and if each sound were spelled one way. If that were true, we wouldn't have so many second-class citizens or have to spend billions of dollars each year trying to teach the most difficult of all alphabetic languages.

Please mark this well. I am repeating myself, but there must be no misunderstanding. Of course it would be unwise not to teach the sounds our letters spell most often. But this is not an either-or, not an all-or-nothing, situation. We can have the best of two worlds; we must combine the two approaches, with phonics being introduced gradually and at the proper time, that is, when pupils are ready and able to deal with abstractions that are new to them—and unreliable. Because some 70 percent (or possibly 65 or even 80 percent, depending on the page) of our *letters* on a page spell the sounds they should represent, then we'd be foolish not to teach letter-sound relationships. But because there are faulty sound-word relationships in some 80 percent of the *words* on a page—and it is words we read, not letters—then it follows that words must be taught as effectively as possible. Several researchers have concluded that the introduction of phonics ought to be postponed at least to the end of the first year; and a number believe it should be introduced much later, as I will soon report.

What Are the Alternatives?

It goes without saying that the reading and listening program will not start without considerable preparation in the classroom. Initially, neither electronic equipment nor books will be used. Perhaps the method will work out something like this. The publishing company whose books have been adopted will provide filmstrips or about two dozen wall charts (or a choice) to be used for introductory practice. (I'll assume wall charts because filmstrips take more time to display.) On two or three of the charts will be words which most children already recognize, such as those suggested in the preceding chapter. Then on perhaps a half dozen charts will be well-known nursery rhymes; and on another half dozen will be well-known songs (which will be spoken, rather than sung, at least not sung later when training with earphones starts). And on a third group of perhaps six charts will be lines taken from well-known stories, such as "The Three Little Pigs," "Little Red Riding Hood," or more modern ones. Possibly a story might be distributed over two or three charts.

A good beginning is an absolute necessity. Using the charts, teachers will use pointers in the same manner as the bouncing ball is used in a sing-along. They will say the words as they indicate them on the chart, not working on letters at all, but on whole words. Thus, they might underline or circle the words, often pointing out differences in configurations. After they have read all the words on a chart three or four times, they might have all pupils repeat each word in unison after them. Then they may point to two words, say them aloud, and have the class repeat them. Individual children should not be called on in this exercise. All pupils must feel comfortable and secure and enter into the group action. Teachers will stop when interest begins to lag.

Of course old material will be repeated in each session, and there would be two, three, or even four short "reading" sessions each day. It will take quite a few days to introduce all the material on the charts. Then after a period of from two weeks to two months, a tape recorder or cassette (I assume cassette playbacks will be used) will be brought into the classroom, and children will be told that the early tape periods will all be review periods. Children will not yet have headsets; they will hear the voice(s) through the speaker of the cassette. Again, teachers will use charts and pointers and follow the voice(s) from the cassette.

After the children have heard all of the material printed on the charts through the cassette speaker, books will be issued. In them on the first pages children will find the same material they have seen on the charts, and again they will listen to the cassette. After they have completed this operation, headsets will be used; and again the familiar materials will be read to them while they follow in their books.

Haste makes waste. But from this point on progress will be faster for many pupils, who will be ready to move on to new material. Of course in practice other plans or ideas may prove to be more effective or feasible, but I must stress this point: The first few weeks will be the crucial period in children's school lives—or, for that matter, in their entire lives.

Authors of the books must give their readers all possible help to assist them in matching correctly the spoken words with their printed counterparts. Although the writers will definitely not be as severely restricted as writers of Basal series readers are, they must not be reckless or extravagant in introducing new words. Editors and authors will compile a master list of all the words on the charts, and with these words as a reservoir they may tell other well-known stories or offer nursery rhymes or songs. New words will be interspersed, as they naturally would be, but the known words will serve as tracks or a road that children will know, and they will be sure they are proceeding in the right direction.

But even this assistance might not prove sufficient for slower and less capable learners. Surely the minds of good teachers and authors and editors will come up with other thoughts and plans. Perhaps in the first book or two (or three) it might be found necessary to use colors. I do NOT mean that colors would be used as with the teaching method, Words in Color. Rather, the lines of the early books may be printed in various colors, e.g., the first in black, the second in green, the third in blue, and so on. Then when the reader on the tape comes to the end of a line and is moving to the next line, he or she might say in a soft voice, "green line" or simply "green." A chime might do the job. But when children have learned a nucleus of words, there really should not be any problem.

The early books should have fairly large print, as in present series, but very soon small print and longer lines can be used. And when the reading matter leaves the familiar areas of well-known stories and rhymes and songs, the danger of children being unable to follow will be slight because not more than three to five new words will be found in a hundred running words. The greater the number of known words, the less likely it will be that children will associate words falsely. After a nucleus of 200 to 300 words has been reached, the task for the writers will be smoother and less arduous. An advantage is that if a word is needed only once or twice in a selection, it need not be used in following selections. Children will NOT be expected to learn every word as they move along. As far as that goes, it may be that not every child will learn every word on the charts.

With the generally accepted set notion that children must learn every word as they go along, some readers, especially some teachers, may question the wisdom of such a procedure. But I suggest that readers who subscribe to that idea should take a red felt pen in hand and circle in

What Are the Alternatives?

their reading for a week all words which they come to and cannot define. If they read the *Atlantic Monthly, Harper's, Saturday Review,* the *New Yorker, Sports Illustrated,* and a weekly newsmagazine, they will conclude that we are all in the same boat.

Besides, the theory that all children must learn every single word as it is introduced runs contrary to nature and common sense. We do not all learn at the same speed, and we do not all learn the same things at the same time. Certainly we did not and we do not learn words aurally that way. If you have had the pleasure of watching children learn to talk, you have observed how they suddenly catch on to a word, one they may be hearing for the first time or may have heard ten or a hundred times.

No matter what method of teaching is used, teachers have the problem of individual differences in children. In this program there will be some children who will come to school knowing most of the words on the first chart, perhaps all of them, and some won't know ten of them. There are children who are slow to learn to understand the spoken language and to talk, but sooner or later they learn to the extent it is necessary. Why, then, should we assume all children must learn to read at the same speed? The SR&LM enjoys the great advantage of allowing faster children to move faster and for slower children to catch up, even if it takes more time. Under current methods the slower learners have no hope.

In an ideal situation, there will be a room set aside in each elementary school for the SR&LM program. In the front of the room there will be five or six playback cassettes placed on shelves at table height (for ease of operation by the aide) in separate lockers. Tapes will be on shelves above and below the cassette players. Children will not, must not, have access to the tapes or to the cassette players. The control panel, in a separate locker, will enable the aide to change channels for any particular child without changing the seating location of the child. The machines will be operated exclusively by an aide or a paraprofessional or, if absolutely necessary, by teachers. This type of activity does not require much training or any knowledge of electronics, such as circuitry. Scheduling will allow classes to work in the room as needed. All classes will use it on an assigned basis only.

Now if you visualize this room to be the center of chaos and confusion, and if you imagine the din of a sheet metal factory, you are in for a pleasant surprise. The atmosphere of the room will be one of serious purpose, and the entire project will provide an excellent environment for unrivaled, complete attention. Children will be seated at assigned places at tables; and, ideally, they will be facing into carrels, that is, semi-booths. To either side will be bare blank walls, and in front of the children will be only blank boards and their books. They will put on headsets, open their books, and read what they hear. They will read silently at all times. When not in use, the earphones will be hung on a hook on a carrel wall to the side. Children will *not* be able to change channels or to listen to tapes other than the ones assigned to them. The carrels will have no ceilings, so that separate lighting will not be necessary. The walls will be high enough to discourage children from peering over them; and because the carrels will have no ceilings, aides (or teachers) will be able to keep an eye on the children to see they are at work. In this arrangement outside distractions will be reduced to a minimum. There will be no stage for a class clown, and here children will learn to concentrate.

For the schools the aim will be the teaching of reading; but children will look upon the reading and listening experience as a means to an end: to enjoy what they read (and hear), to live new experiences vicariously, and to gain information. Isn't that what reading is all about?

If there is a separate room for the program and aides are used, teachers can work regularly with one group in the usual classroom, offering special help needed on various levels, the groups rotating, as you would expect.

Critics who wonder if children will just listen and not try to read must realize that under present conditions vast numbers of children are inattentive and do not follow the instruction. But surely teachers could and would devise ways to motivate children to want to capitalize on an opportunity to learn to read in the easiest and pleasantest way, to work actively on the process of matching sight with sound. It might be advisable, for example, early in the program when the cassette unit is still in the regular classroom as a foretaste of things to come to let the pupils hear an especially interesting and entertaining tape that will be used later as part of the regular program. On that one occasion children would simply listen and be entertained; and if the recording is really fascinating, children will have an incentive to do the matching work. (Note I did not say "play the matching game." Learning to read must be an active and serious process.)

If a room can be set aside for the reading and listening program, but there aren't sufficient funds to develop the plan for a control panel and channels, which would allow unlimited flexibility, and if there isn't enough money to provide tables with carrels, the separate room would still have considerable merit. Good habits are invaluable, and having one definite place to go to achieve the greatest goal in the elementary school, the ability to read—or to improve one's ability—would serve as an aid to promote learning. There could still be as many as six groups, one at each end of the room and two groups at each side wall. To decrease distractions, children would not face toward the center, but toward the walls. There are also nonteaching advantages. The physical problems would be fewer if all cassette players and tapes were centralized. Cleaning, maintenance, and security problems would be fewer and more easily taken care of. Then, too, there would be fewer "stray" cassette tapes.

Shrinking enrollments may make it possible to set aside a room for the all-important task of teaching reading. But if ideal conditions cannot be met, the program could and should still go on. Cassette recorders could be placed on carts (with headsets hung on hooks in front and at the ends), and the carts could be rolled from room to room. Two or three cassettes could be placed on each large cart, possibly five to six feet long. With a low budget, it might be necessary to get along with one cart and only three operable cassettes. In that event, classes could still be divided into four or six groups, two or three working on the reading and listening tapes at the back of the room, with their chairs facing the rear, where possible, and the other children in the class could be working with the teacher in front. Naturally that arrangement would not be ideal, but we must teach more children to read.

These statements and this description cover most of the objections, but I have not touched upon what might well be the greatest one, the cost. Let's see how much money has been spent in the past. According to a Rand Corporation report (*San Francisco Chronicle,* August 29, 1978), the U.S. government between 1966 and 1978 poured 80 billion dollars into public education, of which a considerable portion went to an unsuccessful effort to eliminate illiteracy. Furthermore, local and state governments have expended many additional billions. But still we are left with millions of nonreaders and many other millions of marginal readers.

Currently, the federal government is budgeted to spend ten billion dollars a year for a five-year period on public education. Now I ask, what proof is there of any improvement in reading? Since none has been seen in the past, it behooves us to look for new ways to teach an exceedingly difficult skill, reading. I repeat: What guarantee do we have that there will be any change if we don't experiment? Money used to try out the Simultaneous Reading and Listening Method could be the best investment ever made in elementary education.

In fairness, I will point out that there would be many additional costs:

1. Far more books will be needed because pupils will read incredibly more than with any other method.

2. An aide or paraprofessional for each school (but not for each room) should definitely be employed to take care of the mechanics, and this would be true whether the program operated in a separate room or in regular classrooms. Teachers can be much better used, for their time is too valuable to devote to this routine operation. The aides would not require credentials or special training, and their work could be taught to them easily and quickly.

3. Each elementary school would need a minimum of four cassette players, one of which would be held in reserve to use when one of the other three becomes inoperable. Ideally, in the room set aside for the program there should be seven. The many tapes—and I do mean many—would be supplied by the publishers, but in the final analysis, school districts would have to pay for them, for their cost would be included in the price of the books. And tapes would be expensive. Authors would have to be compensated for writing many times as much reading matter as is found in current books, and all tapes would have to be made with the utmost care. Readers (speakers) would have to be carefully chosen; they must be people with clear, distinct, and pleasant (but not saccharine) voices who could and would read at proper speeds, with vivacity and interest in their voices. Some tapes would require two or three voices to fit into situations in the stories; they would give variety and an added spark to the reading material. It goes without saying that the tapes themselves would have to be of high quality.

4. There would have to be a minimum of 20, but preferably 40, headsets, say 1.3 per child, the extra ones to be used as replacements when children drop one or one is broken and needs repair.

5. In the separate room there would be the initial expenditure for the building of closets and for the installation of six channels and the necessary control panel. Cupboards (closets) for cassette recorders and shelves to hold tapes would be needed in any event, as would outlet plugs for every child expected to be listening at any one time. Wall outlet plugs here or in each classroom would obviously be needed. Carrels on the tables would be of importance in the program, but they need not be expensive ones.

6. Maintenance costs must be considered: headsets would have to be cleaned (and teachers would not be expected to use their time doing that work); and broken and badly twisted cords would have to be replaced. We must take into consideration additional insurance that would be required against burglary and vandalism.

But now comes the good news:

1. Schools would begin the program only on the first grade level in the first year.

2. After the first book or two, for which there would have to be a copy for each child, only a half or a third as many copies of any one book would have to be purchased because faster learners would move ahead and be using, say, book four or five while the slower ones would still be using book two or three.

3. Books need not be of the same quality as current books. Fewer pictures would be needed because word pictures will replace visual ones; and after the second or third book, margins at the top, bottom, and sides could be reduced substantially, and more and longer lines would be printed

on each page. Even the print would become smaller as children begin to get more interested and involved in what they are reading.

4. Tapes will last a long time, and their fidelity will remain good for many years. Very few replacements would be needed, and surely school districts would be given permission to make a limited number of copies as replacements.

No lay critics of my plan have foreseen the greatest problem that will confront teachers when they put the new method into operation. It is the fact that not all children are equally ready to start to learn. Most lay people are inclined to scoff when educators speak of "reading readiness." Nevertheless, it is true that whereas a few children can already read when they first go to school as well as the average child can after three or four (or more) months of training, there are at the other end of the scale children who simply aren't ready to cope with either letters as symbols for sounds, or printed words as symbols of spoken words.

Does this mean the upper 40 to 75 percent of the children will be held back and denied for many months the opportunity to begin to learn the proposed efficient way? No, we can't accept that. We will simply have to come up with ways and means to meet the problem. In schools where there are two or more first-grade classes, teachers could cooperate and one could initiate the children who are ready into the supplementary SR&LM program, while the second teacher works with other children on a reading readiness program. In schools where there is only one class of first graders, an aide could work with the children who aren't ready to learn to read, while the teacher was starting the other children off on the new program. I may be overly optimistic, but I imagine the new program might be much more natural and so much easier that there would be very few children who wouldn't profit right from the beginning.

The motivation will come, I feel sure, from the children themselves because there will be a tremendous incentive to get ready fast since the slower children will want to be engaged in the same activity as their peers. This would be doubly true if the program were to be conducted in a special room. While I see the question of varying degrees of reading readiness to be a major problem and one which educators will have to meet and solve, still I look upon the new program as being a more natural approach than the methods used in the past. We must again remember how children begin to understand oral language. We do not wait to talk to children until they are ready to understand. Learning oral language is a slow, continuing process; and learning to read is also a slow, gradual, and continuing process. What I am trying to say is this: Admittedly, there surely is such a state as not being ready to learn to read, but if the simultaneous reading and listening process is introduced exceedingly carefully and slowly, and if the learners do not feel frightening pressure, the method will surely reduce the time taken to help children to be ready to learn to read.

The details of the method after ten or twenty years may be quite different from my description, and some of them I might not recognize if I were to see them—which will be quite impossible in twenty years, unless a life-stretcher or extender is invented very soon.

There remains a question. At what grade level do I think the program should stop? Let me first say the program is needed in the first three years, as most people would agree if they believed it should be started in the first grade. But it is urgently needed in the fourth grade, when a variety of subjects is introduced, and new words and new concepts are thrown at them from all sides. A great many children who are not very good readers at the end of the third grade fall far behind in the fourth. The help of the SR&LM program could enable them to keep abreast.

In addition, if you remember the chapters on "The Price We Pay," you know how much more difficult it is for our children to develop adequate vocabularies than it is for children speaking other languages. Thus, if the program is an intelligent one, it would benefit all learners to get the most efficient instruction we can provide them. I do not know how long the program should last, but as of now I think it would be highly profitable to offer it through the sixth grade at least, but it wouldn't have to be daily after the fourth grade; possibly two days a week would be enough. Much would depend upon publishers' willingness to tape certain of their books beyond primary grades.

Using a few phonetically spelled words, I'll reveal why I think we should not stop formal reading instruction at the end of the third (or fourth or fifth) grade. Using nine words, I'll illustrate how great the discrepancies are between our spelling and our sounds, and why our children need as much help as we can give them.

These words are spelled phonetically:

1. /än′ trā/   2. /âr′ĭs/ or /ĕr′ĭs/   3. /fānz/
4. /lōzh/   5. /nô′ tē/   6. /ô′ gyə rē/
7. /pĭrs/   8. /shə nĕl′/   9. /vĭt′ ′l/

For at least two years, *The Real Paper,* a Boston weekly, had a contest to see how many readers could arrive at the "correct" (conventional) spelling of words when they saw them only in phonetic respellings. The above words were taken from the August 12, 1978 issue. Of course the way to get the answers is simply to say aloud the sounds spelled phonetically. Here are the words: 1. entree; 2. heiress; 3. feigns; 4. loge; 5. naughty; 6. augury; 7. pierce; 8. chenille; 9. victual.

If you consider the phonetic spelling (from a college dictionary)

What Are the Alternatives?

irrational and hard to read, you need no further proof to show how thoroughly conditioned you have become to our faulty spellings; and you can see how much help our children should be given to assist them to become excellent or at least good readers. We are all /ârz/ or /ĕrz/ (or /âr′ ĭs ĭz/ or /ĕr′ ĭs ĭz/) (heirs or heiresses) of a language whose spelling leaves so much to be desired that we are compelled to call upon electronics to help more of our children learn to read.

CHAPTER 27

Help for Our Adult Illiterates

This book was written to reveal the real reasons why Johnny can't read. But in the process of writing it, I have many times considered the sorry plight of our many millions of adult illiterates. Can't we help them? I have known for a long time why most of them do not attend evening classes to learn to read. They are ashamed and they don't want to be seen going to school for that purpose. They feel it is a disgrace not to be able to read.

Thirty years ago I taught remedial English classes at night. Enrolled in the classes were apprentice plumbers, carpenters, and electricians who were obliged to take and pass the course as one of their requirements to become journeymen. In my classes I had men ranging in age from around 20 to 30; and a good many of them were concerned, fearing that I would discover they were either illiterate or barely literate. Early writing assignments proved them to be right; a number wrote and read on second-grade level.

Those classes were not easy to teach. The men were tired after having put in a full day's work, and they didn't like having to spend 75 minutes twice a week doing what they had not chosen to do. A good many felt the requirement was unfair, not having anything to do with the work for which they were preparing. In the beginning, at least, there was little motivation, and I could easily detect antagonism. Naturally the level of confidence in some class members was low. And we did not have suitable textbooks. For the reading portion we tried the *Reader's Digest* at first, because it is quite generally assumed the *Digest* provides easy reading. Very soon we discovered, however, that the vocabulary range was much too wide. Different authors writing on different subjects use too many words for poor readers.

William Saroyan's *Human Comedy* was recommended to me. It had just become available in paperback, and I read it right away. It proved to be an excellent choice. In the dedication to his mother, Saroyan says he had written the book "as simply as possible," hoping that she would be able to read and enjoy it. Her native language was Armenian, and

Help for Our Adult Illiterates

her English was poor. My students, the best as well as the poorest, liked the book very much, and they were rather proud to be reading a well-known author.

The first writing assignment to a group of plumbers was to write out in complete sentences directions for changing a water heater. This presumably easy assignment was not easy for several, and for three class members it proved to be too difficult. So, contrary to explicit instructions, they got help; in each case a wife had done the writing, one even doing the handwriting! I wrote on each paper they had turned in that I wanted to see the writer for a minute after class in my office. Three crestfallen young men knocked on my door, and the minute turned into an hour. The men felt a real crisis had come into their lives. They couldn't read at all well, and their writing was bad. They wondered if they should drop out of the apprentice program, but I reassured them, saying I would work with them. I asked if they were married. They were. Then I recommended that they ask their wives, all of whom could read, to read each page of the reading assignment three times aloud to them while they looked into the books and followed what they were hearing. Then they were to read the assignment silently two or three times. They were dubious, feeling perhaps that such a procedure was quite embarrassing. Nevertheless, they followed my suggestion, and within two or three months they showed remarkable improvement.

By the way, a few years later, one of the three men came up to me in a large department store, introduced himself, and reminded me that I had "taught him to read"! Of course I hadn't done anything but make a recommendation. At all events, he thanked me profusely and told me he had become a good and avid reader. He suggested that I might take out a patent on my reading method! In subsequent sections I made an announcement the first evening that there were probably a number of poor readers in the class and told how spouses had helped their husbands to learn to read. I recommended to unmarried men that they get their mothers or an interested party to help at least three, preferably four, times a week. I know a few men did use the method.

Now you may wonder why I didn't relate my experiences with those men in evening classes before when discussing the SR&LM. The answer is simple. Whenever I have talked about it, my listeners have believed the method which might be suitable and work with adults who are conscious of the values of being able to read would be too much for youngsters to handle.

Now I am not going to propose that we develop a mass movement and get spouses to help nonreaders. Not only is it an awkward situation, but there is too much emotion involved. Besides, it is inefficient. Finding the proper materials would be a major obstacle. Finding mutually satisfactory times would be another, and soon the project would be abandoned.

Friends and acquaintances have suggested the use of television. But that is basically wrong. "Sesame Street" and "Electric Company" amuse and entertain children, and they watch by the hour. But primarily they are being amused and entertained. Their getting ready to read is a bonus. But adults want to see results. Illiterate adults don't need motivation; they want to be helped, and they already know how much it means to be able to read.

Reading is an active process and requires textual material on a page or sheet in front of the learner. Movement and action on television screens are not the same as reading. If you have read this book, you will not be surprised at my suggestion:

THE RADIO IS OUR BEST HOPE

Cf course I believe in teachers, but I have also considered the travel time to and from a school or college and, above all, the amount of courage it takes to show up in classes where reading is taught to native-born adults. The plan I propose is essentially the same as the one I propose for children, but with these major differences:

1. Because there will be no teachers to turn to, writers will have to take that fact into consideration, and explanations will have to be complete.

2. The reading material must be on an adult level. We err if we assume all nonreaders are unintelligent. To give them childish reading matter would be insulting and would "turn off" listener-readers.

3. The selections, even in the beginning, should be much longer than those for children in the first grade because adults have longer attention spans.

4. The beginning vocabulary should be somewhat larger because semi-literate adults can read more words than beginning pupils can.

5. Listening would take place in the home or room of the learners, in a place where they can develop and exercise complete concentration.

We should learn from and profit by the mistakes made in Britain, when Parliament instructed the British Broadcasting Corporation to attack the illiteracy problem. A program on TV such as was begun in October, 1975, is not my idea of teaching reading. To prepare a program here that would be good enough to be shown in good viewing time(s) would cost an exorbitant amount. But TV is not the place to teach reading. Admittedly, the British series "On the Move" would and did motivate readers to want to learn to read; but this I maintain: If nonreaders can be convinced that the ability to read is within their grasp, that assurance will be more than ample to motivate them. Spot announcements on TV and radio will make the project known, and they would be necessary because illiterates very obviously don't read newspapers.

From what I have been told, the British program was designed to motivate nonreaders to want to learn and to enlist tutors to help them. But to me untrained tutors are a grave weakness in the program. Some tutors doubtless would be well prepared and able teachers. But there must be a whole lot of tutors whose knowledge of the spelling of sounds and teaching performance are not matched by their willingness and enthusiasm to help. So they know too little about their subject and don't know how to put across either what they know or what they don't know. Besides, who is to decide what reading matter is to be selected? And that is of major importance and must not be left to whims or chance.

I want professional, high-quality reading matter developed with the utmost care, with words chosen as carefully as pearls on a string. And I insist that the reading matter be intensely interesting to learners of both sexes, even though there are more male than female illiterates. These two aims are not unreasonable. I worked with two master craftsmen—superior writers—when we "constructed" the reading matter in two German grammars, and it had great appeal to men and women students. The vocabulary we used was strictly limited, and new words were carefully woven in and then repeated in at least five subsequent lessons. Only my coauthors, our wives, and I knew of the countless hours we devoted to our projects. But the end product was richly rewarding, for we received innumerable compliments from both students and colleagues in many institutions, and a half million students read those selections.

In other words, fascinating reading matter can be written with as few as 250–300 words, and the cause is so important that learners must be driven to want to continue to learn and progress.

As good as it is, I am sure the *Human Comedy* should not be used to start off the radio programs. Possibly Saroyan's heirs and/or his publisher would allow the writers to use the story as a base, using as many of the original words as feasible and replacing unusual words or paraphrasing where necessary. But even that plan would probably not be desirable at the outset. In the second grammar we told an original story in letter form of an unhappy love affair, unhappy because the young man was hooked on heroin. (We wrote the story in 1957, long before drugs played such a big role in students' lives.) We had only 315 words which we could use to begin to tell our story and we had only 420 at the end. When we came to our last story, we elected to retell *Brigadoon*, which was originally a German story written about 1845. By then we had 600 words at our disposal.

What I am saying is that expert professional writers can surely do what my colleagues and I—three amateurs—succeeded in doing. But I must not give the wrong impression. Reading matter need not always be stories, even though by their very nature they have more restricted vocabularies and words are repeated more easily and logically. In one grammar we had an article about the time sense of bees, and over three lessons we told the history of the English language. But we always reserved space for continuations of our stories.

The one thing our writers must NOT do is to copy in any way the first book used in the BBC program. It was ill-conceived and was insulting to all who bought copies of it. They paid a pound for something which should never have been published. It has excellent cartoons, but in my opinion that is its only redeeming feature. It is a paperback about 8½" by 12" and is very much like reading readiness books designed for children. A good friend in London sent me a copy, along with the accompanying *BBC Adult Literacy Handbook* and the *Handbook for Literacy Tutors*. Although I find much to criticize in the latter two books, I'll restrict my reactions to the one illiterates work with.

It is an extremely poor beginning. Adults cannot help but be insulted by much they find there, especially the childish approach. For instance, the book has 156 pages, and the alphabet is printed a total of about 130 (!) times, on some pages once, and on some pages twice. A good many pages have just letters printed in dotted lines, and learners are supposed to fill in the blank spaces and make whole letters!

Many pages have four cartoons and then just one word appearing one time in each cartoon. And that represents an entire page! Still worse, nearly every native-born adult would already know all or at least most of the words on those pages and indeed in the entire book. Here are samples of single words on a page, appearing three or four times: "parking," "street," "road," "avenue," "full," "lift" (elevator), "food." Two words are often taught on one page: "off," "on"; "tea," "toilets"; "pay," "here"; "slow," "stop"; "new," "news"; "in," "out"; "up," "down"; "on," "under"; "boys," "girls." It takes two pages to teach "push" and "pull," and two more pages to teach "hot" and "cold."

There are just words, usually one or two, and cartoons on a majority of the pages. The short sentences which finally appear are about as inane as the poorest ones in our first Dick and Jane readers.

In the *Handbook,* which all tutors are supposed to read, we find the E. W. Dolch list of 220 words "which make up 50 to 75 percent of all ordinary reading matter." (p. 24) But I estimate that not more than 25 percent of those words are found in *On the Move!*

Now that we know what we must *not* do, let's see what we can do and how we can go about accomplishing the goal of decreasing appreciably the number of our illiterates. The private sector could not or would not develop such an ambitious undertaking. Because we live in a democracy and we respect the individual, the Federal government should and must take over the operation. It need not, should not, and must not develop

Help for Our Adult Illiterates

into a huge bureaucracy—or even a bureaucracy of any kind. There should be only a small cadre at the top, and the person who heads it must be carefully chosen, a person who has the ability to run the show, a person who is well acquainted with the relationship between symbols and sounds, one who knows quite a bit about teaching, especially of older and slower students. Yes, this is a real order, but the person will be pivotal to the entire project. The small cadre of specialists should come from a number of fields: (1) the English language; (2) the teaching of reading; (3) adult education; (4) educational psychology; (5) human or public relations; (6) the preparation and recording of tapes.

These top people must develop a sensitive and intelligent program, one which will appeal to the broad spectrum of adult illiterates and keep them motivated so that they will continue in the program until they can read satisfactorily.

The program must not be hastily thrown together and hurriedly put into print and on tapes. There is too much at stake. The end product must not be grim; there must be considerable light-hearted humor, and the listening-reading program should be a pleasant one, something to be looked forward to with anticipation. There must be a pilot program, condensed, to be sure, but it will show up areas of weakness and where improvements must be made. It is absolutely essential. The quality of the writing will probably be the decisive factor, along with the choice of words to be used at the outset and the number of words to be added in each listening period. Too heavy a burden would discourage those who start the program, and too light a burden would require too long for the learners to attain their desired goal. Finally, the quality of the tapes must rival that of the printed material.

The government should bear the costs, both for the preparation and printing of the material and for the preparation of the tapes. The latter will go out on loan to radio stations, which will be expected to broadcast them free of charge at satisfactory hours. Stations are granted the privilege of broadcasting, and they should have the responsibility of earning that privilege by performing an important public service, that is, by playing the tapes on a regular, prearranged basis. Both AM and FM stations must cooperate.

Details can be worked out, but in many areas there are several stations, and if each one runs through the entire series once, that would be sufficient. Say, for instance, station A begins the program. It could broadcast the material at a certain hour three times a week and rebroadcast the same material at a different hour on three other days during the week to catch as many listeners as possible. Then a little later, say three months, station B could use a similar pattern but choosing still different hours. Station C could start three months later, and so forth. In that way all who can't read would have the opportunity to participate, and repetition by different stations would take care of those who were late in hearing about the project, were ill or missed some of the listening-reading periods.

It is not clear in my mind whether the reading material should be offered free of charge, sold at half the printing costs, or at a price high enough to pay the printing. It is claimed that people do not appreciate things that they get free. I wouldn't know. I appreciate many things that cost me nothing: sunshine, nature, liberty, sight, hearing, good music, and many other blessings. Certainly the paper would not have to be of high quality, and bindings would be as inexpensive as possible because the printed material would be used by only one or two persons.

Even though the project will cost a good deal of money, it is cheaper than other plans which have been tried, and cheaper than any other plan I can think of. And when it comes to reaching those who need it, it will win hands down. The other plans which have been tried—and I am aware of them—have been failures, as evidenced by the great numbers of adults who still can't read. If no better and no less expensive program can be devised, we must wait no longer.

Give the proposed plan a chance.

CHAPTER 28

The Truth—at Long Last

Two important topics remain to be discussed. One will be taken up in this chapter, and the other one in Chapter 30.

A number of people have told me they had read or heard somewhere that whenever experiments have been conducted to see which of the two methods, phonics or word recognition, is more efficacious, phonics had come out on top every time. That is not true. This misinformation first gained general currency when Rudolf Flesch made that claim in his book, *Why Johnny Can't Read.* Indeed, the false claim was reinforced not long ago when Mr. Flesch wrote an article for a magazine which has one of the largest circulations of all American magazines, *Family Circle,* November 1, 1979. He gave his article the title, "Why Johnny *Still* Can't Read." He still blames the teachers; utopia lies in abandoning the Basal teaching method and adopting intensive phonics. Any number of people have quoted Mr. Flesch to me, and they have acted as though he were the final authority.

If you have read this book, you can't believe the misleading claim. But you'll have a hard time convincing those people who have read Flesch's *Johnny* book or his more recent article that he was wrong. His easy, chatty, informal style and his positive and self-assured attitude lead his readers to believe he truly is The Great Authority. His consummate skill as a journalist makes them forget to read his writings critically. He has capitalized on misconceptions and prejudices of lay people, and he has played on their emotions. He has caused many readers to believe a prophet by the name of Flesch has arisen who can lead all children out of futility and failure to the promised land of literacy.

He wrote the book mainly to and for parents whose children were not learning to read, at least not fast enough to suit the parents. They learned that all the schools, all the teachers, and all the textbooks were wrong. (p. 2) Parents were relieved and happy to learn their children were not stupid; the teachers were at fault; they were too stubborn to return to the instructional method which, he claimed, had been used everywhere in the world, including the United States, until about

1925. If teachers would use phonics exclusively and completely abandon word recognition, there would be no reading failures. I have previously reported how the word recognition method had been used for long periods, here and elsewhere.

In the first chapter I told you how Edith Efron in the *TV Guide* named Flesch as her authority for her statement that "Earlier generations read perfectly well." And so even a whole lot of people who have not read the *Johnny* book believe the false information.

A number of Flesch's erroneous claims must be considered, and we'll begin with a pivotal one. As I said, Mr. Flesch claimed that phonics had won out over word recognition in all studies when the two methods have been compared. He repeated the claim in the *Family Circle* article, and it is high time that it be refuted. In the book Flesch described briefly eleven experiments, saying they were the only ones that had ever been conducted, and then he stated he had "left out nothing" and he had "misrepresented nothing." (p. 68)

Lay readers assume Flesch built an impregnable case, but I state here unequivocally that:

(a) Mr. Flesch did *not* report on all experiments made up to the time of his book.
(b) He left out important conclusions of researchers.
(c) He misrepresented much when he left out those significant conclusions.

If you will read an article by Professors Paul A. Witty and Robert A. Sizemore, "Phonics in the Reading Program—a Review and an Evaluation," you will find that Flesch failed to report on half of the studies which had been made before 1955, the year the book appeared. (See *Elementary English,* 1955, pages 355-371.) The conclusions of Witty and Sizemore differ sharply from those of Flesch.

You decide if Flesch "left out nothing." In the eleven studies which Flesch did tell about he left out important conclusions from six of them. I'll give statements from three of the six. The following quotations were taken verbatim from the reports. (The emphases are mine.)

1. Researchers: Sexton and Herron (1928): *"The results clearly indicate that the teaching of phonics functions very little or not at all with beginners* in reading during the first five months. It seems to be of some value during the second five months, but is of greater value in the second grade." (Mr. Flesch believes phonics should be used exclusively, beginning on the first day.)

2. Researchers: Garrison and Heard (1931): "In the teaching of reading it seems probable that *much of the phonetic training now given*

should be deferred to the second and third grades." (This statement is diametrically opposed to Flesch's theories and claims.)

3. Researcher: Tate (1937): *Regular periods for phonics instruction are not desirable . . . Overemphasis on phonics hinders rapidity and thoroness of comprehension."*

If you are wondering about the other studies, I'll take the space to tell you about two on which Flesch reported. In Scotland a man set up an experiment using only Greek letters! He gave children a little practice, some with individual Greek letters, and some with Greek words. Then he gave the children an English passage written in Greek letters. The children were supposed to decipher the passage. The letter children won out, and that, presumably, proved the phonics method is better than the word recognition method! Are we to take the experiment seriously? Mr. Flesch called it "brilliant." What controls did the "researcher" use? Why would one resort to such a weird way to prove something so important as a method of teaching reading, where English letters are used? Another study was made with children whose I.Q.'s ranged from 30 to 75. I assure you that among the studies Flesch did not report on there were more logical ones.

Mr. Flesch told the readers of his book that teachers had completely abandoned phonics and were using the word method exclusively. This was not true. You can read the facts in one of the most highly respected books ever written in the United States on the subject, *Learning to Read.* The author was Professor Jeanne Chall (Harvard University). She wrote, "Though Flesch stated flatly no phonics was taught in 1955, a mere perusal of the pupils' workbooks and teachers' guidebooks of these series shows that phonics was indeed a part of the reading program." (p. 6)

In at least a dozen books or articles written between 1940 and 1955 we can read that phonics was used in conjunction with other methods. The strongest statement was made by Professor Emmett Albert Bates, Director of the Reading Clinic, Department of Psychology, Temple University. Here are his words: "For the past 150 years the phonics fad has come and gone. Now the fad has taken over reading." (*Education,* January, 1954, p. 326)

Finally, in an article in *Time,* January 9, 1956, from which I have previously quoted, we read this: "Flesch's accusations that the public schools have abandoned phonics . . . are ill-founded." Incidentally, ten phonics readers or practice books were published between 1940 and 1953. (*Elementary English,* May–September, 1953)

Here is still another preposterous claim. Mr. Flesch reported that Horace Mann observed the *phonics* method being taught in Prussia in 1834 and returned home and "praised it highly." (p. 128) I have read in at least ten places that Mr. Mann opposed the phonics method and favored the word approach. I read it in his own words in his *Report on an Educational Tour,* in biographies of Mann—for instance in one by E. I. F. Williams (p. 258)—and in several books on the teaching of reading. As a matter of fact, Mitford Mathews in *Teaching to Read* gave Chapter 7 the title, "The Word Method Endorsed by Horace Mann." In 1955, hundreds, perhaps thousands, of educators knew that Mann was loud in his praise of the word method, and they must have been flabbergasted to read the Flesch claim. The refutation to this claim and to many other false claims was made in educational journals and in two monthly magazines. But the damage was done. I ask you this: If phonics was used everywhere in the world before 1925, why would Mann be surprised to find it in use in Prussia and why would he return home and praise the method? He praised the word method, of that there is no doubt whatsoever.

It is humorous and incredible, but Flesch disqualified himself. If he believed what he wrote, he had no right to write a book on the subject of reading. He said only individuals trained in psychology or linguistics were qualified to write on the teaching of reading. (p. 123) He neglected to tell his readers that his specialty was in neither field! For instance, we read what a linguist, Robert C. Pooley, had to say about Flesch and his knowledge of linguistics in the Preface to *Let's Read—A Linguistic Approach* by Bloomfield and Barnhart. He wrote, "What Dr. Flesch lacked or at least did not utilize, is a command of the science of linguistics, which would have provided him with an understanding between sound and the written forms."

In this connection, here are two examples showing that Flesch did not know enough about the subject of his book. (1) He said the letters *au* in P*au*l and *aw* in cr*aw*l spell a diphthong (two sounds). In his native German *au* in *Paul* spells a diphthong. In English it does not. Nor does *aw* spell a diphthong. (2) Gratuitously, Flesch offered to show his readers what phonetic spelling is like. He gave "phonetic transcriptions" of "bazzite" and "periclasia": "*baz* ight" and "perry *klay*zha." My goodness! No wonder he made the claim that 87% of English words are spelled phonetically. What Mr. Flesch does not realize is that he offered conclusive and incontestable proof that he has no idea what phonetic spelling is. When we see his transcriptions, we still do not know if the *a* in b*a*zzite represents /ă/ or /ā/ or /ä/. Even worse is the fact that he used "silent" letters—and *g* and *h* are not sounded in "-*ight*." "Silent" letters do not exist and cannot be tolerated in phonetic spelling. In "periclasia" the second and last vowel letters spell schwas, and the phonetic symbol for the schwa, /ə/, is and was in 1955 what you will find in any acceptable dictionary. Language experts, including linguists, of course, used the schwa symbol and only that symbol for the sound long before 1955.

The man we are talking about, who pitted himself against all of the teachers, professors, and writers with their combined centuries of experience, knowledge, and acquired wisdom told parents they would be well-advised to take over the teaching of reading to their children. He repeated the suggestion—or admonition—in his recent article.

In my opinion, the most indefensible, the most unconscionable, part of the *Johnny* book is Flesch's absolute and unequivocal promise that *all* parents would succeed in teaching their children to read if they would use the method and material in the second part of his book, which he called a "primer." These are his words: "The method is *guaranteed*." (p. 32) On page 115 the author reaffirmed the claim, saying, "The method is *certain* to work." In both instances the italics are in the original. It made no difference if the child was only five or if the son or daughter had been a failure in school for many years. We even learn that perhaps the operation won't take a whole year! (p. 112) (We are not thinking of gifted or even average children; we are thinking of Johnny, who will be fortunate if he learns to read in four or five years.)

What right did Mr. Flesch have to "guarantee" success with unproved materials, using an untried method, to untrained parents, most of whom know precious little about how to teach and about our written symbols? They run the risk of further confusing a child who is already behind, and they can easily make matters worse. Parents have no right to experiment with their children in this significant matter. There are trained reading specialists, and they are not so stupid as to guarantee parents that all children, especially those who have reading problems, will learn to read well. They know how complex the reading process is, and they know vastly more than the average parent about the teaching of reading and about our mixed-up writing system.

You have to see the material in Flesch's primer to realize how bleak the chances of success with it actually are, especially with five-year-olds, who don't even know many of the words and can't handle abstractions: marks on paper to symbolize sounds that symbolize things or ideas. There isn't a single story in the entire primer, not a single paragraph, not a single sentence, and not even a single phrase. Just isolated words, nothing but columns of isolated words, 72 pages of columns of words. I submit that untrained parents working with Flesch's uninspired, deadly dull material are not going to find the success which Flesch so cruelly promises them, certainly not in a great majority of cases, either with five-year-old tots or with children who already have reading problems, hangups, blocks, fears, misconceptions. The lists of words can only bore children, who need to be motivated; they have to have something to capture and hold their attention. I can imagine the irritation and anger of parents when their child shows less than the desired (and promised) improvement. Parents aren't about to blame themselves, and Flesch states so positively that the method will work. The blame, therefore, must rest on the defenseless child, the "stubborn" or "stupid" child. I can also imagine the child's feelings of bewilderment, bitterness, despair, frustration, helplessness, and hostility. I can also visualize the tears.

Pedagogically, the reader is unsound. Would a specialist in psychology ever write one like it? Children can't see or feel the need to learn to read those "dumb" words, one after another, one after another. Flesch himself said the child would be cured once he had taken his medicine! (p. 115) What will result from this total lack of compelling interest? Short attention spans, fatigue, squirming, yawning, wiggling, scuffling of feet, gazing out the window, the desire to be released from this irrelevant stagnation.

Learning has to be made meaningful, interesting, rewarding. These endless columns of words are none of these things. From everything I have read about the teaching and the learning of reading, I'm sure that reading is much more than long columns of unrelated words. Reading goes beyond the sounding out of words. Reading is for meaning. Mr. Flesch inadvertently put his finger on the difference. As a high school pupil in Austria he had studied Czech for a semester. Years later he could still remember the pronunciation and he could pronounce words. That would be possible because most Czech words are spelled phonetically. Once he "read" aloud from a Czech newspaper, and a native of Prague asked him if he knew Czech. He replied he didn't, that he didn't understand a word of it, and that he could only read it! (p. 23)

To Flesch, reading is the ability to sound out words. To me, it is much more; sounding out is mechanical, merely a phase. Reading is communicating, the transfer of thought, the grasping of ideas, seeing mental pictures, often moving pictures.

If you were to read down forty or fifty columns, I believe you would also find them lifeless and insipid, just as children would, only the children would take a whole lot longer and would, therefore, be bored longer. These lists simply cannot interest the average child. Lasting, involuntary interest cannot be aroused and held by their use. There is not one single factor of interest in the whole procedure. Working endlessly on unrelated words is self-defeating; they haven't anything to say to the learners.

Worried parents would naturally assume their enthusiasm would rub off on the children, but imagine the expression on the faces of uncomprehending children, for whom such an ordeal would require more than concerned parents' constant encouragement. Working with meaningless abstractions isn't any fun; it certainly isn't interesting. The children can communicate orally, and someone can read to them or, better still,

The Truth—at Long Last

they can watch TV. And believe me, those short, look-alike words on page after page are monotonous. (Most children learn more quickly the very long and very short words because they are more easily identified.) Parents' eager and fervent desires will not prevail. Variety is not only the spice of life; it is a means of holding attention.

If you are wondering why I would devote so much space and attention to the Flesch book, it is because it is so widely accepted even today—by lay people—as offering the best hope to eliminate illiteracy. In my opinion, it, more than any other book, has done much damage to the cause of literacy. It has developed divisiveness and abrasiveness between parents and teachers, and it has caused confusion in the minds of parents, many teachers, and, indirectly, even schoolchildren. The article compounds the confusion. Flesch's false doctrines are not dead, buried, and forgotten; they continue to affect literacy adversely. Articles written in 1955 and 1956 in rebuttal did not, as I said, have the wide readership of the book and certainly had only a fraction of the impact. The book is still in print and may be found in thousands of libraries. Flesch called attention to the book in his *Family Circle* article; parents were to use it to teach their children to read.

A grave weakness of the primer is a lack of sufficient repetition. To be sure, 22 of the 72 pages are used for review, but the amount of repetition which might be barely sufficient for gifted children isn't nearly enough for average learners—not by any means. And how much would Johnny and Ichabod require? I thought the book was supposed to be directed toward children of Johnny's ability. But more repetition would have meant a larger book. Naturally. The whole *Johnny* book is short, not more than 250 pages of printed material. The second part, the primer, takes up only one-third of the total number of pages. Instead of offering just 72 pages of lists of words, Flesch owed it to the children and their parents to give *at least* five times that many pages. The entire book would then have run about 500 pages. Books were not expensive in 1955, and there should have been a realistic attitude toward the most important intellectual achievement of most people, the ability to read.

To avoid misunderstandings, I must make this point: There is ample repetition of the easy words in the first fourth of the primer with such words as *bet, let, set, bed, red, web,* which are all listed at least eight times. But there is far too little repetition in the last third when the spellings (words) get harder and much more repetition is sorely needed. For instance, the spelling of the /sh/ sound by *sh* is easy and needs little repetition. But the spelling of the sound by *ci, si,* and *ti* is a disaster. After the group in which they are introduced, *ti* spells /sh/ in words only fourteen times, *si* only five times, and *ci* only four times!

The primer falls far short of what the author claimed. He said it was "reasonably complete" (p. 27) and that upon completion children would be able to read *The Reader's Digest* and *Treasure Island*. That is a great promise. But if you have read the preceding chapters in this book, you know that such a rash promise, even for average learners, is unattainable and impossible. It was inhuman to make it. If you have a gallon of liquid, you know before you try that you won't be able to pour it into a pint container.

If English sounds are spelled more than 600 ways, and they are, you know that you'd have to introduce 12 spellings a page if you have only 72 pages and use 22 of them for review. Mr. Flesch said English has only single letter spellings and "some fifty combinations." (p. 111) But if he had bothered to count, he would have discovered he had introduced 75 combinations. (Remember also how many sounds the single letters spell.) He didn't begin to use all he needed for a primer designed to accomplish his announced goal.

How can a primer be "reasonably complete" and prepare children to read "anything" (p. 32) if upon completion of it children are not able to read such essential words as these:

you	have	woman	love	eye	friend	Monday
they	are	heart	any	one	receive	buy
their	been	blood	son	two	people	move
there	says	ocean	shoe	to	money	build
would	of	again	sure	who	English	language

If you have been reading this book carefully, you must be wondering how anybody could possibly write a beginning reader and use a pure phonics approach, when not one of the thirty-five words in the above group can be sounded out. I agree. It cannot be done, and Flesch couldn't do it either. He could fool his readers (and, perhaps, himself) because they don't know what phonetic spelling is. If you were to ask a hundred literate nonteaching adults how many of the thirty-five words are spelled phonetically, nearly all of them would say they all are. I repeat: Not one is.

For the most part, what Flesch put together might be called a "pattern" approach. Children had to be told how the words at the top of the page, the samples, are pronounced, that is, the sounds the letters spell. Mark this well: That wouldn't be necessary if our words were spelled phonetically. Children followed the patterns offered, not because they were necessarily logical, but words on those pages fitted those patterns.

Thus, at the top of the page of group 24 we find the digraph *ea* spelling /ē/, as in "m*ea*l." In the columns on that page are other words in which that sound is spelled by *ea*, e.g., b*ea*n, *ea*st. However, later, in group 65, we find three additional spellings by *ea*: /ā/ in br*ea*k, /ĕ/ in head, and /û/ in learn. In the columns we find, intermixed, great, bread, heard, dead, pearl, steak, etc. Now if those words in group 24 are spelled phonetically (which they aren't), then what about every single word in group 65? The author doesn't even provide a clear-cut pattern for the spelling of each sound. So we can't even call his method a "pattern" approach. You may well imagine the guessing that would go on in group 65. Children have learned read /ē/ and then see bread and they are supposed to be able to sound out both words. They might well see "eat" in "sweat."

Similarly, ou is offered in group 31, and we find a number of words in which the diphthong /ou/ is spelled by ou: cloud, count, and proud. The ou combination is found again in group 67, where it spells /ŭ/ in young and /ə/ in famous. So of the nine spellings of the combination ou Flesch introduced three. The spellings of the other six sounds are nowhere to be found in the primer. That is why the word "you," in which ou spells /o͞o/ was never once introduced. Similarly, "your" and "four" are never used, not introduced because the spelling of the sounds was not given.

Now if you were to look at the last page, 72, you would find what appears to be a showcase demonstrating what children will be able to read when they have completed their "course." (In the last eight words of the preceding sentence, "to do when they have completed their course," children will be able to sound out only one, the word "when.") So children will be able to read "anything"? That is not true. Furthermore, a good number of the words have no right to be on the page because the children would be unable to sound them out. Unstressed syllables are given shabby treatment; in the 80 words there are 112 unstressed syllables, and children will not know how to handle them.

You see "banana" and "vanilla" on page 72. Children will quite logically put the stress on the first syllable. Nowhere in the primer are children helped with the spelling of schwa sounds when they are the first or a middle element in a word. Unfortunately, about 70 percent of all the words in the primer are words of one syllable, and fewer than five percent of all words have three or more syllables. But even many of the words that are stressed on the first syllable will be too much for the learners. Take, for instance, "vinegar" and "miserable." Children sounding out "vinegar" will come up with /vīn gär/, not /vĭn'ə gər/, because they know "vine" and "bar," "car," and "star." And in "miserable" they will see "miser" and "able." And why not?

"Mysterious" is also on the list. In the primer we learn that y spells only /y/, as in "yes," /ē/, as in "happy," and /ī/, as in "my." So the child gets off to a bad start, and there is no help for the spelling of either e or i, since here e spells /ĭ/ and i spells /ē/, and neither spelling is given in the long lists of words. I would say the word is out of place.

Please permit me one more statement. There is no doubt about the tone of the *Johnny* book. (The recent article is belligerent.) In the book Mr. Flesch said he was "mad." (p. 18) He played to an audience that wanted to believe him; and a calm, judicious approach would not have stirred up his readers and made them angry. He made vitriolic attacks on all educators and he belittled psychologists, especially educational psychologists. How could a person claim *all* reading specialists were wrong? He tore down; he did not really build up, and what he did build on was sand. Fanned by the flames of his own, self-induced fury, Flesch sowed seeds of suspicion, doubt, distrust, and divisiveness. Like weeds, they have kept on spreading.

CHAPTER 29

The Teacher Is All

This message must come in loud and clear: The proposed complementary teaching method will in no way supplant teachers—supplement, yes, but *not* supplant. If you have read this book carefully, you know what a difficult task it is for large numbers of children to learn to read our language. So a great many youngsters will continue to need all the help they can get. Besides, teachers lend an indispensable quality: the human touch. Teachers will still be needed to teach, to lead, to direct, to motivate, to develop high morale, to keep order, to encourage, to be supportive, to praise, to offer comfort, to console, to sympathize, to cheer up their charges, to settle disputes, to be surrogate parents, to reprimand when necessary, to watch for illnesses of children, to protect children from danger, to exercise gentle but firm authority, to be a calming influence, to be even-tempered, to display a sense of humor, and so on and on.

Oh yes, indeed: They will continue to perform many mundane tasks, such as making evaluations, having conferences with, and listening to, parents, helping find lost articles, helping little tots with their boots and jackets, even wiping runny noses, and so forth.

In short, teachers will, in the future, as now,

BE ALL THINGS TO ALL CHILDREN.

CHAPTER 30

It Is Up to You!

If you now appreciate the problems confronting Johnny and Ichabod, you may feel somewhat thwarted when you try to tell others in a few words what our slower-learning children face. Because the computer plays such a significant role in our lives, you might tell about the computer study in which the electronic brain, using 308 rules, was able to spell only 49 percent of 17,310 words. (Chapter 4) Words that are easy to spell are generally easy to learn to read; conversely, words that are hard to spell are hard to learn to read. Everybody knows that we have huge numbers of words that are hard to spell.

Or you might refer people to a page in the *Random House Dictionary*. On one page they can find 380 "common English spellings." They are listed and then exemplified in sample words. If anyone says some of the 380 spellings are not common, I'll be happy to replace them with other spellings that are. The "Table of Common English Spellings" is found on page xxxii of the College Edition and on page xiv of the Unabridged Edition.

Or tell how relatively few of our words are spelled phonetically. If you were to take an hour or two and actually do what I suggested earlier, that is, make your own count of words which are and words which are not spelled phonetically, then you'd be able to speak from your own experience. The most interesting aspect of the operation will occur when you tell the results of your personal count. The people to whom you give the information will not believe you! You have support from Professor Falk Johnson, who, as you may recall, wrote that it had been reported only about 20 percent of our words are spelled phonetically.

Or you might tell about a comparison of twelve English and twelve German words that I am about to make. We'll simply use the cardinal numbers from one to twelve. The unphonetic spellings will be numbered and explained.

It Is Up to You!

ENGLISH	GERMAN
one /wŭn/	*eins*
1. Where does the /w/ come from?	No problem (The combination *ei* always spells /ī/.)
2. *o* should spell only /ō/ and /ŏ/.	
3. The *e* serves no phonetic function.	
two /to͞o/	*zwei*
4. *w* serves no phonetic function.	No problem
5. *o* should spell only /ō/ and /ŏ/.	
three /thrē/	*drei*
Good!	No problem
four	*vier*
6. *ou* should spell the diphthong, as in *ou*r.	No problem (The digraph *ie* always spells /ē/.)
five /fīv/	*fünf*
No problem (Note that *-ive* spells /-ĭv/ in at least 500 words, e.g., creat*ive*, expens*ive*.)	No problem (The vowel sound is "short" because two consonants follow *ü*.)
six /siks/	*sechs*
Note the phonetic spelling.	No problem (*e* spells a "short" sound; two consonants follow. When followed by *s*, *ch* always spells /k/.)
seven	*sieben*
7. The first *e* should spell /ē/, as in *e*ven.	No problem (The final *e* spells a schwa, as it should in an unstressed syllable.)
8. The second *e* spells /ə/.	
eight /āt/	*acht*
9. *ei* is one of our 53 digraphs which spell sounds 180 ways. (Cf. *ei* in h*ei*ght.)	No problem (When *ch* follows a back vowel sound [*a, o, u*], the combination always spells a guttural sound.)
10. *g* and *h* are both unsounded.	
nine /nīn/	*neun*
No problem. (But see *-nine* in femi*nine* /ĭ/ and mezza*nine* /ē/.)	No problem (The combination *eu* always spells a diphthong.)
ten /tĕn/	*zehn*
No problem. (But see of*ten* and sof*ten*.)	No problem (The letter *h* is a sign that the preceding vowel spells a "long" sound.)
eleven /ĭ lĕv′ən/	*elf*

English	German
11. The first *e* spells /ĭ/;	No problem (*e* spells a "short" sound because two consonants follow.)
12. The second *e* should spell /ē/. (See *seven*.)	
13. The third *e* spells /ə/.	
twelve	*zwölf*
14. The final *e* serves no phonetic function.	No problem (*ö* spells a "short" sound because two consonants follow.)

Summary: In the twelve English words there are fourteen unphonetic spellings; in the German words there are none. (Without going into details, the *ei* and *ie* spellings are truly phonetic because German phoneticians consider that the combination *ei* spells a diphthong, and *ie* is the standard spelling for /ē/.)

Our unreliable symbols were the reason Professor John Dewey recommended that we should wait until children are at least eight before we should start teaching them how to read. I have quoted him before, but I believe with the suggested supplemental Simultaneous Reading and Listening Method we have at last a valid answer. He asked, "Is the child of six or seven years ready for symbols?" (*The Forum*, 1898) He deplored the teaching of reading as the end in itself. He wrote, "Reading is made an isolated accomplishment. There are no aims in the child's mind which he feels he can serve by reading; there is no mental hunger to be satisfied. The book is a reading lesson. He learns to read not for the sake of what he reads, but for the mere sake of reading. When the bare process of reading is made an end in itself, it is a psychological impossibility for reading to be other than lifeless." Dewey wanted children to read for meaning, just as we adults read for meaning.

With respect to the teaching method, he said all methods in use then and before "lack the essential of any well-grounded method, namely, relevancy to the child's mental needs. No scheme for learning can supply this want. Only a new motive—putting the child into a vital relation to the materials to be read—can be of service here."

If we are not going to heed Dewey's advice and postpone the teaching of reading until children are at least eight, we can be thankful that we are living in the electronic age: With tapes we can whet mental hunger and we can give relevancy to children's needs; with the Simultaneous Reading and Listening Method we can develop the new motive and can put "the child into a vital relation to the materials to be read." Obviously, the writers of the new material will face a challenge and will have to make their material come alive and create reading matter that will be meaningful in the minds of the young learners. The success of the

It Is Up to You!

program will hinge on their ability to appeal to young minds and make the children eager to return again and again to the SR&LM program.

In conclusion, I think we must ask ourselves these five questions:

1. Isn't the most important task of elementary education the teaching of reading?
2. Don't we have an exceedingly difficult spelling (writing) system?
3. Have we not failed in the past to teach many millions of children to read up to a functional level and hosts of others to read as well as citizens in a democracy should be able to read?
4. Do we really wish to help all of our children to learn to read?
5. Are we willing to make an affirmative and positive experiment which might well be a momentous and memorable one—the Simultaneous Reading and Listening Method—to see if we can do a better job in helping all of our learners?

It is up to you.